12.7.08

KISS OF DEATH

Tobias Churton is a writer, composer and film-maker. He has a Master's degree in Theology from Oxford, and is an Honorary Fellow of Exeter University where he lectures on Western Esotericism. He has proved himself to be a bridge-builder between scholarship and the general reader, with the television series and best-selling book *The Gnostics* and several successful books on the history of Rosicrucianism, Freemasonry and alchemy. He is a keen and objective commentator on the contemporary and historical Gnostic phenomenon.

I dedicate this book to my wife and daughter,
and to the memory of my beloved father, Victor Churton,
who taught me everything essential to the path of life.

KISS of DEATH

THE TRUE HISTORY OF THE GOSPEL OF JUDAS

TOBIAS CHURTON

WATKINS PUBLISHING

LONDON

This edition published in the UK 2008 by
Watkins Publishing, Sixth Floor, Castle House,
75–76 Wells Street, London W1T 3QH

Text Copyright © Tobias Churton 2008

Tobias Churton has asserted his right under the Copyright, Designs
and Patents Act 1988 to be identified as the author of this work.

1 3 5 7 9 10 8 6 4 2

Designed by Jerry Goldie

Printed and bound in Great Britain

British Library Cataloguing-in-Publication Data Available

ISBN: 978-1-905857-39-5

www.watkinspublishing.co.uk

CONTENTS

ACKNOWLEDGEMENTS

When publication of The Gospel of Judas was announced in early 2006 amid a storm of exaggeration and distortion, I itched to say something about it. By dint of providence, an opportunity came in the form of a suggestion from Tuvia Fogel to write a book about it for Cairo Publishing of Milan. Tuvia did the business and helped to translate the book into Italian.

Thanks to my agent Fiona Spencer Thomas and editor Michael Mann, *Kiss of Death – The True History of the Gospel of Judas*, can now be read in its original language.

While my understanding of *gnosis* has matured over the years, the cup is by no means exhausted. I have been privileged to engage with excellent minds, some of whom have, sadly, departed this life. Hans Jonas, Gilles Quispel and Kathleen Raine – all irreplaceable talents – are much missed by all those who knew them. Elaine Pagels still holds the torch of serious and exciting scholarship aloft, as do the growing number of scholars associated with Joost Ritman's amazing *Bibliotheca Philosophica Hermetica* in Amsterdam. I shall always be grateful to the *Bibliotheca* for the many happy times when the flower of my interest grew in hot-house conditions during the 1980s.

I should also like to thank Professor Nicholas Goodrick-Clarke for his tireless efforts in organizing Britain's first MA course in Western Esotericism at the Department of Humanities and Social Studies, University of Exeter, and for asking me to lecture to the growing number of students there.

FOREWORD

Kiss of Death is the considered assessment of one scholar to the phenomenon of interest and recrimination surrounding the publication of The Gospel of Judas.

Critics of the gospel have eagerly pointed out that the gospel's title has been known to scholars since the late 2nd century AD. Those critics have been less eager to state that the literal contents of the gospel have not been *read* for at least 1,600 years. The gospel is, indeed, new to our eyes.

In order to offset the force of this fact, opponents of the gospel have asserted that its contents nonetheless conform to long-since discredited doctrines associated with the heresy of *Gnosticism*. The gospel has nothing of any real value to offer people today.

In contrast to this position, some scholars have noticed that even among the known genres associated with the alleged 'heresy', The Gospel of Judas exhibits many characteristics unique to itself. It is a special work; the gospel's sudden appearance in our era is worthy of widespread attention – and not a little wonder.

According to its automatic critics, The Gospel of Judas is little more, at best, than a quaint survival of a bygone era – a mere footnote no one need bother themselves with. Its value, critics assert, should be entirely confined to the world of scholarship. Only scholars, in fact, can be trusted with it – especially *believing* scholars. The gospel is, they say, not deserving of impacting on people's spiritual beliefs. It is an issue for scholars, not for believing or non-believing members of the general public: a mere sensation. Critics hope or expect the matter will just go away.

The coolly dismissive approach, widely disseminated by the Churches into the media, seems hard to square with the quantity of vitriol aimed at the gospel and those who believe it might be of interest to the general public. If the work has no value for non-specialists, why expend so much energy on denouncing it? What are critics afraid of? These seem reasonable questions to objective observers of the wave of international bickering that came in the wake of the gospel's controversial publication in Spring 2006.

Kiss of Death has been written from the conviction that The Gospel of Judas is of great interest and significance to believers and non-believers alike. Its implications deserve to occupy all thoughtful people; public interest is not simply a matter of sensationalist curiosity.

Kiss of Death explores not only the message, but the global *reaction* to the message, asking questions that have occurred to many who have observed the spectacle, encouraging readers to ask their own questions.

The intended audience of *Kiss of Death* is the general public. The book has not been designed, primarily, for academic debate. However, many issues raised in the book may appear to scholars and clergy as straying into 'their' specialist territory, with respect to which the author is reassured that within our dynamic society, neither churches nor academics have special possessive rights to dominate the terms of public interest and debate. While the gospel's original audience was probably a self-defined élite, suspicious of the limits of 'common knowledge', its message can now be brought before the consciousness of everybody.

Even with all of the benefits of the best international scholarship on the subject, no one can claim to understand definitively every word of The Gospel of Judas. However, the reaction to its appearance suggests that what *can* be understood may be as disturbing to some people today as it was to those who first read 'Judas' gospel' over 1,800 years ago.

Chapter One

TIME BOMB

Less than a month after terrorists bombed the US Embassy in Beirut in 1983, killing 40 innocent staff, a very different kind of bomb was prepared in a Geneva hotel room.

On 15 May, a small group of American scholars gathered off the Rue de la Servette, Geneva. This was no ordinary day for experts in ancient Coptic and biblical history. In fact, there was something distinctly shady about the circumstances, but there were rich pickings for those who stayed the course.

First to be jettisoned from the team was Astrid Beck, a graduate student completing her PhD on comparative religion at the University of Michigan in Ann Arbor. Her supervisor, Professor David Noel Freedman (general editor of the prestigious *Anchor Bible Dictionary*), and his manuscript-collecting colleague Ludwig Koenen, advised Astrid that since they were meeting Arabs, her gender might be cause for offence. Suppression of femininity was not an auspicious start to proceedings. Perhaps there was already confusion about what to expect.

Two men did arrive at the Hotel de l'Union, the pre-arranged rendez-vous. Neither, however, was an Arab. Mr Hana A Airian was an Egyptian Christian – a Copt – from Cairo. Yannis Perdios, the middleman, was a cultured Greek from Athens. Both men were in the antiquities trade. Both were familiar with Koenen's reputation and neither objected to meeting women in the course of business.

More importantly, they had goods they wanted swiftly assessed, and swiftly sold.

The scholars were whisked away to a second, unknown hotel, without Ms Beck, who was left behind, deeply disappointed.

Koenen, the 'connection' between the Cairo antiquities market and the University of Michigan's manuscript-buying programme, had hoped to secure the presence of the world's most influential authority on ancient Coptic manuscripts. In spite of the poor-quality photographs of the papyrus for sale, Ludwig Koenen knew the manuscripts were important, and he knew the man to contact. The man in question was Professor Emeritus James M Robinson from Claremont Graduate University, California's Institute for Antiquity and Christianity. Robinson was general editor of the largest ancient Coptic Library of papyrus books ever discovered: the amazing 'Nag Hammadi Library', a collection better known to the world as 'The Gnostic Gospels' – 52 previously unknown texts from the early centuries of Christianity.

Robinson could not come. Instead, the Professor Emeritus sent Stephen Emmel, a former student of his. Emmel had also been Robinson's co-worker on the painstaking assemblage of the Nag Hammadi Library at Cairo's Coptic Museum during the 1970s. Stephen Emmel had a great deal of experience with fragments of papyrus lifted in mysterious circumstances out of the sands of Egypt. Emmel now holds the only permanent chair of Coptic studies in the world, at the University of Münster in Germany – so you could say Robinson was a 'good picker', both in terms of giving Emmel a job as his assistant in Cairo and, later, as his emissary to Geneva.

The point for Robinson was that while Emmel was working in Rome at the time – a train journey away from Geneva – he, Robinson, was far away on the other side of the world. Had Robinson not taken the more economically viable option of staying put, the story of The Gospel of Judas may have turned out very differently.

There is an old adage for the requirements of magic: *be willing to buy the egg of a perfectly black hen without haggling*. Sometimes it is best to pay; money is not everything. This was certainly the view of the Cairo antiquities dealer trying to make his fortune that morning in a Geneva Hotel. Hana (the name means 'John') did not like too much haggling; he was prepared to wait as long as necessary for the right price where serious goods were concerned. The value of history was beyond ordinary computation.

Stephen Emmel was a good choice – but the younger man had no authority to promise money. Emmel was there to make a report, if that was possible. In fact, a proper report was not possible. Hana Airian stipulated there were to be no photographs, no writing implements – no records of any kind. If the assembled scholars reckoned these manuscripts were important, then the price would be justified. What is money?

Middleman and translator Perdios took a different view. He was curious to know what the scholars thought of the manuscripts, if for no other reason than to more accurately assess their value. There were several and so far nobody appeared sure what the documents actually were. However, more accurate knowledge might 'up the price'; the scholars would be loath to say much.

The meeting lasted about an hour – and there was no escaping the tension. Hana seemed nervous. Emmel reckoned this was probably because someone had smuggled the goods out of Egypt. In Egypt, all finds must be registered with the government and any export without the government's consent is forbidden. While Koenen and Professor Freedman talked money in the hotel suite's bathroom, Emmel tried to get a closer look at the papyrus pages as they lay exposed in the bottom of three shoeboxes. This was his chance. Playing against time, he used tweezers to prise the leaves apart. A sudden movement could damage the papyri forever.

Meanwhile in the bathroom, Koenen and Freedman did not have much to play with. Discomfort with the setting added extra pressure. The owner of the goods, Hana, was no less uncomfortable than the potential buyers. Hana would have preferred to negotiate with professional dealers who knew the ropes and spoke his language, not US university representatives with letters after their names. Still, Koenen was known in Cairo and regular purchases had helped make dealers better aware of the value of manuscripts. A problem with buying such wares can be that the buyer's own enthusiasm creates the very market that ultimately pushes him or her out altogether. In antiquities, being first frequently means being last. Hana was usually ready to wait as long as necessary for the right offer. He had already gone to a great deal of trouble to be in a position to sell the manuscripts sitting on the hotel bed. He wanted recompense for that trouble – justification for the pain suffered – as well as a return on his initial investment.

James Robinson, like all professors, would prefer ancient manuscripts to come straight out of official archaeological digs, thence to land intact on his work table. He knew from experience that the more clandestine the nature of the discovery and delivery process, the more likely was it that this shadowy world would follow the text in its frustrating journey towards academic light. Important documents could be 'lost' (to all but exclusive study) for years.

The Nag Hammadi Library (which included the famous Gnostic gospels) stood as a flagrant case in point. The 13 leather-bound codices (papyrus books) had been unearthed a few months after the first atom bombs exploded in Japan in 1945, but were not published in an edition suitable for the general public until the Sex Pistols sang *God save the Queen* 32 years later.

That the complete Nag Hammadi Library had been published at all at this time was thanks to Professor Robinson's determination and success in breaking what he considered to be an unhealthy scholars' monopoly – when translators held on to their particular texts for years and years. His view was that the material was too important for human knowledge to be left in exclusive hands – that was his view.

The values of the marketplace are not supposed to be the values of academe. But everything has a price. Robinson knew the owner of the new material would be anxious to turn a good profit. Knowing his institute did not possess the acquisition funds required, Robinson turned to Harold Attridge, one of the editors of *The Nag Hammadi Library in English*[1], a professor of New Testament studies at the Southern Methodist University, Dallas. Attridge reckoned he might get $50,000 from the Perkins School of Theology's Bridwell Library if the cache proved to be sufficiently special.

Koenen, on the other hand, felt a figure in the region of $50,000 to $100,000 could be raised from the Dorot Foundation which supported the Michigan University papyrus collection – for which Koenen was chief buyer – as well as the Israel Museum and its world-famous Shrine of the Book. However, the foundation's preference was for rare biblical items; they were less interested in works not found in the Jewish and Christian Bibles.

Despite these shortcomings, Koenen and Freedman appeared to make some progress in the hotel bathroom. They were satisfied that the material under offer was genuine and of interest to their backers, and exchanged words with Hana through his intermediary. But even Perdios' ample charm and personal stake in the negotiation could not surmount one glaring difficulty. As far as price was concerned, the owner and potential buyers were speaking on completely different wavelengths; they might as well have been living on different planets. Stephen Emmel's heart must have sunk when he saw the older men emerge from the bathroom. The faces told it all: *No deal.*

The material was swiftly covered with old Egyptian newspaper and removed from Emmel's purview. A late, tentative offer of $300,000 from Professor Freedman only served to insult the owner. Hana A Airian wanted $3,000,000, *minimum* – and that was that.

Or was it? In spite of the disappointment, not to say insult to his dignity and professional reputation, the Cairo dealer offered the team of experts lunch. Perhaps Mr Airian reckoned the group might have a fallback position. Anyhow, they might at least go home and think more seriously about the price once they got a chance to discuss its contents amongst themselves. Buyers often come back with better offers. He may have wished to satisfy one appetite while stimulating another – a good old dealer's trick. It was perhaps best that they remember a nice lunch along with the memory of amazing objects all-too-soon nipped from view.

As the lunch went on, Emmel realized he had better make as good an inventory of what he had seen as he could, now that the restriction on writing implements was lifted. True to the spirit of the morning's negotiation, Emmel went to the restaurant men's room to commit his anxious thoughts to paper. These notes were written up and sent to Professor James M. Robinson a fortnight later. In the long travelling history of the cache, Emmel's report affords a tantalizing snapshot of one moment in the half-life of the contents of the dark shoeboxes.

The State of the Texts

From Emmel's report we learn that on that morning in May 1983, the collection comprised four manuscripts derived, he surmised, from the Roman Egypt of the 4th century AD. Within the manuscript bundles, Emmel observed a Greek version of part of the Book of Exodus, a manuscript (also in Greek) showing how to use mathematics and geometry to solve practical problems, some letters of St Paul in Coptic, and three Coptic Gnostic works. These works comprised what Emmel called the 'gem' of the collection. Two of the Gnostic works were known from different versions in the Nag Hammadi Library, these being the Letter of Peter to Philip and the (first) Apocalypse of James. The presence of parts of Paul's epistles to the Hebrews, Colossians and Thessalonians should have pleased both the Bridwell Library at Dallas and the Dorot Foundation. The Coptic Gnostic works, however, were of special interest to Stephen Emmel, a young veteran of the Nag Hammadi project, soon to be awarded his doctorate at Yale University.

The third of the Coptic Gnostic works, beautifully written in a local (Middle Egyptian) dialect of Sahidic Coptic, was what looked like a dialogue between Jesus and his disciples. Emmel compared it to some known works in the Nag Hammadi Library, but did not think it was a copy. This work was new to him. In it, Emmel observed the name 'Judas' repeated several times.

Emmel was later extremely annoyed to realize that this was not, as he had thought at the time, a reference to 'Didymos Judas Thomas' (Judas 'the Twin', associated with the famous Nag Hammadi Gospel of Thomas), but was in fact none other than Judas Iscariot, the infamous betrayer of Christ. Emmel just wasn't expecting to see a gospel of Judas. *Who was?* Even in Gnostic studies, the very idea would not, in the natural course of things, spring to mind.

Two long-forgotten references in ancient sources (see below) to a gospel of Judas were just that: long forgotten. We were not supposed to know about such a work; possession of it had been forbidden. The lid had been closed on that subject a very long time ago. Fortunately, or unfortunately, depending on your viewpoint, that lid had been opened again – by grave robbers.

Limited time did not permit the Coptic specialist to examine carefully the final page of the Gnostic codex. Had Emmel done so, he would have been able to inform Professor Robinson that the long-lost Gospel of Judas had been discovered after a 1,700-year absence from the historical record.

It is perfectly possible that Stephen Emmel's utterly innocent oversight contributed significantly to the sad adventures that would befall the papyrus leaves of the gospel as subsequent years rolled by. That is not to say that Emmel in any way underestimated what he had had the opportunity to examine. Far from it. His message to Robinson, back in California, was unequivocal. Emmel urged Robinson to acquire a collection that was 'of the utmost scholarly value, comparable in every way to any one of the Nag Hammadi codices.'

Emmel also observed that the manuscripts had been badly handled. While he reckoned the work, when discovered, had all its margins intact, in the intervening time half of the codex's leather cover had disappeared and a number of pages had broken. The individual leaves measured 30cm by 15cm, while page numbering, he observed, went into the 50s (more than 25 leaves). However, Emmel reckoned that perhaps half of the codex might have been missing, along with the back cover, since he was used to Nag Hammadi codices numbering up to about 100 pages (50 leaves).

In fateful anticipation of what might befall the collection, Stephen Emmel signed off his report with a plea that the material be swiftly acquired and delivered to a library or museum. The collection urgently cried out for proper restoration, conservation and evaluation. Without such measures, further deterioration would render the work difficult or impossible to assess.

A time-bomb was ticking. Readers experienced in worldly affairs will already have guessed what, in broad outline, happened next. But before we fill in the detail, perhaps we had better look at what had happened *before*. How had this beautiful, but fragile, papyrus worth $3,000,000 (disputed), rudely dressed in newspaper, come to be sitting on a hotel bed in Geneva in the first place?

A Voice from the Grave

Grave robbing is now called archaeology when it is authorized by a state or dignified by academe. Of course, advocates of either activity will tell you there are significant differences. Grave robbers violate 'ancient sites' for cash (to feed their families), while archaeologists investigate such sites for the benefit of humanity. Grave robbers don't care about the historical or cultural value of the sites, only the cash in hand value of the choicest artefacts. Archaeologists keep strict records of what they have done – and what they have removed.

Nevertheless, many of the most significant discoveries to the benefit of human knowledge come from violated graves – and if it was *your* grave, would you care who had broken in? *Rest in peace?* You'll be lucky! Of course, many people today probably don't think the dead are in a position to care about anything.

Not infrequently, the medium between archaeology and grave robbing is the antiquities market. While archaeologists can occupy the moral high ground, antiquities dealers sometimes have to get their hands dirty – not *too* dirty, mind you. Most of the dirty work has already been done further down the supply chain. Everyone wants a middleman. Everyone wants to be respectable.

Some time in the middle to late 1970s, a grave was discovered at the foot of the cliffs called the Jebel Qarara. The cliffs were situated across the river from the village of Maghagha (pronounced *Mu-rair-a*), 120 miles down the Nile, south of Cairo, in the province of Al Minya, middle Egypt. It should be borne in mind before we go on that no story of grave robbing can be taken as an objective portrayal of the facts of the case. Those involved are often nameless and the stories change according to circumstances and the audience. Verification of such stories is an inexact science, to say the least. After all, it is understood that what enquirers require is a good credible story – and that means *no one gets into trouble*.

It is fair to say that the likelihood of 'getting to the bottom' of a story is minuscule since the bottom dropped out of the story long before. The process of telling and re-telling means that facts become negotiable: science is for scientists, truth is for sale. The more you pay, the more you get.

In this case, the story goes that a cave was hidden down among rocks at the foot of the Jebel Qarara. A skeleton was found in a shroud. Near to the remains stood a white limestone box. Inside the limestone box were papyrus manuscripts and a leather-bound codex. There were also glass flasks of Roman type. It sounds like a film set, but film sets are based on stories like this, and, presumably, *vice versa*.

Whoever discovered the grave knew that the way to make some money was to contact a local scout, a middleman for the antiquities market. In this case, the middleman – now deceased – shall remain nameless. He was a garlic farmer and a Copt – an Egyptian Christian, whose fellow believers constitute about 15 per cent of the population in this part of the Arab Republic of Egypt.

The Egyptian government is alert to the value of archaeology in Egypt, since tourism is vital to its economy, and tourists are more interested in Egypt's past than its present. The government must think of its future, and so sends wardens out into the field to keep an eye on what might turn up, and who might be responsible.

An additional antiquities law of 1983 gives Egyptian dealers six months to register finds (foreign export is prohibited), then the government may compensate the dealer for the object at a value designed to benefit the state, but not ruin the dealer.

If you are at the bottom of the supply chain, falling into the hands of the law is almost certainly going to be more awkward than if you have the benefits of a more cosmopolitan lifestyle, in Cairo, say. The middleman concerned was not at the bottom of the chain, but he was close. He was the kind of man that Joanna Landis, a modest dealer in folk art based in Alexandria, might seek out when looking for interesting pieces – ancient textiles, for example: the sort of thing that might be found – or even discarded – in old graves.

In 1978, Landis was informed by the garlic-farming middleman of a recent sale of ancient manuscripts. The Copt had done very well out of the deal, for a man in his position. He had bought a car and his family was more comfortable. Initially relaxed about the whole thing, he was delighted to take Landis to a series of catacombs, unknown to the Antiquities Authority or to the world of archaeology. Carved out of the limestone, within the jebel (mountain), were squared pillars supporting a series of burial alcoves. The bones of a skeleton were strewn about the place. Apparently it had been recently visited by less scrupulous grave robbers, the sort who would kill to protect their interest.

The Copt told Landis that the books had been wrapped in newspapers and sold through contacts in the jewellery shops that existed in the provinces and which were linked to bigger dealers in Cairo. He had made 8,000 Egyptian pounds from the deal.

After his death, Joanna Landis pressed the Copt's colleague (called 'Mahmoud' in the printed accounts, but you can take that with a pinch of salt) for more information. These enquiries proved to generate diminishing returns. By the time the colleague had spun his last evasive answer, the find had no longer been made where she was told it had been made. Rather it was miles away and completely inaccessible to foreigners. It was all too dangerous; other interests had become involved. Even natural inquisitiveness and determination failed to secure a definitive account.

And so it has remained to this day. Of course, had the find and its setting been reported to the relevant Egyptian authorities, the story might have been very different. But it would still have been a story, albeit for a different audience. The truth has effectively died with the warm-hearted garlic farmer and his pious colleague of the Coptic Church.

The Cairo Dealer

Another layman of the Coptic Church would become the beneficiary of the discovery – though he would soon come to the conclusion that this particular cache of antiquities brought with it a hideous curse, revocable only by divine intervention.

The plot – and the air – thickens. Enter chain-smoking Hana A Airian, a respectable Cairo antiquities dealer who entertained serious clients in the second floor apartment of his property in Heliopolis. We first met him in a Geneva hotel-room on a rare, discomfiting excursion beyond his native land.

Hana, no expert in papyrology, had become aware of the sales value of papyrus artefacts due to the presence in Cairo in the mid-70s of Ludwig Koenen, manuscript buyer for Michigan University's collection. Another papyrologist, Peter Manfredi, had also given advice to Cairo dealers on how to spot valuable items in the field.

The price of obtaining the good stuff involved simply 'upping' its monetary value. It may have been Manfredi who suggested to Hana a price tag of $3,000,000 for the manuscript collection. One wonders if the suggestion was entirely serious. The seller can, of course, always say that there's 'someone out there' who will pay practically anything for anything. The value of a thing is often expressed in what the buyer paid for it; the only hope for the show-off purchaser is that he does not meet someone who will tell him straight what it is worth – especially in the company of his friends.

For a dealer, the price involves a personal investment. At a certain point in a negotiation, to question the price is to question the judgement of the seller: the bigger the dealer, the bigger the pride. Big dealers expect to get big money. When big dealers sell to big dealers, they both expect to make a profit. At the end of the line, a fool and his money are going to be parted – unless, of course, the client can classify his purchase as an 'investment'. The price goes up, even after the 'final sale'. An antiquity, properly cared for, should have a shelf life of a few more thousand years. The only thing you need is a rich buyer. Socialism will never favour the antiquities market; the cause of 'humanity' comes too cheap.

So, the question now for Hana was: *who had the big money?* Where could he locate the big buyer? Hana did what he always did. *Don't rush; leave it till the right person comes along.* Let the buyer come to him. Trust in Providence.

Providence came, but with a sting in its tail.

Three Dealers

We now introduce a brace of fresh names to this account of the buying game. Hana A Airian had in the past done good business with one of the biggest and cleverest antiquities dealers in the world, Nicolas Koutoulakis, an impressive character with connections in London, Paris and New York, like a fashionable perfume. Originating in Crete, Koutoulakis' highly profitable skills had earned him a beautiful villa on the Rue de Florissant, Geneva and the widespread respect of his peers.

Frieda Tchacos was a young student of Egyptology attending the École du Louvre in Paris when she was invited out for an evening's rich entertainment by the older and more worldly Koutoulakis. This charming glimpse of the good life made its mark on her. To Koutoulakis' surprise, the ingénue would in due course become a friendly competitor, opening her first gallery in Paris, later relocating business to her Nefer Gallery in Zurich. Switzerland will play a large role in this story. Perhaps it's the air.

In Switzerland, Frieda Tchacos married a jeweller, Werner Nussberger, and became Frieda Tchacos Nussberger, a mighty name for one who refers to herself as 'little Frieda', an innocent abroad in a perfidious world. Like Koutoulakis, Frieda knew Hana before he bought the precious Jebel Qarara manuscripts. She had been a business guest and friend of the family at his apartment in Heliopolis. The world may be large but the world of antiquities dealers is very small. Just *how* small we shall now see.

It's a Crime

In March 1980, Hana's varied collection of prize antiquities, gathered unusually in a single location, was stolen. The collection included the barely examined cache of ancient Coptic papyri. First it was stolen from the grave, now from a respectable apartment. One might wonder how its previous, long-deceased owner had acquired it. It has been mooted that the person whose grave was robbed might have been a monk, a mystic, a kind of early Freemason – certainly a devoted reader of manuscripts. But the nearest ruined monastery is two hours' walk from the area where the manuscripts were discovered. Perhaps the ancient Copt had himself been in the codex business – who's to know?.

We must beware of romance in the telling of this story, even if the story itself has become something of a romance. How could it not be so, with characters like those we have briefly met, telling it? It is nonetheless an undeniable fact that Hana's precious collection of textiles, jewellery, gold pieces, statues, glass inlays, Ptolemaic artefacts, Byzantine, Roman and Greek coins, faience amulets – and papyri – was stolen. Who would do such a thing?

It was not unknown for Nicolas Koutoulakis to turn up in Cairo accompanied by two attractive women: one of whom, known as 'Mia', or 'Effie', sometimes 'Fifi', spoke fluent Arabic. Perhaps it was ease of communication that made Hana suggest to her that she might herself sell some of his wares for a commission. Had Koutoulakis known of this, he would have been offended – how dare Hana set up deals using Koutoulakis' own representative when he, Koutoulakis, had always dealt with Hana personally?

'Mia', apparently unbeknownst to Koutoulakis, came back to Hana with an interesting possibility. According to a colleague of one of Hana's relatives, Mia was in touch with some wealthy persons whose yacht was anchored in Alexandria's harbour. They were, according to Mia (if that was indeed her name), interested in anything Hana had got.

The clients duly arrived at the apartment where Hana had assembled his treasures. They noted down everything they found, did not haggle over prices, and expressed an Olympian enthusiasm for everything before their delighted eyes. In point of fact, they were prepared to purchase the entire collection for a very large sum of money indeed. Hana's future was assured, at a stroke.

Imagine Hana's feelings when he discovered, the following day, that his property had been ruthlessly ransacked of every item on the inventory. He could expect little help from the police. None of the stolen items had been registered; there was no paperwork to identify them or their value. He had no legal proof to speak of that they were his property in the first place. The bottom fell clean out of Hana Airian's world.

It is said that Hana retired to a Coptic monastery for six days to recover his sanity. He then employed soothsayers, Coptic magic and prayer to locate the items. The items remained lost. He was angry, convinced that Koutoulakis' Mia was the architect of his professional despoliation. He took to carrying a gun; Hana, a peaceful man, meant business. And still he believed in Providence. Did the Cretan Koutoulakis have a motive for so vexing the Egyptian? Could he have been trying to teach the Cairo dealer a lesson?

The story goes that Hana had previously sold Koutoulakis an ancient Egyptian statue. Koutoulakis then found reason to doubt its provenance; it could be fake. It very likely was a fake. But Hana would not hear of refunding the money; he insisted the statue's provenance was what he had said it was. Hana's intransigence seemed unprofessional and spoiled relations.

Furthermore, there was the issue of Mia. Hana had effectively gone behind Koutoulakis' back in suggesting she bring him clients. She was there primarily for Koutoulakis' advantage, not that of *his* clients.

Could there have been other reasons? The Koutoulakis angle dies without evidence. But the role of Mia seems less doubtful. As Professor James M Robinson has observed, 'Mia' is the feminine of the Greek numeral *one*, and can mean a female *someone*. That is to say, it is not necessarily a name at all. There are, in fact, grave doubts as to Mia's provenance. She seems to have been a fake herself. But who would take her back, and what was she really worth – and to whom?

And what had she to do with the little golden statuette of Isis suckling Horus-Harpocrates that was bought from Koutoulakis' villa five years later? Confused? So was Hana, but he had Providence on his side. Of that he was sure. The provenance of Providence is God, and God knows the secret of every human heart. He knows where all the buried treasure is, and he is, believers believe, prepared to pay the highest price to redeem the lost.

In late 1981, Hana turned to another Greek for help. Yannis (John) Perdios had a pad in Cairo and Perdios was on good terms with Koutoulakis. Perdios met up with the bereft Hana, absorbed the impact of the story and agreed to play middleman with the Cretan giant of the antiquities trade. Koutoulakis confided in Perdios that he thought Mia might have been in on the theft, but that he himself was innocent. The contact led to a tense meeting in Perdios' apartment in Cairo. Hana faced Koutoulakis and a highly fraught Mia. She had brought her daughter, apparently to secure special understanding, if not sympathy. Fretfully asserting her innocence, Mia communicated to Hana that she and Koutoulakis would come to his aid. He was not without friends in the business.

In 1982, Koutoulakis was still phoning around his global contacts to locate the elements of Hana's lost trove. He and Perdios got wind of a necklace that had come into the hands of Dr Jack Ogden, a London gem specialist. Ogden revealed that he had bought a necklace from one 'Effie', a redhead. Effie and Mia seemed to have more than hair colour in common. 'Effie' can be short for the Greek name *Ephthimia* – Joy – or one can shorten the name to its last part: *Mia*.

Ogden was happy to surrender the doubtful goods into the hands of Perdios and Koutoulakis' son, Manolis. In the summer of that year, with New Romantics and old punks swanning about the capitals of Europe, a meeting was held at Koutoulakis' villa in Geneva, watched over by a formidable array of security cameras.

Hana's manuscripts, thanks to detective work by Koutoulakis and Perdios (and Mia), had been recovered. Since the manuscripts had been valued at some $3,000,000, surely Hana would not object to a deal that compensated for the considerable trouble expended on his behalf by Nicolas Koutoulakis. And so it came to pass that a relatively trifling $50,000 worth of other returned goods (including the beautiful, gold statuette of Mother Isis) would remain in his host's care, to his host's profit and satisfaction. Providence had provided. It is interesting to note that Manolis Koutoulakis maintained that relations with 'Effie' were strictly curtailed after this meeting.

And what of the Codex? Perdios suggested to Hana that

(presumably now that the manuscripts were already out of Egypt) it would be best for these items to be secreted in a Swiss bank vault, where no one could rob them again. In Switzerland, they would be safer than the grave.

Perdios' interest in the cache did not end there. While enjoying the Swiss air, he called on Frieda Tchacos Nussberger in Zurich. Could she find a client for the precious merchandise? He gave her some photographs of the manuscripts. This was apparently Frieda's first notice of the texts' existence. She made a few enquiries but was soon distracted by other business. In late 1982, Yannis Perdios decided that confirmation of the texts' authenticity and collectible value might assist a sale. He sent some photographs to Ludwig Koenen, the expert purchaser for the University of Michigan's papyrus collection, whom we last met in a Geneva restaurant in the company of Professor Freedman and Stephen Emmel.

The scholarly gathering in the Geneva hotel in May 1983 came as a result of Perdios' sending photographs of the manuscript to Koenen. And we know how it turned out: a disappointed Hana, a disappointed Koenen, and Emmel's scholarly report of the goods dispatched to Professor James Robinson in California.

Hana Airian put the manuscripts back into the Geneva vault and considered his next move.

New York, New York

It's a hell of a town, and it's the obvious place to shift goods into a realm that combines culture and money in equal, heady doses.

And so, in 1984, Hana braved US customs, carrying the vulnerable papyri wrapped in newspapers, bundled into his hand luggage. He headed for people he could understand and who would understand him; Hana's English was inadequate to clinch a deal by himself.

On West Side Avenue, Jersey City, New Jersey stands the Coptic Orthodox Church of St Mark. There is a sizeable Coptic immigrant community in the area, whose spiritual needs were met at the time by the popular, distinguished Father Gabriel Abdel Sayed. Father Gabriel would accompany Hana to a meeting with the famous rare book and manuscript dealer, Hans P Kraus, at his five-storey head-quarters on East 46th Street in Manhattan.

In order to assure the safety of the merchandise, the two Copts arrived with a coterie of substantially built men, darkly dressed. Looking perhaps like a scene from Martin Scorsese's *Goodfellas*, they made Kraus feel distinctly uncomfortable; he thought he was in the presence of armed bodyguards. Kraus did not care that he was being made an offer he could not refuse. This was not how he liked to conduct business.

Hana heard something said in English between the priest and the king of the New York antiquarian book trade that seemed to kill the deal. Nevertheless, a subsequent meeting was set up to establish the authenticity of the manuscripts. On the morning of 27 March 1984, the somewhat farcical proceedings proceeded. The office of classicist Roger Bagnall, on the sixth floor of Hamilton Hall, Columbia University was the chosen venue. On this occasion, Bagnall thought Hana and his Egyptian partner were the bodyguards! Things did not feel right. Bagnall did not think Father Gabriel was a real priest. The manuscripts, on the other hand, looked genuine enough. Kraus, however, was not convinced by the price. Hana had come down to a cool million for the whole package, but Kraus reckoned restoration costs could add a great deal to the initial investment cost. He may also have had doubts about legality and provenance. He passed on the deal.

Fed up with the lack of progress, suspecting the priest had somehow killed the deal, while aching to get back to his homeland, Hana left the manuscripts in a safety deposit box. There was no point in taking the goods back out of the USA now they had got safely in. Like the sun, the price rose in the East and set in the West.

A deposit box had been set up at Citibank in a strip mall in

Hicksville, Long Island, four days before the Columbia University meeting. The lid was once more shut on the codex; darkness and stale air would envelop its fragile leaves as menacingly as the flames that embraced Rosebud at the climax of *Citizen Kane*.[2]

Sixteen years of disintegration would visit the decaying papyrus fibres in safety deposit box no.395, Hicksville, Long Island. *Hicksville!* Was this farce or tragedy?

The Professor Strikes Back

It should not be thought that Professor James Robinson had lost interest in the elusive texts after having heard from Stephen Emmel in May 1983. He just did not have the money, a cause, doubtless, of great irritation. As far as Robinson could see, the texts had disappeared.

Having now completed his final volume introduction to the facsimile edition of the Nag Hammadi Library, Robinson turned his attention to this tantalizing 'new' material. From Emmel's report, the material clearly belonged in the same orbit as his last 20 years' work: late antique Egyptian Gnosticism. The issue for Robinson was how to lure the owner of the texts back into the open where he might be approached by the right funding source, and the material come under the homely umbrella of his old editorial team.

Robinson's method was low-cost, but was perhaps too low-key. Had he known, of course, that the cache included the long-lost Gospel of Judas, he might have been able to raise significantly more press coverage and, consequently, interest in funding the project. But as things looked at the time, the material was not up there with either the Dead Sea Scrolls[3] or the less well-known (though no less significant) Nag Hammadi Library. Really the material looked only of serious interest to Coptic scholars and historians of religion.

So it was that at the third international Congress of Coptic Studies in Warsaw, Robinson and Stephen Emmel announced the existence of a new papyrus codex. Delegates were informed that the codex contained new versions of the First Apocalypse of James, The Letter from Peter to Philip, and a dialogue of Jesus with his disciples (the one that mentioned a Judas on a number of occasions).

Robinson also alerted Hans-Gebhard Bethge at the Humboldt University, Berlin, to the existence of this alternative version of the Letter from Peter to Philip. Bethge was writing a dissertation on the work, whose readers were now able to observe that a parallel version was 'so far not yet available for scholarly evaluation'. This was something of an understatement. It was slowly rotting in a box in Hicksville.

For all Robinson's careful moves, his method for raising interest in the cache caused no ripples, as far as we know, neither in Cairo, nor Geneva, nor in Yannis Perdios' home in Athens. The trail of the texts went mysteriously cold for the next six years. Robinson realized the only way he was going to get access to the texts was not to rely so much on the academic funding network, but to get face to face with a big buyer. Robinson's efforts in this direction proved fruitful.

Martin Schøyen was a cultured, wealthy Norwegian who possessed one of the world's largest private manuscript collections. Once Robinson had made the connection with Schøyen, in 1990, Perdios found it worthwhile to agree to meeting Robinson at his Athens base. Knowing the manuscripts to be still in New York, Perdios suggested there as the proper place for an encounter with the owner, without giving his reasons why. Robinson intuited that New York was where the manuscripts were located. He left Athens thinking he was at last getting somewhere.

What Robinson did not know, however, was that Perdios and Hana had fallen out. Hana had decided to negotiate with Hans Kraus in New York without Perdios, the man without whom Hana would never have retrieved his precious nest-egg in the first place.

The likelihood of Robinson and Hana being brought together was further frustrated by international developments. President Bush was in open conflict with Saddam Hussein. Feverish speculation in the souks and coffee houses of Cairo had reached such a pitch that Hana was afraid to leave his new family in Cairo lest

World War Three erupt the moment he got on the plane. By 1992, Robinson had found additional backers to rescue the texts from obscurity. Again he tried Perdios. Perdios said he would contact the owner, but he never did. Robinson tried yet again five years later when he was back in Europe teaching in Germany. He suggested a meeting between the owner and the Norwegian collector Schøyen. This time Hana was interested. Even a workable price had been suggested, yet for some reason the encounter never materialized.

Schøyen did not need Robinson in order to view the manuscripts. He had deep inside knowledge of the dealers' world, a world to which Professor Robinson was an outsider, even a supplicant. A few years later, the Norwegian collector would obtain leaves of the biblical texts contained in the Jebel Qarara cache through contacts of his own. The dealing process undoubtedly exasperated the biblical scholar in California. This time Robinson had the money, but where was the owner?

Enter Frieda Tchacos Nussberger (Again)

In the Spring of 2006, National Geographic published Herbert Krosney's *The Lost Gospel* [4] – an account of the provenance of The Gospel of Judas and its significance for Christians, Western culture, and National Geographic. In some respects, the book constitutes an amusing vindication of the saving role of Frieda Tchacos Nussberger in the affair of this 'lost gospel'.

However, with (at least) two knights hunting for the Holy Grail, things can get complicated. Who was going to save The Gospel of Judas – the scholar Robinson, or the dealer, Frieda? We kind of know the answer, because the codex is now called the *Codex Tchacos*, which is a bit like landing on the moon and signing it. Like Galahad in *Parzifal* [5], Robinson is presented as having some curious fatal flaw that prevents him reaching the prize. Was it the case that, like the magician Clinschor in this romance, he just *didn't have the balls*? Frankly, the dealers ran rings round him.

From Krosney's text, we learn that in 1999 a Greek telephoned Frieda and offered photographs of portions of manuscript. To establish their authenticity she sent the photographs to Robert Babcock, curator of the Beinecke Library at Yale University. He recognized them as being parts of a cache examined by the experts from Michigan in a Geneva hotel back in 1983. Frieda in turn remembered the visit of Perdios to Switzerland in the summer of 1982, when the Greek middleman had suggested she find a client for Hana's manuscripts after their owner had recovered them at Koutoulakis' villa. Time had not dulled Frieda's initial vague interest in the manuscripts. For some reason, possibly supernatural, she was intrigued to know more. She decided to follow up the phone call with a meeting.

Frieda met up with the dealers. She did not like them; her usual clients had class. These men looked like opportunists. They wanted $100,000 for the papyrus leaves. She was having none of it. She had $25,000, take it or leave it. Being the kind of people they were – as the story goes – they took it. Frieda took the isolated sheets from Hana's collection and placed them in a vault. But who had taken these leaves from the collection? Could it have been Perdios? No, it must have been Mia; she must have retained objects from the 1980 robbery.

Close inspection of the photographs Frieda had sent to Yale backed up the supposition. Newspapers behind the leaves were from Greece, dated October 1982, the time shortly after Hana had recovered (most of) his manuscripts. Frieda subsequently discovered that one of the dealers she had just paid was Mia's boyfriend. QED. Now Frieda wanted the rest of the collection.

She went to Egypt to celebrate the new millennium. There she met up with her old friend Hana Airian. He had the key; she had the money. Perhaps tired of the longstanding psychological burden that possession of the manuscripts entailed, or perhaps in honour of this historic marker in the Christian calendar, Hana succumbed to Frieda's negotiating skills. Where everyone else had failed, she succeeded in buying the rest of the collection for a figure in the hundreds of thousands. Now all she had to do was to get hold of the goods themselves.

For this, she would need to get Hana back to New York. He was unwilling to leave Cairo unaccompanied. She said there was no way she would go to Cairo first and pick him up. Frieda contacted Hana's wife, urging her not to let her husband miss out on this great opportunity for the sake of a little anxiety. Two women's collective will is enough to move most men off their perch. Hana was no exception.

Arriving in New York City on 3 April 2000, Hana drove to Hicksville with Frieda's sister Deda and husband Alec's daughter Sybil, while Frieda waited at the Stanhope Hotel, Fifth Avenue. Armed with a large cardboard box, the party arrived at Citibank, Hicksville. Hana had his old receipt but the locks had been changed. The bank asked if they could return later while the problem was sorted out? *No way*. It would cost over $100 to call out the locksmith on the spot. But what was a hundred bucks when the future of religion was in your hands? Unfortunately, on opening the box, there was no orchestral fanfare of global significance – only an unpleasant odour. The manuscripts were in a pitiable condition. The baby was still alive, so to speak, but would need intensive care and a new, loving mother.

Frieda Tchacos Nussberger also believed in the guiding hand of Providence; perhaps such a belief is a requirement of antiquities dealing, for despite all the hard salesmanship, there was often a touching faith too.

Frieda officially bought the manuscripts on 4 April 2000. Taking her new charge straight to the Beinecke Rare Book and Manuscript Library, Yale, she left the manuscripts with 'foster parent' Robert Babcock (who, of course, had seen the photos of the missing leaves), and offered sale to Yale at a very modest price. Yale had the where-withal, which Frieda did not, to restore the manuscripts and raise the tattered pages to the lights of science.

A few days later, Frieda's faith was justified by ecstatic news from Babcock. Those sad, miserable, uncared-for manuscripts contained nothing less than *The Gospel of Judas Iscariot*! The rewards of faith should shortly be forthcoming. And lo, soon there were more magi at the cradle! Coptologist and Nag Hammadi team editor Bentley Layton backed up Babcock's judgement. This judgement in turn was supported by another old colleague of James Robinson, Harold Attridge, a Yale professor. Now, where was the restorative frankincense, the preservative myrrh – and, above all, the revivifying gold?

On August 21, Frieda received a report from experts at Yale. This was no ordinary baby. She possessed unique versions of the Letter of Peter to Philip, an Apocalypse of James and, 'totally unknown to the modern world', The Gospel of Judas. She was assured that these works were comparable in importance to the astonishing Nag Hammadi Library. She had indeed struck gold!

At or around this time, the figure of Judas Iscariot seemed to come alive in Frieda's mind, in conjunction with a certain sense of destiny. So she tells us, and so we must believe, for our deepest convictions cannot be questioned. Without them, what do we have? If we cannot believe our deepest convictions, then we can believe nothing. Judas had been misunderstood; he was crying out for understanding, dignity, rehabilitation. He was tearing himself from the very fibres of his own gospel. Judas somehow needed to 'move on'. Perhaps he should become the patron saint of antiquities dealers, for when he sold his merchandise for 30 pieces of silver, did he not refuse his commission, even as he was commissioned? His motive was no fakery, his claim was genuine, his provenance good. His were not the values of the mere gallery of life; he served a *Higher Power*!

Alas, the higher powers at Yale were blind to their opportunity. They would not make an offer for the manuscripts. Their provenance was uncertain. Could Frieda's entitlement to possession of the manuscripts be upheld in law? Yale's reputation, befitting its status in the Ivy League, must be squeaky clean, unimpeachable, pure as the driven snow of a New England winter. Curiously, in spite of being out of pocket and personally unable to bear the restoration costs and long-term responsibilities of possessing the manuscripts, Frieda does not appear to have approached the associate editors of the Nag Hammadi Library who had examined her property. They would surely have led her to James Robinson, who, we must believe, would not have tarried in his enthusiasm for obtaining the collection.

No, on picking up her cardboard boxes from Yale, Frieda modestly claims to have made one of the biggest mistakes of her life, for which she blames only herself. Perhaps it was the sheer weight of responsibility – a world treasure in her personal care, deteriorating every second – that made her do what she did. Time was running out. She had to get *Judas* to a safe port. After all, one might conclude, the Good Samaritan did not take the battered victim of robbery home for life, rather he was left in the care of the nearest well-stocked hostelry.

Nemo to the Rescue

In June 2000, a London-based antiquities dealer, Bill Veres, visited Frieda in Zurich. He told her about one Bruce Ferrini. Bruce, from the Midwest, had been obtaining antiquities for James Ferrell, Chief Executive Officer of *Ferrellgas* in Liberty, Missouri – a global combatant in propane gas provision. Ferrell seemed the man to buy the Jebel Qarara cache. But he was not the only client Ferrini had in mind. Ferrini had mentioned the name Bill Gates, a veritable *open sesame* of fiscal excitements. Gates was mentioned as being, in some undefined manner, linked to Ferrini's business activities. Then again, so long as most of us employ *Windows*, I guess we're all linked to Bill Gates' business interests too. But Ferrini had other cards up his sleeve.

Having collected the cardboard boxes from Yale, Freida headed for a New York plane to take her to Cleveland, Ohio, where she would meet Bruce Ferrini, the one-time opera singer, culture enthusiast and now antiquities dealer to boardroom America.

A bad omen. The airline would not permit Freida to carry the boxes with her. As indignity mounted indignity, the papyri were loaded into the plane's baggage compartment – hardly the controlled conditions required by such tender artefacts.

If first impressions count, Freida's one of Bruce was that he was not the man for the job. If I understand her account correctly, she thought he possessed the kind of swagger better suited to selling shares in a Florida hotel complex than handling the world's most precious documents and dealing with folks who expected a cool coating of class and conversational finesse. And he looked like an American football player. Poor Bruce. Nothing he said – and he was voluminously enthusiastic about ... well, everything – could break down Frieda's feelings of foreboding. Even Ferrini's company name failed to impress. It was called *Nemo* – that is *Nobody* (in Latin). How apt, she thought.

And yet, she went through with the deal. As she said, it was the biggest mistake of her life. On the other hand, the deal would bring with it certain advantages. Frieda had decided to revive Hana's old notion that the manuscripts should raise over two million bucks, especially now it was known they contained what must surely be the world-shattering revelation of Judas Iscariot. Judas would have them queuing round the block. This was a transgressive age, and Judas was nothing if not a transgressor. Or was he?

Ferrini, for his part, seemed to have ideas of his own. On 9 September 2000, he gave Frieda two post-dated cheques, each for £1.25 million. This was, of course, because he expected to sell on the works very quickly. One was dated January, the other February 2001. Anyhow, he had got the stuff, and so far it had not cost him anything.

Another mistake. In spite of feeling foreboding, and with only the promise of a vast profit to show for her efforts, Frieda did not demand that their contract stipulate the retention of her title to the goods until she secured payment. It is tempting to think of a lamb to the slaughter, but somehow the image does not seem to fit. Perhaps it was just the mysterious workings of Providence, providing, in this case, for Bruce Ferrini.

In retrospect, it is difficult to know which was the bigger mistake: dealing with Bruce in the first place, or overestimating his ability – or willingness – to pay. Nevertheless, it may be to the recently bankrupted Bruce that we owe the brilliant idea of commercializing the whole Judas project. Yes, *get that word*. It was a *project*.

Flogging Judas

The decaying manuscript was to be groomed for stardom. Judas was going to get the full treatment. Bruce drew up ambitious project directives. There would be an expansive programme including a 'Team to Sensationalize and Romanticize: Process of Discovery, Recovery, Translation and Dissemination', using expensive photography, translation, preservation, prestigious book cataloguing, public exhibition and exploitation through film. This marketing exercise was to be headed by Ferrini himself, along with one Dorothy Shinn, art and architecture critic for the local *Akron Beacon Journal*. That's Akron, Ohio, folks.

Amazingly, things started to go wrong almost immediately. Ferrini had become aware of Martin Schøyen's continued interest in the manuscripts and alerted the Norwegian collector to their new whereabouts. Only two days after making the deal with Frieda, Ferrini was contacted by Schøyen with an appraisal of the kind of price he was willing to pay. He based his pricing on a suggestion from Hana which in turn reflected a proposed meeting with James Robinson – one which, as we know, never took place.

This figure of Hana's Schøyen referred to in his communication with Ferrini. It must have dulled his enthusiasm somewhat.

Whatever Ferrini had agreed to pay for the manuscripts, the only kind of figure the Norwegian was interested in was that suggested by the their previous owner. The figure was $986,000. One can only wonder what Bruce thought of Frieda at that moment. Had the diminutive Freida Tchacos Nussberger 'got one over on him'?

If that morsel of news was not chastening enough, the next arrival on Bruce's doorstep really set the cat among the pigeons. Ferrini had been looking forward to a 'good meeting' with James Ferrell, human gateway to lucrative antiquities deals with the Midwestern plutocracy. Indeed, Ferrini had got into a business association with Bill Veres of London to maximize the profit potential from antiquities dealing. That is why Veres had recommended Ferrini to Frieda Tchacos Nussberger. All roads lead to cash.

Ferrell duly arrived, but not with a cheque to patronize the Judas project. Ferrell was accompanied by his financial advisor who brought some accounting anomalies to Ferrini's, no doubt astonished, attention. Ferrell was not satisfied that monies paid were going where he had thought they were going. Ferrell was not satisfied. Court action followed.

Meanwhile, things were looking pretty grim for the manuscripts too. It seems Ferrini had some pretty original ideas about the best way to preserve ancient manuscripts. He had approved their being placed in a deep freeze. This procedure, he said later, resulted in no harm to the manuscripts and would enable the pages of the codex to be separated. Why did Bruce want to separate the pages? We shall see.

Of course, deep freezing The Gospel of Judas and the other documents was, to say the least, a very bad idea. The process of freezing brought moisture from the depth of the papyrus fibres. The result was that the papyri turned, one might say generously, *blackish*, and the ink that gave them their interest value was thus contaminated, rendering the texts even harder to read, and at the same time hastening their degeneration. Bruce really was the kind of guy you would want entrusted with the world's treasures.

Alarm bells began (at last) to ring in Frieda's mind. Judas was calling her again. He was losing his sparkle. He had to be saved. She realized that the chances of redeeming cheque value from Ferrini were remote, and yet he still had the manuscripts. Worse than that, he was trying to sell them without having paid for them. In the words of a lawyer whom we are just about to meet, this behaviour was characteristic of a thief and embezzler – and lawyers should know. Poor Bruce. Poor Frieda!

On 15 September 2000, a perturbed Freida discussed the matter with her Swiss lawyer, Mario Roberty. Roberty got the picture straight away. The manuscripts must be recovered. It was not going to be easy. The contract was a bummer. As they say, possession is nine-tenths of the law. Frieda was in Switzerland. The manuscripts were ... in the deep freeze.

Dealing with the Dealer

Mario Roberty now became a major player in the fight for possession of the baby. In the process, the baby, perversely echoing Solomon's famous judgement, would literally be pulled apart.

A meeting was arranged between Roberty, Ferrini and Ferrini's New York lawyer, Eric Kaufmann. Kaufmann was clever. He saw the issue of provenance as the Achilles' heel in Frieda's case. Did she have the right to own the documents? Had they not come out of Egypt? What might be the position as regards Egyptian law? And how had they been brought into the United States in the first place?

This issue added new pressure. It is not surprising that Roberty's memorandum of the discussion insisted on 'utmost secrecy' being observed by everyone involved. Ferrini could really screw things up if he was pushed too far. Handled correctly, on the other hand, there was profit to be gained from the sensational nature of the material – profit, cultural and fiscal, for all concerned.

Roberty tried to get Ferrini interested in a cultural foundation to promote the codex. Its aim would be to make a decent profit (to reimburse the considerable amount of private money already spent, and more) and to bring the remarkable documents to the safe zone of pure culture – before they might, advisedly, have to be returned to Egypt. The concept went under the name of 'The Logos Project'.

How history repeats itself! Back in 1982, I launched plans to make a film series about the Gnostic gospels and subsequent Gnostic tradition. We called the initial company *Logos*. In the beginning was the Word, indeed! We were lucky, of course. In our case, the precious manuscripts were already back in Egypt, and their contents had been revealed to all who wished to read them, thanks to the efforts of Professor James Robinson and his team of editors.

By mid-January 2001, there seemed to be an understanding reached by which Ferrini would return the manuscripts, except for the mathematical treatise and the Pauline epistles. The garments were being divided. The post-dated cheques Ferrini had given to Frieda were rendered void. While Ferrini was expected to pay Frieda $300,000 for the manuscripts he retained, the decision to divide what was in fact an integral collection hardly set Ferrini a good example. The varied character of the collection is in fact one of the most interesting things about the Jebel Qarara discovery. What kind of person would hold together such a collection? What does it tell us about the mentality and culture of the deceased?

If Ferrini's division of the collection could be tolerated (presumably as a sweetener), why not remove the odd page or two of the codex as well? Ancient papyrus could be sold by the page. Business is business. And this was business.

Not surprisingly, Ferrini stalled on returning the manuscripts. He wished to pursue other avenues for paying off his mounting debts. Ferrini's declining finances made him vulnerable and Roberty saw a way of piling pressure on the troubled and troublesome dealer. It was, however, a risky strategy. Time was running out. The tick was becoming audible.

Blogging for Judas

Michel van Rijn, a self-appointed moral watchdog hailing from the Netherlands, set up a website to report on nefarious activities in the arts and antiquities trade. Roberty contacted van Rijn. This story was right up his sarcastic alley. Van Rijn would ruffle Bruce's feathers like no other could.

In an email of 5 February 2001, Roberty thanked the internet blogger for his work on Ferrini. This 'greedy' and 'maniac dealer' was standing in the way of a humanitarian foundation for 'parts of our history'. It should have been obvious that anyone who could turn on the venom so quickly against someone he had never met was either a mischievous journalist or a very loose cannon. Van Rijn got the bit between his teeth and unfortunately started releasing information unhelpful to Roberty's negotiations with Kaufmann.

On the other hand, van Rijn also furnished Roberty with information. For example, Roberty emailed van Rijn on 6 February, remarking on titbits about one of James Robinson's contributing editors to 'his' *Nag Hammadi Library in English*.[6]

Apparently, this editor, Charles Hedrick, had received from Ferrini 164 low-calibre digital photos from which Hedrick had been able to identify the name 'James' from the (first) Apocalypse of James, and the title of the Letter of Peter to Philip. The disclosure of this information seriously discomfited Roberty's plans both to profit from the manuscripts and to facilitate their first appearance (since Roman times) on the great stage of the world. What if Hedrick were to make the text available to, well, just about *anyone*?

Apparently, Roberty had heard something about Hedrick and the texts. Hedrick was now Professor Emeritus of Religious Studies at Missouri State University. His PhD thesis had been tutored by James Robinson. True to his calling, and the good example of Robinson, Hedrick passed on his material, including translations, to his circle of contributing editor colleagues on Nag Hammadi: Birger

A Pearson, Douglas M Parrott, Hans-Gebhard Bethge, John D Turner, Wolf-Peter Frank – and James M Robinson.

In Robinson's own account of what he calls 'the peddling of the Gospel of Judas'[7] Robinson laments that similar co-operation was not forthcoming from those 'who have a monopoly on it!'. Hedrick published reports of his photographs in 2002 and 2003 in those journals of note, *Bible Review* and the *Journal of Early Christian Studies*. Hedrick gave clear notice that The Gospel of Judas was now available on the antiquities market. Now pressure was building on Roberty. It was going to be difficult to maintain the 'utmost secrecy', especially with Michel van Rijn's website spilling the beans.

On 8 February 2001, van Rijn's insinuations led Kaufmann to complain to Roberty that both his client's reputation and income were being adversely affected. He spoke of 'injury' to his client. Negotiations with Ferrini, difficult enough already, were being muddied. Roberty tried to get van Rijn to tone it down, but he was enjoying himself too much; he had found a cause. Roberty was merely part of the fabric.

By the end of the second week in February, a deal was finalized with Ferrini. Ferrini would now only retain the mathematical treatise, for which he would pay $100,000. Recovery of the manuscripts took place on 16 February 2001. Frieda attended. Since she had not photographed the collection when it was in her possession, she had no way of knowing that the fragmentary items displayed on Ferrini's dining table in Akron, Ohio, constituted the entire collection. Yet, she would have to sign a document indicating her satisfaction that her items had in fact been returned, if not entirely in the same condition in which they had been delivered the previous September.

Through the unpleasantness of the occasion – Ferrini's celebratory champagne was 'warm and tasted sour' – Frieda could nonetheless glimpse the outlines of Providence: 'Judas didn't want to let me go. He was holding on to me and torturing me.' Frieda's romanticism came once more to the surface. 'Judas chose me to rehabilitate him. He was leading me, pulling the strings to put me on the right path. But the unworldly forces which had kept him in the dark for thousands of years were fighting his restitution.' She had a friend in Judas. He was leading Frieda 'through the labyrinth to the final salvation'.

Yes, the end was in sight. Roberty made an agreement with Frieda that the works should come fully into the embrace of the law. That is to say that Freida would turn the collection over to a responsible foundation. In fact, Roberty had one ready-made for the purpose: his own creation, the *Maecenas Foundation for Ancient Art*, named after an ancient patron of culture. The idea was that the foundation would generously return the manuscripts to Egypt after restoration and publication.

The thorny issue of provenance, like the 'higher power' in Shakespeare's *Romeo and Juliet*, 'hath thwarted our intents'. Such could have been the cry from Frieda and Roberty! Provenance was the snake in the grass, the undoing of one kind of deal and the beginning of another. As Professor James Robinson sees it: 'The fact that the manuscript could not be sold for a profit, but rather has to be returned to Egypt, made the commercialization of the contents of The Gospel of Judas the chosen path to riches.'

The issue of provenance was bound to come to the surface. For example, Hedrick observed how Ferrini maintained to him that he, Bruce Ferrini, had paid for the codex, but when the issue of provenance came up, he 'called his money back in' and returned it to the seller. To give his story an extra bit of spice – and self-justification – he then added a shocking detail, whether true or not, readers may judge. According to Hedrick, when Ferrini returned the codex to the seller, the person he dealt with slammed it on the table. Fragments of papyrus flew about the room, whereupon adding insult-to-culture to injury-to-codex, the seller gathered up the papyri in a strop, saying 'Maybe I will just burn it.'

This does not seem credible to me and I am sure it would not stand up in court. Charles Hedrick made the point that, 'The person who slammed the book on the table was not Frieda, but no names were used.' I am not surprised. In trying to do himself a favour and extricate himself from impending ruin, Ferrini sold the mathematical treatise in two parts to different buyers. According to classicist and papyrologist Roger Bagnall at Columbia University (who in 1984, you will recall, asserted somewhat nervously in the presence of Hana that the manuscripts were authentic), this act was scandalous. Bagnall had hoped to publish the complete text in 2008, only to find the portion allotted to him for scholarly assessment was not complete. But the collection should never have been divided up in the first place.

Just how important was the connection between the texts was illustrated in 2005 when Bagnall found a tiny reference on the mathematical treatise to *Pagus 6*.

Jane Rowlandson's *Landowners and Tenants in Ancient Egypt: The Social Relations of Agriculture in the Oxyrhynchite Nome*[8] shows us precisely what *Pagus 6* meant. *Pagus 6* was a strip of land designated thus for Roman administration. It stretched from the area around Oxyrhynchus towards Maghagha – the very area where the manuscript cache was allegedly discovered. This vital fact enables us to date fairly accurately the treatise and gives us a good idea of the general dating of the assembly or writing of the texts. This is because we know that *Pagus 6* replaced earlier administrative divisions in either AD 307 or 308. The cache should be seen as a whole.

It was not only the mathematical treatise that had been broken up. Frieda soon discovered, after the texts were returned to her from Ferrini's care, that pages and fragments both from The Gospel of Judas, and other texts in the collection, had disappeared.

In March 2001 another papyrologist who had seen the codex earlier (presumably during its brief sojourn at Yale) found that four or five pages from the Letter of Peter to Philip and the Apocalypse of James had gone missing. In January 2006, surviving parts of two pages from The Gospel of Judas reappeared. A New York collector had received them from Ferrini, that is, after he had returned the collection to Frieda. It was pointless bringing Ferrini before the law over the issue. He had filed for bankruptcy in an Ohio court in September 2005.

Old Scores

These episodes are by no means the most shameful in this cautionary tale. One might have thought that on recovering at least the greater part of the collection, Frieda – or Roberty – would have made haste to contact Professor Robinson. Robinson is not only the world's leading name in Egyptian Gnostic literature, but he is also a very well-known, highly effective organizer of editorial strategies regarding public and scholarly access to this special kind of material. Robinson has the best track record in the business, and he has earned it. As they say, 'a tree is known by its fruits.' Robinson has opened the Gnostic world to the world. That he has trodden on some scholars' toes in the process should only serve to remind us, the public, that often otherwise good and respectable people stand in the way of progress through the inevitably narrow focus of their personal interests.

Yes, one might have thought Frieda and Roberty would make haste to contact Professor Robinson – a man who had spent years trying to gain access to the texts, and funding for them. One would think so, if, that is, the chief motive of the players had been to enable, for the sake of human knowledge alone, the swiftest publication of the texts.

Robinson had long since established as a demonstrably good and effective principle that new discoveries with a broad potential of scholarly and public interest should be published quickly in their original language, so all scholars would have a chance to work on them. Working translations should then swiftly be made available to non-specialists. The possibilities of the internet have made this dissemination process even easier and considerably more immediate.

There really is no excuse for keeping copies of important new material under lock and key, as if they were state secrets.

It is perfectly clear that while Frieda and Roberty have shown themselves to be anything but blind to the requirements of education and enlightenment, the need to garner a return on their financial investment was equally motivational. In order to maximize returns, it was deemed necessary to control strictly the whole process.

However, the process resulted in the subtle tarnishing of a distinguished and innocent man's reputation. It is, in fact, fairly obvious to me why James Robinson was excluded from the programme of restoration, translation and dissemination. Not only had he been effectively a competing purchaser of the manuscripts – Frieda succeeded with Hana where Robinson had 'failed' – he also had a powerful, pervasive reputation as one who would not tolerate the monopolizing of texts. Was Robinson perceived to be a 'problem'?

Robinson's influential and controversial paper, *The Jung Codex: The Rise and Fall of a Monopoly,*[9] published in 1977, makes his determination to break scholarly monopolies clear. The professor had previous experience of one of the most scandalous situations known in history regarding ancient Coptic texts. He demonstrated what could happen to a discovery of global significance when its contents fell among coteries of competing scholars and private interests.

To be sure, Robinson has sprung to his own defence and that of the principles he has espoused. His book *The Secrets of Judas*[10] was published by Harper San Francisco in 2006 to coincide with the 'official' publication of *The Judas Gospel*, funded by the National Geographic Society and controlled by National Geographic's deal with Roberty. Robinson's book makes his stance clear from the beginning:

> The Gospel of Judas, a long-lost second-century fictional account that elevates Judas to hero status in the story, has been rediscovered! But it has been kept under wraps until now, to maximize its financial gain for its Swiss owners.

The grand exposé is being performed by the National Geographic Society, timed for the greatest public impact, right at Easter. Those on the inside have been bought off (no doubt with considerably more than 30 pieces of silver), and sworn to silence on a stack of Bibles – or a stack of papyrus leaves.

My narrative is not expurgated, sanitized, cleaned up to make it an appetizing story, and you have a right to know what has gone on.

Unfortunately perhaps, the power of the professor's first broadside is somewhat weakened by his book's heavy dependence on Swiss and German newspaper reports, and upon the eccentrically expressed 'revelations' to be found on van Rijn's website (on which, more later). But this was doubtless a result of the professor's having been kept outside of the walls of 'what has gone on'. He is not an investigative journalist and has had to build his edifice from what scraps have become available to him – the story of his life, perhaps. Had Robinson seen the text of Herbert Krosney's *The Lost Gospel* (2006),[11] he would have found considerably more ammunition for his outrage at the fate of the Jebel Qarara discovery.

Krosney's account – in all innocence for all I know – lays quite a lot of stress on establishing a motive for what is, effectively, an underlying dispute between Robinson and the Maecenas Foundation. It would appear that Robinson's motive is called into question as a means of deflecting any criticism Robinson might wish to make about the motives of Frieda Tchacos Nussberger and Mario Roberty. Krosney's well-researched narrative reads in parts like a legal submission. Robinson's motive for disapproval is shown to be a severe case of sour grapes, and his professional judgement is subtly called into question several times, with gathering potency.

Readers unfamiliar with Robinson's work and reputation would probably not notice the number of insinuations that occur throughout a text which, one would have thought, was intended to be something of a glorious celebration of the finding and eventual revelation of the 'lost gospel', intended for the broadest possible public.

The subtitle of the book is *The Quest for the Gospel of Judas Iscariot*. *Whose* quest is not made clear, but there is no doubt that Frieda Tchacos Nussberger is presented as a heroine, albeit fallible and reassuringly human, but nonetheless guided by a supernatural or spiritual light – if not by the mysterious being of Judas himself.

Robinson, on the other hand, is presented as a spoiler, and in some ways as a *naïf*, lost in the hard, real world of professional dealers. He is an 'ivory tower' kind of guy but ambitious, and that is the problem. He does not know when to shut up. Let's have a look at what I am getting at.

On page 156 of Krosney's book we learn that 'He [Robinson] wanted that *editio princeps* [first edition], which he maintains is the principal scholarly achievement worth pursuing when it comes to ancient manuscripts, and the prestige that it would bring.' This is a clear statement that Robinson wanted supreme credit for bringing The Gospel of Judas to the world.

In the list of contributors to the English translation of the Nag Hammadi Library (1977), Robinson is one of 32 scholars listed (in alphabetical order), while the Managing Editor's name is given as Marvin W Meyer. This all seems reasonably democratic, courteous and fair to me. Robinson was the acknowledged head of the Committee of UNESCO and Egyptian Antiquities Organization charged with publishing the Nag Hammadi Library. At no point has Robinson made sole claim to this particular *editio princeps*. On the contrary, he puts himself over as the member of a team, whose names appear next to each work in the Nag Hammadi Library.

So where does all this opposition to Robinson come from? It has long been established that Robinson has been motivated by nothing less and nothing more than a powerful desire to see the Coptic Gnostic inheritance made widely available. If he has gained personal satisfaction from that process, then good luck to him. He has succeeded – until, that is, this late outbreak of Gnostic textual fever.

On page 246 of Krosney's text, the author states Robinson's well-known policy on the matter of textual availability – that nothing should be kept private or be monopolized by individual scholars. Krosney then makes a statement that seems motivated by some unaccountable sourness, the source of which is not apparent: 'Since he [Robinson] did not qualify as a Coptic translator, it was easy enough for him to advocate a free-for-all on publication and translation matters.' A 'free-for-all on publication' – who would think in these terms? '... Easy enough for him ...', '... did not qualify as a Coptic translator' – Who is setting the admissions standard here? There is something in this statement resembling a slander, and its roots seem to go back to an earlier, fairly muted section of Krosney's account.

Again, the general public may not be well versed in the stakes involved, and goodness knows, there is no particular reason why the public, to whom Krosney's book is addressed, should even be interested in this veiled dispute, but for some reason it is there in the text. Robinson 'did not qualify as a Coptic translator'. He is primarily a theologian and historian of religion. Whose gripe is being voiced here? This is the gripe of a Coptic translator.

When Robinson first got involved in Gnostic scholarship in 1966, over 20 years after the discovery of the Gnostic gospels, the Nag Hammadi Library had been distributed to a number of scholars. A few of the ancient works had been translated and published, notably The Gospel of Thomas. Extracts had appeared in other works, notably by French writer and scholar, Jean Doresse. As an historian of religion, Robinson was anxious, as were many others in the same field, to learn what the whole collection had to say.

In order to gain an overall understanding, Robinson would have to jump over the work of scholars who were looking forward to the eventual publication of their translations and notes. *These* are the chaps who know that the *editio princeps* of a new text is the holy grail of academic scholarship and peer-group status.

Since Robinson encountered resistance to calling time on the amazingly long study period, Robinson decided to go to the source. He went to the place where the original papyrus codices were stored: the Coptic Museum in Cairo. Under his wing, he took the young graduate, Stephen Emmel – one of the first scholars to get a look at The Gospel of Judas – even though he did not realize in 1983 that that is what it was.

Krosney, you might say, gives us the 'other guy's' point of view. What happened to the poor Coptic scholar who had slaved for days and nights over a text in the hope that a shining name might glow at the end of the long tunnel – only to find his work gathered up and published independently of his control, by *an American*, a late-comer – not even a virtuoso in Coptic?

Krosney writes: 'In what could be interpreted as a self-serving stance, Robinson's view was that the text materials in the original language should be published through the UNESCO committee on the project, of which he happened to be secretary. He decided to attack what he called "academic fiefdoms and monopolies" in order to give all scholars, not just those working on particular sections, the right to inspect and translate the text.' ... *of which he happened to be secretary* ... ? ... *self-serving stance*? Yes, the caveats are there. I mean it is all *arguable*, but so are the insinuations. Whom does this argument serve?

On the rights to translate, Krosney seems to imply that the academic culture in Europe is different to elsewhere, that somehow Robinson did not respect the time-honoured practices of those with whom he was dealing. Again, what could be the source of such a peculiar point of view – especially in a popular work?

The alleged 'rights' are simply common conventions and are generally and politely observed. The legal value of polite conventions is questionable, to say the least. By and large in academe, people do not like treading on other people's toes, though it happens often enough. However, let's not pussy-foot here. In the case we are talking about, these 'rights' had been enjoyed – or even exploited – by scholars for *decades*! Let's be clear about this. The Nag

Hammadi Library was discovered by Muhammad Ali al-Samman near al Qasr, Egypt in the December of 1945. The collection only reached non-specialist readers – and that was done thanks chiefly to Robinson – in *1977*!

This incredible delay was a scandal. Its absurdity cannot reasonably be defended on the basis that the breaking of a scholarly 'monopoly' might upset some individual scholars. It was an outright scandal, no less than that. And what do we find in the case of the Jebel Qarara discovery? Found 'some time in the late 70s' and published in 2006. Of course, Robinson was interested in what had happened – and so are we!

Things now start to get nasty. *What?* You thought things were already getting nasty? Fasten your seatbelts. Let's have another look in the ivory tower.

Robinson's very full account of his investigations into the provenance of the Nag Hammadi Coptic Gnostic Library occupied the final volume of his facsimile edition series, which included photographs of the individual pages and thorough notes and annotations. That work took Robinson's team until the mid-1980s to complete.

One of the scholars, a brilliant Coptologist, whose work on the so-called Jung Codex had to some extent run into conflict with Robinson's efforts to publish the entire corpus, disagreed with Robinson's account of the provenance of the Nag Hammadi Library. His name is Rodolphe Kasser. Kasser thought that parts of Robinson's account differed, at the expense of truth, from that of an older account by French scholar Jean Doresse. Kasser was angry that Robinson took no note of Doresse's interpretation of the eyewitness accounts the Frenchman found 'on the ground' in Egypt when Robinson came to finalize his definitive account.

Robinson had spent a lot of time meeting people in the vicinity of the discovery, and had built up a comprehensive picture, with detailed photographs and anecdotal support. It was too detailed for Kasser. In his view the people of the region cannot be trusted or expected to tell the truth accurately in such matters. There is money in the story and personal advantage counts most in communicating with foreigners. Their memories of such distant events must also be regarded as unreliable. Kasser was contemptuous of the younger man who had rocked the boat: 'At the end of several months, he [Robinson] had his history, a true novel ...'

Just out of interest, I can say that when the team of which I was a part made the TV documentary series *Gnostics* in 1986, we bumped into Muhammad Ali al-Samman in a street in al Qasr. He was happy enough to talk about what happened but it did not bother him much. He remembered the events vividly for they were linked to a spell in prison for having killed his father's murderer in a local blood feud. He did not seem the kind of man who cared what other people thought of what he said. He had no vested interest in the matter, they were just a few old books. He had been paid 11 Egyptian pounds for the codices and that was the end of the matter as far as he was concerned.

Muhammad Ali al-Samman's account confirmed Robinson's version, which was also accepted by leading Gnostic scholar, the late Professor Gilles Quispel, who was glad to have the opportunity to shake the hand of the man who had found what was later called the Jung Codex (Quispel joined the TV team in Egypt). Quispel it was, incidentally, who took the codex to the psychologist Carl Jung himself in Switzerland. 'All my life,' Jung said to Quispel when he was presented with the text, 'all my life I have been seeking for the secrets of the psyche, and these people [the Gnostics] knew already.' High praise from Jung, one of the two most important psychologists of the 20th century. Hence the manuscripts discovered at Nag Hammadi were named the *Jung Codex*.

Maybe Kasser had good reasons to doubt the man who found the collection, and whose memory of the time seemed good enough, but you cannot do better really than speak to the 'man on the ground'. Kasser was not there; Muhammad Ali al-Samman was. He even showed the film crew where his mother had burnt some of the books as kindling for the bread oven! He did not ask for money. Either way, it does not seem particularly scholarly to call Robinson's relating of events a 'novel'. Sour grapes here, I think.

Krosney goes on to quote Robinson himself on the matter: 'I know that Kasser hates my guts because of the article on the Jung Codex.' (That is the article mentioned earlier on the *Rise and Fall of a Monopoly*.) According to Krosney, 'His [Robinson's] sense that he owned the field would later exasperate some of his rivals, not least Rodolphe Kasser, who shrugged his shoulders and said, "Robinson believes it all belongs to him."' Whereupon Kasser shrugs his shoulders again, adding, *'What can one do?'* It is difficult to square this opinion with the facts of what Robinson has actually achieved for all scholars and the general public.

But in case we did not fully get the message on this occasion, Krosney cites a few, chosen words from Robinson's fellow scholar Roger Bagnall, high up in the very bosom of professional competence. Bagnall states, in a phrase whose fuller context is missing, that Robinson tended to 'become proprietorial about 4th-century finds in Egypt'. That kind of lays the case, doesn't it? Just a hint of megalomania!

One might have hoped Robinson and Kasser might have patched up their differences by now, but that looked less likely than ever. Why? Because we are now approaching the final chapter in this particular account of how The Gospel of Judas ultimately came before the purview of the wide world, and the revelation might astonish all but the most cynical, experienced and worldly readers of this book.

A Miracle

Do you believe in coincidence, serendipity, destiny? Your inner answer to that question might have a bearing on how you will interpret the next piece of this jigsaw.

Let's go back to the year 2001. Frieda and Roberty had got most of the collection back from Bruce Ferrini. What were they going to do with The Gospel of Judas? The papyrus leaves had got to be restored. There were hundreds of fragments. The whole thing was a mess. Which bits fitted where – and, above all, *what did this text say*?

Some honest advisors might have suggested Frieda and Roberty got in touch with those nice people who translated the Nag Hammadi Library. After all, some people reckon the Jebel Qarara cache is in some way linked to the Nag Hammadi find. It might even be a missing codex. Maybe this was the bit Muhammad Ali *did not* leave for his mum to immolate in the family bread oven. Anyhow, you would think that was a pretty good way to start.

And *whom* would you contact to make sure you got in touch with just the right people for the job? *Right.* James Robinson, that guy with the abiding interest in the texts, the permanent secretary of UNESCO's International Committee for the Nag Hammadi Codices. The one who, if only he had been luckier with the Cairo dealer, could have saved Frieda Tchacos Nussberger a small fortune, and all this terrible trouble with Ferrini, lawyers, restoration costs and some kind of supernatural encounter with the departed spirit of Judas Iscariot.

Now, Frieda and Roberty were in Switzerland in July, and there was an expert on the doorstep. He was Professor Emeritus of Coptology at the University of Geneva. What was his name?

Rodolphe Kasser.

It's a small world! Krosney catches something of the flavour of events: 'Kasser translating The Gospel of Judas would represent a tremendous victory.' For whom, and *over whom*?

Frieda and Roberty met Professor Kasser, now an old man in declining health, in a Zurich coffee house. Old he may have been, but blind to the significance of the opportunity he certainly was not. Taking in the wretched state of the papyri, Kasser called his colleague, Florence Darbre, chief restorer at the Martin Bodmer Foundation museum in Celigny, a suburb of Geneva. Rodolphe Kasser was senior advisor at the museum.

Another Coptic scholar soon joined the team: Martin Krause,

head of Münster University's Coptology department. By a strange coincidence, Krause was another critic of Robinson's account of the discovery and transmission of the Nag Hammadi Library, but Krause was old too – too infirm as it turned out – and recommended Gregor Wurst, senior Coptologist under Stephen Emmel who now held Krause's Chair at Münster.

Three years later – on 1 July 2004 – over 100 scholars associated with the International Coptic Studies Association assembled at a lecture hall in the Institut Catholique, on Paris's Left Bank, for a special announcement. 'A New Coptic Apocrypha Becomes Available to Science' was the main title of Rodolphe Kasser's paper on The Gospel of Judas, whose discovery and preservation he described as a 'miracle'. Listening to Kasser's dramatic account of the gospel's significance was Stephen Emmel's old PhD supervisor, Bentley Layton. He had seen the codex when it was available to science at Yale four years earlier. Managing Editor (under Robinson) of the Nag Hammadi Library in English, Marvin Meyer (holder of the Chair in New Testament Studies, Chapman College, California) was also there, along with his old colleague James Robinson.

Having listened to Kasser's paper, Robinson predictably challenged Kasser as to the veracity of his paper's title. A *new* Coptic Apocrypha? Hadn't Stephen Emmel seen the codex over 20 years previously? Hadn't Ludwig Koenen obtained photographs of it, and hadn't Koenen sent them to him, and hadn't he, Robinson, sent what he could read of the blurred photographs to Marvin Meyer? In other words, hadn't every effort already been made to make the scraps of information available to the circle of Coptic scholars?

In Krosney's account of the occasion, it is the temerity of Robinson voicing these concerns that becomes the subject of censure. His question was 'a classic attempt at a put-down'. We are told, without context for the statements, that 'one of Robinson's closest colleagues said later' (how much later? And who was the very close colleague?) that 'Jim lost his dignity. It was totally unprofessional.'

I guess Jim was fed up. Open sparring with fellow academics is supposed to be a part of lively debate at the top of the profession. The implication seems to be that Robinson lost control, revealing that he was simply jealous, having learned, as Krosney puts it, 'that he had failed in his quest'. The quest being the credit – the only thing worth having, according to other insinuations in the book – for producing the first edition of The Gospel of Judas.

However, even if this were true, which readers may judge for themselves, it is an indisputable fact that Robinson's serious interest in the texts goes back well before anyone even knew The Gospel of Judas was in fact contained within the Gnostic codex.

We are then presented with an image of disturbed innocence. Kasser, 'the venerable Swiss professor', was 'shaken'. The idea of cruelty is evoked as we are told that Kasser 'had not realized that this newly discovered ancient manuscript had also involved a contest for its possession'. (*The Lost Gospel*, 2006, p.245)

Leaving aside whether the codex in question could properly be described as 'newly discovered', the idea of Kasser's ignorance of other attempts to gain control of the manuscript is straining credulity to the limit. Earlier, Krosney had told us that translating The Gospel of Judas constituted some kind of 'victory' for Kasser. This statement is meaningless without the established context of Robinson's longstanding attempts to bring the material to the purview of science.

Robinson simply could not understand why Kasser had made no reference to previously published information about the codex – for example, that of Harold Attridge (Dean of Yale's Divinity School) and Hans-Gebhard Bethge (contributing editor to Nag Hammadi). According to Robinson, 'It is normally the scholarly way of doing things, to begin with references to previous publications about such a new text. Sure he [Kasser] knew about them, for he was the Swiss representative on the International Committee for the Nag Hammadi Codices. What was in fact the only new thing in Kasser's sensational speech was the title of the last tractate in the manuscript, The Gospel of Judas.'

But, of course, as Robinson knew perfectly well, it was precisely sensation that the owners of the codex were aiming for. Anyone today who has heard of The Gospel of Judas has done so because of the sensationalist treatment of its publication. This chapter has been written to explain how this has come about.

We need to understand the text itself, but we also need to understand the nature of the sensation – and the causes of that sensation. It tells us something about our age and the way we are thinking about things. It will also help us to think more clearly about The Gospel of Judas, if we can sort out fact from fancy.

It is fairly likely that had Professor Robinson's attempts to get the text out of the antiquities market shuffle been successful, the text would not have appeared with such a fanfare. It is possible that readers may never even have heard about it, which would be a shame in terms of public awareness. It would not, of course, have bothered scholars all that much.

Scholars have got used to the idea – whether true or false, or a bit of both – that the general public is not really interested in what they do. For example, the gap between popular faith and the understanding of professional theologians has widened in the past century or so to the position where non-academic believers and theologians are effectively speaking a different language when they discuss the Bible. In fact, most believers probably prefer to leave discussion of the Bible to professionals and those people dismissed as embarrassing religious obsessives.

So long as theologians do not go out of their way to tamper with the basic beliefs of believers (God, miracles, life after death, right and wrong), no one is upset. However, in the case of spectacular finds of documents with messages attributed to Jesus, there are sure to be ripples between the separated camps, though some scholars might rather prefer to defend and shield 'ordinary believers' from worrying too much about the implications.

I remember going to interview the Scots theologian, R McLachlan Wilson at St Andrew's University when making the TV series *Gnostics* in 1985. The kindly Wilson was a contributing editor to the Nag Hammadi project. His parting words to me, delivered with a twinkle in his eye, were: 'You don't have to take this too seriously, you know.'

Professor Robinson has clearly been perceived as a thorn in the side of those responsible for the (ultimately successful) attempts to control the dissemination of the codex. His capacity to spoil the spin around the project may have been over-rated. It is probably the case that the public is not *all that* interested in the details of scholarly and non-scholarly wrangling, so long as it does not affect our lives or income. But I think the current possessors of the codex *are* concerned about their reputation, status and profit-worthiness. It would be very strange indeed if they were not.

And so Professor Robinson's motives and attitude must be persistently shown in a less than perfect light. After all, nobody could prove in court that Robinson is either perfect or without ambition.

In November 2005, Robinson attended a symposium on 'How Nag Hammadi changed the world of early Christianity' at the annual Society for Biblical Literature meeting in Philadelphia. Robinson's fellow panellists were Marvin Meyer, Harold Attridge and John D Turner (fellow editor on the Nag Hammadi) – quite a powerful quartet.

In Krosney's words, Robinson 'erupted again' at this meeting. The image of uncontrollable obsession, motivated by something less than professional academic truth-seeking, is again evoked. But by this time in the Krosney narrative, readers would be well used to the idea that Robinson was rather *too* concerned with the 'new discoveries'. Why was he not simply 'accepting defeat' and minding his own business? Surely, one might conclude, nobody could be surprised that Robinson was not party to the Judas project. His own behaviour somehow alienated himself from consideration!

What Robinson re-iterated at the meeting was his familiar and proven theme that discoveries of ancient texts should not be the exclusive preserve of individual scholars. It is at this point that

Krosney lets loose the statement that, 'Since he [Robinson] did not qualify as a Coptic translator, it was easy enough for him to advocate a free-for-all on publication and translation matters.' I hope readers will now see for themselves what lies behind this particular statement.

In fact, the owners were carefully expanding their team. Perhaps they were aware of the Robinson monopoly jibe. Perhaps they realized that it would simply look better in presentational terms to have a few more experts on hand to cheer on the effort and guide it through.

Furthermore, while the owners were interested in a sensational splash to recoup costs and make a profit, they were also committed to producing an unimpeachably scholarly version of the text. No one man could do this.

It must have been a galling experience for James Robinson to become aware that the Judas project had begun to cherry-pick from his old colleagues, fastidiously avoiding his own vast experience and expertise.

Indeed, the only reason to consider Robinson's report to the Society for Biblical Literature to be an 'eruption' is because what he revealed at that meeting was the lengths to which the secret control of the Judas project was prepared to go in monopolizing the dissemination of knowledge.

In 2005, Marvin Meyer was obliged to sign a confidentiality agreement with the owners in view of their arrangements with the National Geographic Society for the commercialization of The Gospel of Judas. He could not talk about the publication of the gospel, even with fellow academics with attested professional interests in the gospel.

While preparing his report Robinson emailed Meyer for some minimal information about the publication of The Gospel of Judas. Meyer's reply was succinct: 'I'm sorry – but I must say, no comment.' According to Krosney, Meyer, who was working on an English translation of Judas with Gregor Wurst and Rodolphe Kasser, tried to assure Robinson there was neither a conspiracy nor a 'European attempt at monopoly'. The implication here is that Robinson was somehow in a kind of America *versus* Europe culture mentality, on account of past disagreements with Kasser and Krause. I know of no compelling evidence for this idea at all. The original UNESCO Nag Hammadi project was international in scope.

The simple fact was that information relevant to Robinson's work, and that of other colleagues, was being deliberately withheld for non-scholarly reasons.

Meanwhile...

Robinson was not the only one trying to find out all he could about the Maecenas Foundation's handling of the Gnostic codex. One of the worrying sources of Robinson's trawl for information was Michel van Rijn, originally engaged by Mario Roberty to pressurize Bruce Ferrini into surrendering the papyri from his house in Ohio.

It must be said that van Rijn's website treatment of the contest between Roberty and Ferrini can only have raised anxieties in Robinson. As a cool observer might have predicted, it was perhaps only a matter of time before van Rijn, cooling on Roberty, was likely to get together with Ferrini. Perhaps it was destiny; perhaps it was obvious. Both men suffered from the insecurities of entrepreneurial lifestyles.

In 2002, van Rijn spent four weeks living in Akron, Ohio with Ferrini, having secured the American's confidence. They found things in common. Both were looking for a mutual target. They settled on James Ferrell – who, from Ferrini's point of view, had let him down, questioned his probity, maybe even wrecked his plans for the Midwest antiquities big-time.

By March 2003, van Rijn had to promise an Ohio court he would remove Ferrell's name from his website. Van Rijn promptly broke the agreement. In November 2004, he was ordered to pay $1 per contemptuous act. As things stood, that added up to $20,000. But by then van Rijn was back in his Dutch homeland, out of pocket but not out of ideas, as we shall see.

Meanwhile, Professor Robinson was gathering material for his report on The Gospel of Judas to be given to the Society for Biblical Literature in Philadelphia. Eleven days before the event, Robinson got in touch with a French scientific journalist, Patrick Jean-Baptiste who wrote for the French monthly, *Sciences et Avenir*. Jean-Baptiste informed Robinson that National Geographic had paid nearly a million dollars to the Maecenas Foundation for the intellectual exploitation of The Gospel of Judas.

Robinson decided to write a book, to put his side of the story, and contacted his old – and indeed younger – colleague Stephen Emmel in Cairo to check his facts. Robinson was astonished to hear that the monopoly had been broken, though in fact *expanded* into what was now a duopoly: the National Geographic and Maecenas Foundation! Whether this happened because of the reasonable fear that Robinson's point of view on this might tarnish the good name of this duopoly is not known.

Emmel's friendly email to Robinson makes something of a fitting, if slightly anticlimactic coda to Robinson's book, *The Secrets of Judas*. It is revealing, while at the same time both discomfiting and satisfying, especially as it appears under the rubric, 'STEVE EMMEL TO THE RESCUE':

By the way [Emmel writes], I want to tell you that I – with some reluctance – just yesterday agreed to join the National Geographic Society's 'Codex Project Advisory Panel', which means that I have signed an agreement not to reveal information that NGS [National Geographic Society] has given me confidentially. Believe it or not, up until now this information has not (repeat: has not) included knowledge of the contents of The Gospel of Judas. Frankly, I would rather not have any privileged access to that, and I am going to try to avoid having any knowledge of it until my agreement with

NGS absolutely requires it (for instance, if they want my opinion on it at some point prior to its publication). Furthermore, nothing of what I have learned only through my association with NGS (which goes back to fall 2004 or a little earlier) is of any great interest, in my humble opinion, but I am not a member of the innermost circle...

What I want to tell you is this: I have joined the NGS advisory panel and signed their confidentiality agreement as a way – I sincerely hope! – of getting into a position to ensure that the Coptic text of The Gospel of Judas will be made publicly accessible as soon as possible, in any case no later than the publication of the first 'authorized' translation of it. I have been working on this angle for some time now and think that I have now secured adequate assurances from NGS. In return, and to have the best hope of holding them to their word, I had to agree to join the gang. D-Day is still set for around Easter this year [2006], so stay tuned. If things go wrong, I will make at least some kind of a stink...

I have cautioned NGS against sensationalism, and I do think that the principals there want to avoid the stupid kind of sensationalism that the press loves so much. But there are some people involved in the project who do not seem to understand much of anything except stupid sensationalism, and so I can certainly not guarantee that the publication of the text and translation will not be accompanied by some phoney hoopla. In any case, surely the media will try to sensationalise it just because of the title The Gospel of Judas. For my own part, I will continue to try to emphasise the genuine scientific interest of this codex (and every other ancient manuscript), which in a perfect world would be (intellectually speaking) sensational enough.

The inclusion of Emmel on the Codex Project Advisory Panel set up by National Geographic offered Robinson genuine consolation that the project would, or could, in the end, be 'done right'.

It is worth remarking that Robinson, contrary to the image of him built up in the National Geographic's *The Lost Gospel*, does not bemoan the appalling lack of good judgement in not having dealt with him personally at any level. It is clear from Robinson's book that he was unaware that his personal motives in the matter of the long story of transmission from Egyptian grave to National Geographic would, in Krosney's careful text, be subject to such malign assessment.

Perhaps when *The Lost Gospel* was commissioned, it was known Robinson had decided to make his own account, and those involved with commissioning Krosney expected far worse than the good-natured conclusion with which Robinson chose to end his account.

Had there been proper communication in the first place, this kind of shadow boxing would never have had to be thrust before the public in the first place. But as Emmel said in his email, this is not a perfect world. Just how imperfect it may be seen to be, we shall discover in due course from the author of The Gospel of Judas himself.

In the meantime, there are just a few loose ends to tidy up.

End Game

On the same day in December 2004 that a team of experts entered the studio of papyrus-restorer Florence Darbre in the industrial zone of Nyon, Switzerland to acquire material to carbon-date the papyri, van Rijn alerted Roberty to a possible spanner in the works.

He, van Rijn, had photographs of fragments from The Gospel of Judas, either sold by Ferrini or sent by him to the Missouri-based Coptologist, Charles Hedrick. If this material went public prematurely, this could scupper Roberty's plans for a big publicity splash for the contents of the gospel. Roberty got Kasser to contact Hedrick to secure the latter's co-operation and to emphasize how a leak could jeopardize the scholar's painstaking academic translation and publication programme.

Roberty was sufficiently disturbed by the possibilities that he agreed to meet van Rijn, in London, five days later, to discuss what it was that Ferrini had withheld from the official restitution of Frieda's property. Van Rijn was delighted to have got his foot back in the door. His website was already spoiling the image of the Maecenas Foundation's work on the gospel. The website maintained that it was *his* exposure of the Judas project's shenanigans that had led to the decision to return the material to Egypt, following restoration, commercialization and publication.

Van Rijn's aim, the website maintained, was simply to prevent Frieda Tchacos Nussberger, Roberty's client, from profiting from the enterprise, if that was at all possible.

However, van Rijn also wished to profit. His work in bringing to light shady deals in the art and antiquities market threatened to engulf him financially. According to Krosney's account, van Rijn agreed to deliver the images of 'lost material' to Frieda and Roberty, doubtless in the interests of science. His fee for the delivery was a modest €71,000.

On 19 January 2005, Roberty waited in vain for the arrival of van Rijn with the material. He did not show up. In fact, van Rijn had been arrested at Basel airport by Swiss police over charges of maligning a family of Swiss art dealers on his website. Van Rijn reckoned Roberty had betrayed him. *Betrayal*. Had van Rijn caught the *Judas* bug? But if Roberty was playing Judas, could it be that he was really innocent, after all?

Two days after van Rijn's arrest at Basel, a US Court found van Rijn liable to the tune of $157,377.98. Released after a week, van Rijn decided to publish what he had. This would scupper the Judas project! Or so he thought. What had van Rijn got to lay on his target?

Charles Hedrick admitted to having sent a translation of one of 'Ferrini's' fragments to van Rijn, emphasizing that he gave no permission to publish the translation. Hedrick, in retrospect, recognized that sending such material to the internet blogger was 'a mistake'. Luckily for Hedrick, ancient papyri are not (yet) covered by the Official Secrets Act.

Fortunately for the Judas project, the material revealed by van Rijn came from a fragment of a work in the codex given the provisional title, Allogenes, though van Rijn did not realize this. This name means 'Alien' or 'of Another Race' or 'Stranger'. It was a concept beloved of Gnostics throughout the ages. Van Rijn remained, like the figure in his moment of revelation, an outsider.

Those on the inside of the project would proceed apace. Extraordinarily difficult, delicate work had been taking place within Florence Darbre's studio as the scattered fragments of papyrus began to find their place in the book as a whole. Sadly, the codex would never be an entire whole. Some 15 per cent of the original fibres have either decayed to dust or been lost or removed. Matching the fibres of tiny fragments along with traces of ink, parts of letters and words – and often just incredibly fragile and virtually indistinguishable bits of papyrus fibre – took months and months of painstaking work at a microcscopic level.

Slowly the words began to make coherent sense. A narrative began to appear. The long-lost Gospel of Judas began to communicate its message to the minds of its translators, Rodolphe Kasser, Marvin Meyer, Gregor Wurst and François Gaudard.

A year after van Rijn's failed splash, the big wide world began to hear that something extraordinary had been discovered in the deserts of Egypt: an unknown gospel. Jesus, the saviour of Western religion – for those millions who still cared – was in it. And it had been written by... Judas Iscariot: *the one who did it*. The assassin. The fake friend. The hypocrite. The transgressor. The one with holy blood on his hands. The tormented one. The snitch. The thief. The suicide. The outsider.

The climate had changed. Was religion about to be turned on its head? Were we now to believe that Judas was a hero? Had the Christian Church got it wrong all those years? How long would we have to wait? The truth, the world was informed, would be revealed at Easter, 2006: the time of crosses, nails, blood and resurrection, when the world looks for revelation, hope, change, in the pale vellum springtime of bread and new life.

And now, Easter 2006 has passed. The gospel has been revealed. Now the world can hear Judas' one and only confession. Never has a heretic had such a fanfare!

But first remember this: whatever the motives inspiring those who have brought this confession to our collective gaze, we owe them something. They have brought The Gospel of Judas into the intriguing and mysterious world of popular culture. *Alleluia!*

Chapter Two

THE CONDEMNED GOSPEL

You know that every cop is a criminal

And all the sinners saints...

(From *Sympathy for the Devil*, Jagger-Richards, 1968)

Is the text of The Gospel of Judas genuine?

On 10 January 2005, AJ Timothy Jull, director of the National Science Foundation's Accelerator Mass Spectrometer Facility at Tuscon, Arizona, and an expert in carbon-14 dating, produced results from tiny fragments of James, The Gospel of Judas and the leather binding and papyrus attached to the binding. No text was lost in the process.

Carbon-14 dating gives excellent results within parameters of probability. In the case of the Gnostic codex from the Jebel Qarara, the odds were greatest (68.1 per cent) that The Gospel of Judas was put together between AD 240 and 320. There was only a 15 per cent probability that it was created before AD 240, and a 15 per cent probability that it was created after AD 320. A quick calculation gave a mean year of AD 280, give or take 60 years *max*.

However, later in 2005, Roger Bagnall, as we have noted before, found the reference to *Pagus 6* in the mathematical treatise that was part of the original cache. *Pagus 6* was the administrative area code for where the material was probably found. The code only came into being as an area-designate in AD 307 or 308. Of course, the mathematical treatise might have been composed later than the Gnostic codex. The important point is that the precise dating from the *Pagus 6* reference of AD 306 *plus* corroborates the carbon-14 dating.

We can be fairly sure that the Coptic Gospel of Judas was written down on the papyrus leaves and bound into a codex, or papyrus book, around the beginning of the 4th century. This date fits in comfortably with everything else already known about surviving Coptic Gnostic literature.

The Gospel of Judas was originally composed in Greek. Coptic is the old Egyptian language, spoken before Arab invasions led to the dominance of Arabic in Egypt. 'Copt' comes from the Greek word for Egypt: *Aigyptios*, and the Coptic language is Egyptian, written in Greek characters, with lots of words borrowed from the Greek. The Gospel of Judas is written in a Sahidic dialect of Coptic, prevalent in Middle Egypt.

From a letter written by the bishop of Alexandria, Athanasius, in AD 367, we know that Gnostic writings circulated in Egypt and were disapproved of, at least by him. Athanasius was an influential Christian bishop in his day with lots of supporters. In the letter, written at Easter for distribution to the administrators of the Egyptian Church, he declared which books of the Bible (what we know as the New Testament or 'Canon') were acceptable, and said that those who kept heretical or doctrinally unacceptable (non-orthodox) books, would be kicked out of the Church.

This attitude was still dominant in the Christian Church when the *Gnostics* TV team interviewed Pope Shenouda, leader of the Coptic Church, in Egypt at Easter in 1986. He told us that the Nag Hammadi books were 'apocryphal'. They were books of knowledge (like text books), not real gospels, and had no relevance for his

Church, other than as articles of religious history. They had no revelation or inspired divine word to offer. They were something for the scholars, with nothing to say of any value to believers.

In retrospect, I suppose we should have asked him whether or not he would excommunicate anyone found reading the Nag Hammadi Library. It would seem unlikely. Nowadays, it is perfectly normal for theologians operating within the Orthodox, Roman Catholic, Anglican and Protestant Churches, to read heretical books as part of their studies. Studying them is one thing, however; advocating or sympathizing with their message is another.

The Gospel of Judas undoubtedly fits into the mould of the kind of book condemned by Bishop Athanasius and his successors all those centuries ago. Athanasius would undoubtedly see The Gospel of Judas' re-appearance as the devil's work, because by the time he was bishop it was widely thought that the great threat to the orthodox party from Gnostic books and their readers was largely a thing of the past.

There were, of course, persistent rebels, as the orthodox saw them, of many kinds and doctrinal hues, but by and large the Christian message as taught by the Church's bishops and deacons was an orthodox one. That is not to say that the threat was regarded in benign terms. After all, many a new generation seizes upon the condemned ways of the past and uses them as sticks with which to beat the parents, teachers, and figures of authority. Young people were no different fundamentally in the 4th century to what they are today. When the Rolling Stones were marketed to the public in the early to mid-1960s, their manager, Andrew Oldham, deliberately promoted the message that these were the guys your parents would not approve of. *Lock up your daughters!*

Moral ambivalence always appears attractive to a proportion of every generation. Each generation likes to see itself as having something different about it; perhaps some 'hip' insight that the old fools 'at the top' cannot handle. It was just the same in Roman Egypt. Gnostic thought might have been around for a long time by the 4th century, but it still had the atmosphere of danger, of mystery, about it; it promised something you could not get anywhere else. And daddy did not like it. But then, conversely, daddy might have been 'into it', and the youth might have undergone orthodox indoctrination. Repressive institutions attract certain kinds of young people.

Besides, *maybe Gnostic religion had been condemned because it had a special truth about it*: some great secret that could not be spoken of without threatening the powers-that-be. And it had survived, if only just, in the remote places – such as Egypt.

It is interesting that in what has come to be considered the heyday of the Gnostic movement, namely the 2nd century AD, our principal witness against the movement was not bishop of Alexandria, but bishop of Lyon.

The city of Lyon (Lugdunum) was in *Gallia Narbonensis*, or southern France, whose church was in close touch with Rome. When the bishop of Lyon – his name was Irenaeus (from the Greek word for 'Peace') – wrote his very detailed volumes 'against the *gnosis* [knowledge] falsely so-called', he wrote of things going on right on Rome's doorstep – indeed, under the very paving stones of the capital.

Irenaeus was writing in about the year AD 180. In the decades before he wrote, Gnostic types of Christianity had flourished at the centre and were spreading wherever there was an audience. Gnostic interpretations of the Christian message had proved to be so popular that Irenaeus was fearful that the message he had been taught as the religion of Christ might be severely distorted.

At the time of his writing, Christians were being executed for their religion, which was seen as treacherous to the interests of the state. (The worst persecutions took place in AD 177.) Christians like Irenaeus had been trying to say for well over a century the idea that Christianity and the Roman Empire could happily co-exist, so long as Christians were not asked to treat the Emperor as a god.

If Christians were going to die, they had better know what they were dying for. Just as importantly, if Roman magistrates were going to condemn Christians to death, then at least the magistrates should know what it was they had acquiesced in condemning. For Irenaeus, any form of Christianity other than what he was authorized to teach was a false witness. The only martyrdom acceptable to God was the martyrdom of the humble orthodox. The false teachers (as he saw them) were too cocky by far: attractive to women, seducers of the intellect, full of tricks.

Among the people he condemned in his book, later called *Against Heresies*, which became a landmark in the Catholic Church's movement towards self-definition, was a group who suspected, in Mick Jagger's words, that all the sinners were saints. For a start, they recognized that Jesus had been accused of worshipping the Devil, that is, respecting the Devil's power, and using that power for his own purposes. They knew that sinners could be executed. Jesus was a friend of sinners. They had learned this from the orthodox teachers. Those hated by the world had a place in Jesus' paradise (garden).

Following their own logic, these so-called 'false teachers' looked at the scriptures and decided that people who had been condemned in the eyes of the world might have been the real stars! So, the serpent that suggested Eve eat the 'apple'... obviously a hero! *Why?* Because the fruit of the Tree of Knowledge of Good and Evil brought self-consciousness to the first couple. They 'knew they were naked'. That is, they knew *who they were*! They had lost innocence, but gained knowledge. And this upset the god of the Garden who had told them to leave the fruit alone. *Must be something wrong with the deity in the garden of Eden*, the 'Gnostics' surmised.

This god did not seem reasonable. He must have had a problem. Maybe he was jealous. It does say in the Bible, after all, that he is a jealous God. Whom is he jealous of? There must be a higher God. This old God of the Garden was the God of the Law. St Paul had taught that Gentile Christians had been made free of the Jewish Law. Therefore, the group concluded, they must be free of the God of the Law. Those whom the God of the Law condemned might have something positive to offer. You only had to look beneath the surface of the scriptural narrative for the clues.

Adopting this logic, Irenaeus's opponents considered the figure of Cain. Remember the story of Cain and Abel? Cain killed Abel because his god favoured Abel's offering (blood sacrifice). Now, once you have realized there is something not quite right with the deity who is doing all this pushing around, demanding blood sacrifices, things start coming to light which were once hidden, in fact secreted into the story. You're beginning to *get the message*. The secret message.

For example, you cotton on to the idea that maybe this story of Cain being kicked out of his life, condemned to wander around with a nasty mark on his person, is in fact a *cover story*. The mark of Cain is a badge of pride! Cain had dared to transgress. He upset a false god. He was the wanderer, the outsider, the seeker, to whose essential existence, the world was blind. Like Jesus, these guys were the victims of propaganda!

Later orthodox commentators have called these loathed inter-preters (or re-interpreters) 'Cainites', but there is no reason to think they were called this, either by themselves or by people around them. People who think differently are first separated as 'sects', then given names by those who do not like them: 'Jumpers', 'Quakers', 'Methodists', 'Protestants', 'Hussites' – even '*Gnostics*' – all began as nicknames.

Eventually, the nickname becomes the badge of pride. *If that's how we appear to you (the blind world), so well and good – we know who we are.* 'Christian' too was probably a nickname to begin with; Valentinian 'Gnostics' (followers of an influential Gnostic theologian of the 2nd century) said there was something holy about it. It could not be uttered without causing an inner reaction, one way or the other.

The Christians condemned by Irenaeus did not stop with Cain. They had caught the end of a thread and were going to go all the way with it. So, they observed, what is this false deity up to? Was not the serpent an ancient symbol of divine wisdom and health, of rebirth and mystic power? What does the God of Eden do? Condemns it to slide around forever on its belly in the dust!

So the Gnostics identified Jesus with the serpent, symbol of healing, rebirth and supernatural wisdom. And what did Jesus offer? His health-giving venom was *gnosis*: the 'keys to the kingdom', the 'light of the world', as St Paul had called it, blasphemy to the Jews and a folly to the Greeks!

These rebels of the free spirit (as they saw themselves) deconstructed the scriptures and came to some mighty disturbing conclusions. What those conclusions were, we shall now get our first glimpse of, as we proceed to look into the contents of The Gospel of Judas. And by the way, our first known reference to the existence of The Gospel of Judas, was – would you believe? – in the pages of Irenaeus's book. In his 33rd chapter, Irenaeus says that those who regard Cain as a good guy also have a book they have fabricated: a gospel of Judas.

Yes, they had trawled through the Church's gospels and oral teaching and found a figure of great, ambivalent moral status: a true mystery man. Irenaeus himself speaks of a 'mystery of betrayal'. As far as these Christians were concerned, Judas was *all right*. He was *right-on*. Judas was cool. Judas saw what the thick old disciples had not seen. He was the fruit of a very special generation indeed. And what he had, everyone who is part of that special generation can have too.

A last titbit before we enter the catacombs of Judas' gospel. In 1966, John Lennon read a book called *The Passover Plot* by Hugh J Schonfield. The book described a conspiracy around the Crucifixion of Jesus which subsequent generations of Christians had apparently failed to notice. Reading Schonfield's book led Lennon to say in an interview with English journalist Maureen Cleave that 'the disciples were thick and ordinary. It's them twisting it that ruins it for me.'

The literary Beatle reckoned the truth of Jesus' life had been lost in the telling and re-telling. He looked for what was the real truth behind it all. In the process, he decided that the Christianity he had grown up with 'will vanish and shrink', adding that even the Beatles were 'more popular' than Jesus with the new generation. He did not think this was necessarily a good thing, rather a thought-provoking reflection of the truth of the times we were living in.

And guess what? In America's Bible belt, they burned his image and the Beatles' records. In South Africa, Beatles music was banned from the radio. Meanwhile, in Rome, His Holiness the Pope – successor to Irenaeus and the orthodox branch of religion – declared that Christian believers had nothing to learn from 'beatniks'. *Beatnik*. Good nickname. It makes you think, doesn't it?

The Gospel of Judas

The gospel or 'good news' about Judas opens with an unusual statement. You might think you would want to shout 'good news' from the rooftops or in the marketplace to bring a smile to the faces of the sad folks below or before you, but we are straightaway told that this is a 'secret account'. Does it mean some people are not to know about it? Or does it perhaps mean that this story has been kept secret, for mysterious reasons, and can only now be revealed?

Either way, what we are about to hear is not common knowledge. It is about a revelation made by Jesus during 'eight days', 'three days before he celebrated Passover'. So, we have already got a couple of mysteries, and we have not even come to the end of the first sentence.

There is something tricky about this composition. Maybe it is not going to tell us everything on the surface. Maybe we are expected to know things pertinent to its message already. This work needs interpreting, particularly, one imagines, by those who know something of the secret. That, by the way, is supposed to be *you*, the reader.

The 'secret' is, of course, the *gnosis*.

A Greek word meaning 'knowledge', *Gnosis* does not, however, mean just 'facts', like you get in abundance in an encyclopaedia. One might know thousands of facts, but be really quite stupid. No, *gnosis-knowledge* is the kind of sensation of knowledge you get 'when your eyes are opened'. For example, if someone explains that something that happened in a newspaper is only the visible part of an underlying pattern, maybe a conspiracy, suddenly it 'dawns on you'. Suddenly you see it. You get the point. You've got the centre. And from the centre you can suddenly see all sides. Things that seemed far apart suddenly fit together. What looked obscure or dark to you suddenly *makes sense* – a bit like finally getting a subtle joke. In the 1960s, some people used the American slang word 'hip' to express an uncommon awareness. Are you 'hip' to it? *Do you get it?* Do you share the awareness?

Well, I hope you are now 'getting' what *gnosis* means. Whoever wrote this gospel of Judas is, as the vulgar phrase has it, 'in on the gag'. He or she has recognized something the others do not have. And the one with *gnosis*, the gnostic, has 'seen it' for themselves. Once you 'get it', you are free of your former illusion, free of the Lie.

So Jesus said something to Judas. There is a curious phrase. The conversation between Judas and Jesus happened, we are told, 'during eight days', three days before Jesus celebrated Passover. Now this 'eight days' could just be a Coptic phrase for 'a week', that is, Sunday to Sunday. But this is a 'Gnostic' composition, and Gnostics loved using symbols and phrases with multiple meanings. Like poets, they liked making mazes to set the mind off on a magical mystery tour. They used their own 'hip' language and imagery.

Some of it is quite easy to 'get', once you get the idea, some of it remains obscure to others. The feeling you get is that you are meant to reflect on these writings. What it is really all about is not obvious, until it becomes *obvious to you*.

Well, it does not make much sense to us to speak of a conversation between Judas Iscariot and Jesus 'during eight days [or a week] three days before he celebrated Passover'. I suggest that this reference to 'eight days' represents a 'time out of time'. It is well known and well recorded that mystical experiences, when people have communicated with divine spirit, break down our usual understanding or feeling of time. People in love may experience something similar – or even the same. There is a whole canon of love songs that speak of eternity as the natural state of two lovers locked in mutual adoration. When Juliet must wait a few hours before seeing Romeo again, she says 'T'is many days e'er I again behold my Romeo.' We know what she is talking about.

In the many accounts of mystics, and among those who have taken psychedelic (mind-expanding) substances, the feeling of a few minutes seeming like many days or at least hours, is a common experience, blurring the borders of illusion and reality. It is well known that the Gnostic teachers saw our perceived sense of time as being derived from eternal spiritual realities.

According to the Platonic tradition (shared by Gnostics), everything we experience on earth is a kind of deficient *copy* of how things are in a higher, spiritual realm. So, if there are 12 months, for example, then the number 12 represents an eternal spiritual truth, reflected in different things, but especially in time. There are seven planets (as they believed, including the sun and moon); so seven is a perfect number. Each planet has its own 'sphere' or world; and each planet has a spiritual governor or angel, or 'archon' (ruler) as they termed it.

To travel beyond the 'Seven' was to go beyond what they called the 'night-cloak' of the universe. What that garment 'cloaked' was a higher realm of light, beyond the powers of the planets. That is where Jesus had come from, beyond the powers of the 12 zodiacal governors: the constellations. So, it is likely that the 'eight days' referred to as the 'time' when the alleged conversation between Judas Iscariot and Jesus took place, three days before Passover, means that Jesus and Judas 'ascended' to the eighth sphere.

The eighth sphere is understood in Gnostic lore to be a spiritual dimension sometimes associated with the stars, just below the portal to the eternal Godhead, the *ninth*. It would be presumed that anyone who had travelled 'in the spirit' to the ninth, would be unwilling to return to this world. The 'eighth', on the other hand, would offer one both a glimpse of the above, and the true state of the universe below.

This conversation between Judas Iscariot and Jesus is therefore taking place in eternity. This is the power that Jesus has: to look into a person's eyes and show them – even take them – to the realm of eternity, the 'kingdom of heaven'. Judas, as we shall see, is willing to go. He can 'make it'.

There is another point worth mentioning here. If this conversation was taking place in a spiritual dimension, then this state may be regarded as permanently accessible to those who have, or believe they have, risen to the 'eighth'. That people did believe such things were possible – and even wrote about such experiences – is absolutely plain from the inclusion in the Nag Hammadi Gnostic Library of a work called The Discourse on the Eighth and the Ninth, which has just such a description. The launch pad for the experience described in the Discourse on the Eighth and Ninth is plainly Egypt.

Now, one can say that this conversation between Jesus and Judas Iscariot 'never took place' in the approximate year AD 30 (or 33) when Jesus is supposed to have been crucified. But to a sympathetic reader of The Gospel of Judas, this would hardly be a relevant criticism. *Real spiritual communication* does not take place in this world in our time, they believed. Real spiritual communication takes place beyond time, for all time. The fact that the Church's four more famous Gospels were put down on paper some time earlier than the work under Judas' name would carry little weight.

Even on the mundane level, books published today about the Second World War tell us far, far more than the knowledge available to ordinary people during the war or in its immediate aftermath. It takes a long time for things to sink in, deeper perceptions to emerge. Time gives contours and proportion to knowledge. But spiritual knowledge – *gnosis* – is, by definition, held by its exponents to be timeless.

Anyhow, it is doubtful if this historical line of reasoning would appeal to those who read The Gospel of Judas anyway. Jesus was a spiritual being and spirit transcends time. Jesus was not really interested in history, dates and times. He was, Gnostics believed, working on the spiritual level, and that is where he could be found. Rise to the appropriate state of mind and he will appear to as much of your mind as is accessible to him. This was their view. If, like Judas, you are blessed, he will open your mind. That is what The Gospel of Judas is all about.

That is to say, three days before Judas celebrated Passover, he 'tripped off' with Jesus and Jesus opened his mind. This is the 'good news' of Judas. It happened to him; it could happen to you.

We are next given the most perfunctory account of Jesus' ministry. This refers to the ministry many of us will remember from religious studies lessons at home, school or church. The writer is aware of this and knows that we are aware. He or she takes it that we have heard all those things before.

Jesus 'performed miracles and great wonders for the salvation of humanity.' At least we get a clear statement of why this ministry of healing went on. It was not purely an effort of generous social work. He was not setting himself up as a national health service or establishing clinics.

It might be that the writer of the gospel had read The Gospel according to John. In John, there are seven specific miracles or, rather, 'signs', and they all tell us something about Christ, the Word incarnate. Jesus did not do good works just to make people feel better; it was to point the way to how humanity can be saved – from this world, presumably, or rather from its power to enslave the spirit.

We are then reminded that some people walked in righteousness and others 'walked in their transgressions'. Rather ambiguously, we are told that 12 disciples were called for this reason. Were the 12 called because of the transgressions (to save sinners), or because some people walked in righteousness? There may be ambivalence here. Whatever might underlie the phrasing, the writer does not seem terribly interested in what was going on in the ministry, which was generally known, and immediately gets on to his own theological turf. Here the writer could play the game he or she knew best.

Jesus began to talk to the disciples about 'the mysteries beyond the world.' This is what we would expect from a Gnostic gospel. When Jesus' famous words before Pilate, 'My kingdom is not of this world,' were heard by Gnostics, they had no doubt as to what he meant. *Of course it wasn't*, they would say. *You don't even know what the world really is. They* did, or so they were convinced.

Knowing about what this world really is gave Gnostic Christians the clue to understand the other thing Jesus is reported to have spoken to the disciples about, that is to say, 'what would take place at the end'. This lower world has a definite end coming. That alone was cause for relief among those who appreciated the message of The Gospel of Judas. And that end could be pre-experienced, as could the resurrection of the spirit out of this world – for these things were written in eternity.

Jesus the Child

There next appears a sentence so charming in its simplicity, so pregnant with possibility, that it practically disarms the critical consciousness:

'Often he [Jesus] did not appear to his disciples as himself, but he was found among them as a child.'

We have not heard anything quite like this in the Gospels we may have heard in church or school. Now, it may all stem from the famous prophecy in Isaiah, referring to a coming messiah: 'And a little child shall lead them.'

This concept of Jesus appearing in many forms to many people really seems to have excited the imaginations of these Christians. In particular, the manifestation as a child should strike us, because we have all seen suffering through the eyes of a child. We are immediately aware of the archetype of childhood as a sign of innocence, vision, hope, future, truth, creativity. To recapture lost youth is the hope of many. We fear as we grow older that we shall suffer like our ancestors with sclerosis of the conscience. We try to protect our children from the pollution of the adult experience, while at the same time looking to them for hope, even as they look to us, when they are very young, for guidance and strength.

But the idea of Jesus teaching as a child, especially expressed so blatantly and vividly, wipes the smile of cynicism off our face. And yet, many may know of the story of Jesus discoursing with the wise in the Temple in Luke's Gospel. Also in Luke lies the passage that might have inspired the author of The Gospel of Judas to see the saviour as a child. Luke chapter 9, verse 48 tells us: 'Whosoever shall receive this child in my name receiveth me: and whosoever shall receive me receiveth him that sent me: for he that is least among you all, the same shall be great.'

In the theological rush to establish the *manhood* of Jesus we have perhaps omitted the childhood of the saving being. The Gnostics apparently found much meaning and significance in the idea of being instructed by a child. This suspicion of patriarchy – so very strong in Gnostic literature – seems astonishingly modern.

How many of us are loath to surrender Christmas with its image of the baby adored by the wise men, even though theologians tell us it is probably an invention or part of 'mythology'?

It was reported of the Gnostic teacher Valentinus – a couple of decades before Irenaeus wrote his book against this teacher's students – that his Gnostic awareness began when he had a vision of the *Logos* (the 'Word' or creative mind of God) in the form of a child. A similar vision occurred to English gnostic visionary William Blake and may be found in the first poem of his *Songs of Innocence and Experience*.

In the Nag Hammadi Library, there is a work called the Apocalypse of Paul. In it, Paul is on the road, not apparently to Damascus, but to Jerusalem. It is all very symbolic. Paul asks a little child the way.

The little child says: 'Say your name so that I may show you the road.'
Then the little child says: 'I know who you are, Paul.'

Jesus appears in a form appropriate to the spiritual capacity of
the one before him. To the Gnostic, Jesus is not just a person, a fixed
image, he is a power that receives his form from the mind of the one
who seeks him, or who is sought by him, as illustrated in this
incident with the 'little child' on the road. *This* little child is not lost;
he knows the way.

As we grow older, we massacre the innocent.

Giving Thanks Is Not Enough

The scene swiftly jumps to a little vignette that serves to introduce
the main dramatic conflict in Judas' gospel. The conflict picks up
on a theme that is familiar to anyone who has read the New
Testament accounts of Jesus and his disciples. The conflict is one of
understanding. Basically, Jesus understands everything, and the
disciples keep missing the point, forever asking questions that are
either stupid (from Jesus' point of view) or poignant (from ours).

This disparity of vision from the disciples becomes still more
radical in some Gnostic writings, to the extent that you might
wonder why Jesus ever chose these particular 12 in the first place!
But, of course, the conceit is that the disciples represent people in
general who need divine enlightenment and spiritual awakening.

What would you ask Jesus if he invited you to question him?
One might be afraid of making a fool of oneself. The disciples in the
Gnostic dialogues are not afraid to do that. They are like actors,
reading parts. And yet, there is something rather sad about them,
not just because they are, as it were, prepared to 'clown it' for the
reading public, but because they are locked in their roles.

In the passage concerned, the disciples are not asking Jesus
anything. They are happily getting on with something they might
think the sacred teacher would approve of. They are gathered
together, perhaps on a bench or reclining on divans, while offering

a thanksgiving prayer over bread. The scene is somewhat reminiscent of the Last Supper and may even be a parody of it. But Jesus is not at the centre, and the bread is bread, not symbolic or sacramental substance. It might be that the writer is looking at the way Christian communion meals had developed within the Church. But if he or she is, the writer does not seem very impressed.

The disciples are in for a nasty shock. Jesus approaches and starts laughing at them. They cannot understand it. They are upset. 'We have done what is right,' they offer, plaintively. Jesus then reassures them. He tells them he is not laughing *at* them. He is laughing at the scene itself, because he sees it from a different perspective. In his eyes, they are really wasting their time. They are stuck in an illusion. He tells them that the act does not truly come from their own will, rather they think it is through this act that 'your god' will be praised. They have got the wrong idea. The most pious observances mean nothing unless they come first, from the free will, and second, they are directed to the right deity.

This seems a lot to swallow for the disciples, and all they can manage is to declare that 'you' (Jesus) are 'the son of our god'. Before we look at how Jesus responds to what ought to be a great affirmation of faith, it is worth considering this all-seeing, laughing Jesus.

The Laughing Jesus

That the Jesus who appears in Gnostic writings is characterized as a fellow with a sense of humour might appear a bonus. In spite of the fact that some intellectuals regard a jovial demeanour as a sign of weak intellect or lack of existential seriousness, most people's hearts are gladdened when sugar is added to the often bitter pill of reality.

A Jesus who laughs seems more human than the solemn figure most of us associate with a redeemer who tends to be put on altars or high up on walls at some distance from our pathetic individual lives.

Luis Buñuel's fascinating surrealist movie, *The Milky Way* (1968), presented images of a lively and humane Jesus, telling jokes, vivid and physical, his face awash with humanity, lined by laughter. It was a marvellous, compelling image – the more so, perhaps, because it came from a confessed atheist, who enjoyed sitting in cloisters! It might have upset some stuffy religious authorities but to others, his idea of Jesus seemed truly spiritual. That is to say, this Jesus had spirit – and he knew how to let it out!

Now, it may be that the Jesus envisioned in some Gnostic writings is being presented in this way. However, while Jesus in The Gospel of Judas says he is not laughing at the disciples themselves, he *is* laughing at their worldview and the world in which they live. It is not a laugh of pity either; it is a straightforward laugh of someone who is superior. There might even be a nasty edge to it, because the laugh is really aimed directly at the 'lord of this world'.

In a recent lecture (Canonbury International Conference on *Freemasonry and Gnostic Traditions*, 2006), Professor James Robinson seized on this laughter as the all-telling keynote of The Gospel of Judas. Robinson asserted that it demonstrated utter, cynical contempt for the beliefs and salvation of orthodox Christian believers, and for the orthodox interpretation of Jesus' passion through which most Christians believe they find salvation.

Robinson reckoned orthodox Christians had nothing to fear from The Gospel of Judas; what he perceived as its tone of contempt was itself contemptible. The Gnostics, he asserted, cursed life and all created things perceivable to ordinary sense. In Robinson's view, the idea of Jesus himself suffering on the cross for the sake of human beings *as we know them* earned from the author or authors of *The Gospel of Judas* nothing more than sneers of haughty disgust.

Professor Robinson made a strong, moral and almost episcopal case for 'what is wrong' with The Gospel of Judas from the point of view of traditional Christianity – much to the surprise of his audience who had expected a less polemical response from the man who ensured our access to *The Nag Hammadi Library in English*.

In Gnostic writings, the 'lord of this world' (the phrase does appear in the New Testament) is a blind fool, nothing less, nothing more – except, this blind fool has succeeded where other disabled deities might have failed. Blind though he is, he has got humanity in his grip. He has blinded them, tricked them, made fools out of them. When the Gnostic Jesus sees his disciples 'falling for it' he wants to wake them up. As Jesus laughs in the face of the 'lord of this world', he laughs at the disciples. 'Come on!' he seems to say, 'Don't fall for all this rubbish!' 'I know you think you've been told this is the right way to carry on, but if you knew who I was, and who you really are, you'd wake up – and laugh with me'.

In some Gnostic accounts of the Crucifixion, for example, there is the idea that the 'lord of this world' has to be tricked. This is easy enough for Jesus to do, whereas it is difficult for ordinary human beings. Jesus can outwit the world's dark power because he comes from a higher place. And when you are in a higher place you can see more. You have the advantage of height and greater perspective – and, in the case of this Jesus, you have infinitely greater spiritual power.

Jesus comes to earth to show up the lord of this world. He comes to make an ass out of him. He comes to jeer and strip the lord of this world of his pretended authority. Therefore, he comes to free humanity. And is there a greater way of showing you are free than by being able to laugh wholeheartedly? Laughter raises the spirits. A great moment of pure humour is a form of ascension. In *Mary Poppins*, the magical children's story, little Jane and Michael meet a man who laughs so much he, and the children, rise up to the ceiling, only to come down again when someone says something sad.

The laughing Jesus appears elsewhere in Gnostic literature, particularly at the Crucifixion. It is a sign of the extraordinary radical consciousness of some Gnostics that they could take this image of the laughing Jesus and give it a twist that would appear quite blasphemous to an orthodox Christian – then and now.

In The Second Treatise of the Great Seth (the 'Great Seth' being

Jesus) – a Nag Hammadi Library work perfectly in tune with The Gospel of Judas – Jesus describes what was *really* happening at the Crucifixion:

> For my death which they think happened, happened to them in their error and blindness, since they nailed their man unto their death. [...] They struck me with the reed; it was another, Simon, who bore the cross on his shoulder. It was another on whom they placed the crown of thorns. But I was rejoicing in the height over all the wealth of the archons and the offspring of their error, of their empty glory. And I was laughing at their ignorance.

These 'archons' (Greek for rulers) are the real butt of Jesus' cosmic joke. They thought they had him! They govern the world of time and space; they are the chains that bind the spirit of humanity. One of them, 'the lord of this world' is called 'a jealous God' (the phrase comes from the Old Testament, of course). He is jealous of the true indescribable deity above him. He wants to be top god, but he cannot be. Nevertheless, he has managed to get sparks of the higher realm under his control. That's us! Poor, benighted humanity. As we were clothed in bodies and tied to our senses, the spirit went to sleep. Humanity is profoundly unconscious. Jesus has come to wake us up.

In the process, shock tactics are perfectly in order. In the Nag Hammadi *Apocalypse of Peter*, Jesus 'laughs at their [the disciples'] lack of perception, knowing that they are born blind.' The blindness of the invisible (to us) rulers is shared by those under their control ('Lord forgive them for they know not what they do'). But, paradoxically, the archons' cock-up at the Crucifixion serves a purpose: 'But what they released was my incorporeal body' – that is, Jesus' spiritual being: the *Great Seth*. To back this idea up, the 'apocalypse' (or revelation) includes a vision experienced by Peter. In the vision, Peter cannot work out which is the real Jesus, the one seemingly being seized and beaten by his enemies, or the one he sees 'glad and laughing on a tree'. The Saviour says to Peter, 'He whom you saw on the tree, glad and laughing, this is the living Jesus.'

And it is this 'living Jesus' and those who understand him, as opposed to the 'dead image' of him shared by his enemies, that are laughing at the disciples in The Gospel of Judas. The essential point about all this envisioning and recasting of familiar stories in an unfamiliar way is *perception*. This living Jesus is trying to change perceptions of what reality really is. The world is not to be taken at face value. There is, if you like, a spiritual conspiracy going on for the spiritual domination of humanity. One fascinating aspect of the Gnostics' inherent challenge to the orthodox Church was their suggestion that, in important respects, the growing episcopal authority was actually serving – or starting to serve – the conspiracy. Far from liberating the imprisoned souls, the Church was keeping them asleep.

The first step to 'waking up' in The Gospel of Judas is recognizing who Jesus really is. In one sense, the little bit of drama about the thanksgiving meal is just a dramatic device to lead into the main question. The disciples have replied to Jesus' observation that their thanksgiving is directed to appease the will of 'their god', by crying that Jesus is himself the 'son of our god'. How, they ask, can Jesus be critical of their god when he is himself this god's son? He must be joking!

There seems to be a jibe here, at the expense of the orthodox believer who considers himself or herself saved because he or she declares Jesus to be the Son of God. Even this comfort the writer of The Gospel of Judas would like to strip away!

Jesus gives the reply short shrift: 'How do you know me?' He then attacks their generation: 'no generation of the people that are among you will know me.' That means, first, those living in their time, and second, their 'genetic' or family origin. Which god, Jesus is asking, does this 'genetic line' serve? No 'generation of the people that are among you will know me.'

Now, the Gnostics were aware of numerous passages in the New

Testament where Jesus describes 'this generation' as wicked, as a nest of vipers and so on. The generation is roundly condemned – fit for the flames with the tares and chaff.

Again, the Gnostics give this idea of generation a mighty big twist. They assert that they understand the 'gag' behind Jesus' harsh words of condemnation. Furthermore, it is a plain historical fact that the Gnostic writings were not products of the same generation that first tried to express the significance of Jesus. But that's only for starters! The Gnostic identity contained in The Gospel of Judas – as it is in other works of the Nag Hammadi Library – is linked to a unique 'generation', an alternative, gifted genetic line. Just what that unique genetic line is we shall discover shortly.

Now Jesus has really upset the disciples! They are furious and begin 'blaspheming against him in their hearts'. Somewhere in themselves, some part of them knows who he is, but they are, we would say, 'in denial'. Their conscious minds cannot allow this unconscious material to come forth. Rather than face the hidden, suppressed truth, they would rather belittle it, dismiss it, condemn it.

Jesus now speaks in the manner of a Jungian psychologist, diagnosing a neurotic patient. They may be grumbling on a bench, but from Jesus' point of view, they are all 'on the couch'. He wants them to get in touch with themselves and he is quite prepared to challenge their deepest held beliefs – the very things that are keeping them from themselves – the *scotoma* in their visionary faculty, if you like. Like any neurotic, this is the last thing the patient wants, or thinks he wants.

Calmly, without emotion, Professor Jesus probes their sad condition. 'Why has this agitation led you to anger?' The genius soon gets to the root of the matter. The anger in their psyches has been provoked by the 'god who is within you'. Jesus hits the target. One can almost hear a collective '*Ow!*' from the smothered '*ids*' of the disturbed disciples.

Here we get to the heart of one of the most gnomic and suggestive of all Gnostic sayings: 'That which you have will save you if you bring it forth from yourselves.' The disciples are going to have to somehow 'cough up' the false god that has set himself up on the throne of the true.

On the one hand, the false god is causing distress, though the disciples are unconscious of the source of the distress; the false god is apparently within them – it has a grip on their minds. On the other hand, the false can be expelled (that is, the grip is released) *simultaneously* as they bring to consciousness the true hidden deity. If they knew their hidden identity/deity, they would know Jesus.

In a sense, 'Jesus' *is* the hidden identity, which becomes conscious through Man.

We may recall Jung's words to Professor Gilles Quispel, uttered in 1952 when the young Quispel brought the Swiss psychologist the papyrus codex of the Nag Hammadi containing The Gospel of Truth: 'All my life I have been searching for the truths of the psyche – and these people knew already!'

Jesus sets the disciples a challenge. They appear to be 'up' for a struggle; they are ready, they think, to assert their self-righteous pride. So, suggests Jesus, let them try this! Jesus says that if any one of them is strong enough 'among human beings', then let him bring forth 'the perfect human and stand before my face'. *Bring forth the perfect human* ... This 'perfect human' is the hidden identity; it is the inheritance and legacy of the special generation, a generation also known among such Gnostics as 'the immovable race'.

The disciples, misperceiving the nature of the challenge, think it is a question of pride, of raw courage – which they possess in degrees – not spiritual strength. 'We have the strength', they declare. This declaration is reminiscent of the scene in the Garden of Gethsemane in the New Testament, when Jesus asks the disciples if they can stay awake with him. *Awake* ....

If that be the case, it would be an interesting commentary on that famous scene, for in that scene, Judas has already separated himself from the 11 remaining disciples. Perhaps we are about to discover what it is that separates Judas from his peers, for we are next informed directly that while 'their [the disciples'] spirits did not dare to stand' before Jesus' face, Judas Iscariot found himself able to stand before him. However, strong as he shows himself to be, Judas still cannot look Jesus in the eye.

Whether this is just plain fear, or just 'knowing his place', is not made definite. Nevertheless, Judas' next declaration suggests that he knows he is in the presence of a power superior to that conceived by the other disciples: 'I know who you are and where you have come from. You are from the immortal realm of Barbelo. And I am not worthy to utter the name of the one who has sent you.'

Judas has risen to the challenge; he has truly 'brought forth' something from within himself: the truth of his vision.

If this were a TV drama, now would be the time for an advertisement break, while we fix a drink and wonder what on earth Judas Iscariot was talking about.

Barbelo

If there had been any doubt up to this point that we are exploring an explicitly Gnostic work, the reference to Barbelo at such a critical juncture in the narrative should dispel such doubt at once.

There is no way we are looking at a gospel that somehow was left out of the sack from which the New Testament was formed. There was never any chance that the mainstream, orthodox organization was going to adopt this material as being suitable for those they ministered to. Anyhow, as we have seen from the 'secret' character of the revelation, these works were never intended to be read by the 'ordinary' faithful; their writers thought they were writing for the élite: the ones who really understood.

It is no good suggesting this is any more a 'lost gospel' (with its hint that the Bible might just be slightly incomplete) than that the 52 works in the Nag Hammadi Library should also be included in the New Testament. For a start, you would have to know who this 'Barbelo' is. Such knowledge is not given to everyone. In fact, it is not given to me. If 'Barbelo' ever meant something specific, as regards its precise etymology, then the secret has been well kept.

The word sounds like it ought to mean something. It looks like a compound word of Semitic origin. 'Bar' can suggest kinship in Hebrew; 'arba' suggests the Hebrew word for the number four; 'El' is the Semitic word for 'God': the name of the supreme god of the Canaanite religion based at Ras Shamra. 'Bel' (or Baal) was the name of a father god sometimes presented as inferior to 'El', but worshipped nonetheless by Canaanites and Israelites in the Old Testament.

The reference to 'four' has led some scholars to link the name with the *tetragrammaton* the four letters that constitute the name of the Hebrew Godhead revealed to Moses: *Yod, Hé, Vau, Hé*, while another variant interpretation suggests something to do with 'four lights': 'be-arb-orim'.

In the Nag Hammadi Gospel of the Egyptians, Barbelo is linked to the generation of the Four Great Lights, or archangels, so there may be something in that.

There may I think be a play on the Greek word *barbilos*, the word for a wild peach tree. Rooted in heaven perhaps, 'she' gives her fruit to her worshippers or children. One might think of the famous statue of Diana of the Ephesians with her many succulent breasts: authentic nourishment for the faithful. Her 'peaches' may represent the aforementioned archangels. Barbelo in this context would make perfect Gnostic sense of the Tree whose fruit is *gnosis* in an important Gnostic reworking of the Temptation of Eve story (the Gnostic Book of Baruch).

However, if we cannot say with absolute certainty what the name means, we can at least say what 'Barbelo' *represents* in Gnostic writings.

Barbelo is, as it were, the 'Queen of Heaven', a kind of Gnostic mother-goddess. On the other hand, she is bisexual, or rather *perfect*, and so is both male and female. Having said that, the 'mother' idea is the strongest image in Gnostic myth-making, though it is only meant to be an image. You have to know who your Mother is. That is to say, you have to know where you come from – that way, you can find out where you are going back to. *Who is your Mother?* The 'lord of this world' does not know; but the Gnostic Jesus knows all about the Great Mother – and her error.

The basic story goes like this. There was God, the essential, original, indescribable principle of existence. Except, he is so far 'above' anything that has been created that to say he exists means no more than saying he does not exist. You can call him the non-existent. Or the One. Or Father. *Our Father, who art in Heaven...*

The famous Gnostic teacher, Valentinus, an Egyptian, called the transcendent God *Bythos*, which means Depth, as in an ocean. A vast, vast ocean. How deep is He? *That's* how deep! In other words, *unfathomable*.

We might say then that Barbelo is somehow rooted in these ineffable waters: a Great Mother born like Aphrodite in the infinite sea.

Now if they had said 'unfathomable' in the first place, they would not need to say so many meaningless things about God; rather, that anything you *can* say about this conception or non-conception of ultimate deity is meaningless. Still, we are people and we must use language.

For some reason, equally unfathomable, the unknowable Father also expresses his being. This expression is called a First Thought. The first thought reflects the being of the Father, and is the manifestation of his first *Idea*. The potential maleness and femaleness in God's being now becomes actualized. As a result, there is a tension, a dynamic energy. The First Thought was called by Gnostics Barbelo.

In saying that Jesus comes from the realm of Barbelo, Judas Iscariot means Jesus comes as a result of the Father's self-expression in thought: Jesus is the self-consciousness of God, the child of a heavenly mother whose lush fruit is pure wisdom – so heavy is she with fruit, one might say, that her fruit must needs fall.

Barbelo is sometimes called *Sophia*, which is Greek for Wisdom. And Wisdom is a feminine noun. In Gnostic mythology, She behaves like a lot of women have behaved – and misbehaved. In one aspect, Lady Wisdom is the archetypal 'Fallen Woman', and yet she is mysterious, awful, profound, eminently worshippable, adorable, unconquerable Virgin and Whore.

Barbelo, the Gnostics say, is Mother of All. It is quite possible that Gnostics found confirmation of this conclusion while meditating on Jesus' question to his disciples: 'Who is my mother and who is my father?' when they spoke of the arrival of his mortal family.

It is possible, I suppose, that the Catholic Church later insisted that the 'Virgin Mary' was 'assumed to heaven' to take the place of Barbelo, whose devotion had been forbidden.

Judas Is Separated

Judas has recognized the transcendent identity of Jesus. That means he has made the essential first step – for like has recognized like. The identity Judas has perceived in Jesus lurks, as it were, unconsciously, in himself. Jesus is going to help him 'bring it forth', to unlock his spirit.

Jesus knows, we are told, that 'Judas was reflecting upon something that was exalted.' Jesus seizes the opportunity of Judas' perhaps sudden awareness: 'Step away from the others,' Jesus tells him, 'and I shall tell you the mysteries of the kingdom. It is possible for you to reach it, but you will grieve a great deal.'

This instruction stands out as quintessential Gnostic teaching. First, the one who aspires to greater knowledge must be separated out from the common rush or wave of humanity. Ordinary human society is corrosive to the spiritual consciousness of the Gnostic initiate. Jesus is going to initiate him. This cannot be done in groups or by congregations. It is not the common mind that is being addressed; it is the individual. This is Jesus *one-on-one*: a private tutorial. The Master is dividing the wheat from the chaff. Judas is ready.

Judas is clearly going to receive something that the disciples cannot take; they are not spiritually ripe.

This again tells us something about the Christian Gnostic attitude to the religious traditions of the mainstream Christian Churches. Gnostics took the view that simply because a tradition came from one of the apostles did not mean it was necessarily anything more than an early stage of spiritual development – a beginner's gospel: faith for the faithful. Gnostics were convinced there was more to it. A transformation of 'being' could be experienced in this life, not after it.

Since the 'beginner's gospel' was that which Gnostics perceived as being taught by the bishops, priests and deacons, they (the authorities) were naturally offended. In fact their reaction was parodied in The Gospel of Judas in the previous scene. Persons exhibiting such independence of spirit caused the Church's infuriation and rejection.

In psychological terms, orthodox Christians simply could not help themselves. The rational path was closed by the nature of the spiritual *scotoma* that inhibited them. Inwardly blind, they became emotional and angry, like people who cry 'blasphemy' because they have been trained to, or have been told to, rather than finding out what might really be intended with challenging thoughts or statements. The 'living Jesus' is quite prepared to offend the so-called 'religious sensibilities' of anyone. He is interested in the truth, not keeping a phoney peace at any price. States are concerned with laws of offence because they help maintain the *status quo*. In the Gospels, Jesus' enemies accuse him of having disrupted the Roman government's maintenance of law and order.

It had not passed the Gnostics' notice that Jesus was himself treated by some religious authorities in Judaea as a blasphemer and one reliant on the devil. Claiming the 'truth' of his own identity – in however veiled or symbolic a form – elicited an hysterical denunciation.

Jesus' Jewish enemies even allowed him to be executed by a method practised by the Romans against their own fellow Jews, and which was considered as acutely shameful. To be hanged on a tree was seen as being accursed by God.

And yet, the Gnostics envisioned their Jesus laughing at those who thought they had nailed him to 'their tree', laughing at the neurotic follies of those who shout the loudest in any dispute. The enemies of the 'living Jesus' were hanging themselves. The 'living Jesus' is indifferent to the ways of the world. He will 'take apart' the one who knows him; separate that one from the masses and sort him or her out.

Perhaps the reference to 'their tree' also contains a poignant contrast with the tree of which the living Jesus is the divine fruit: Barbelo. The divine child hangs upon his divine Mother. Jesus is a *peach*, the sweetest wine.

Jesus assures Judas – the socially rejected one (and soon to be complete 'outsider') – that he really can 'reach' the 'kingdom' (the highest spiritual being of God), but it is going to hurt. Why is it going to hurt? Well, as any practised yogi will tell you, spiritual exercises are not for the weak-willed or faint-hearted! But there is more to it than that. He is not just being prepared to run the marathon. It is the psychological torture that Jesus is referring to.

The pain is encoded in the well-known narrative about what happens to Judas after he has betrayed Jesus: 'For someone else will replace you, so that the 12 may again come to completion with their god.'

Being taken apart from the crowd, separated from the group, almost re-programmed, we might say, is going to hurt psychologically. His own buddies are going to hate him. Where once he found fellow feeling and the joy and security of being with people he could rely on, where once he was part of an inner group – an élite club or band of brothers – he is going to be sent to the cold outside. He will be 'cold shouldered' – and worse. His truth is going to be blackened by the calumnies of those who have utterly and wilfully failed to perceive what is happening to him. And there will be no revenge, no earthly satisfaction for the one in the will of God.

In taking Judas apart from the rest, he is not doing him any favours from the social point of view. This is going to be very tough indeed. But the goal is there: it is possible for Judas 'to reach it'. If that is what Judas really, truly wants, the prize is winnable; he can make it.

Now, while this is an element in a narrative leading to Judas' climactic act (with which we are all familiar), it is also a meditation on the price all those who follow this Jesus must pay. Yes, we can attain *gnosis*, but it may have painful social consequences; we may experience rejection, outright hostility, slanderous misrepresentation of our deepest motives; indeed, straightforward lies told about us by those we had considered to be our friends. Things that were familiar and comforting may vanish. Livelihoods and lives may be threatened. But fear not.

As the 12 disciples re-bond, it will be as though Judas himself had never existed. His memory is to be all but erased from the record. He is to be a cipher, a nothing. Someone else will replace him. That someone is called Matthias in the New Testament Acts of the Apostles. But there may be even more to the phrasing in The Gospel of Judas. Judas will be replaced. Why? So that 'the 12 may again come to completion with their god'.

Now, this is strange. We can understand that the 12 might want to 'make up the numbers', like an army recruiting after heavy casualties. But here it is to 'come to completion with their god'. Even after all that happens, Jesus is still saying that the other disciples are still going to be following 'their god', that is, a false god.

There may be something in the phrase 'the 12' here. Christian Gnostics well versed in their lore would hardly fail to pick up a nice double meaning in this phrase.

Judas Punctures the Zodiac

The '12' is an expression for the zodiac, the sphere of the fixed stars in the 'night-cloak' that is the visible (at night) cosmos above us. To Gnostics, the lord of the zodiac, who controlled the powers of fate in this world – our world, the lower world – was the false god. The signs of the zodiac, for all their wonder, were yet a copy, or fabricated version, of ideas even more sublime. The perfect idea of '12' existed in the eternal, higher realm. It was one of the higher God's Ideas – like the archetypal principles of geometry.

But the Gnostics believed that the lord of the zodiac suffered – like spiritually unconscious human beings – from a terrible affliction of amnesia. The power of the zodiac was under the impression he was sole lord of everything.

The 'completion of the 12', then, meant for Gnostics the attempt of the false god to repair the damage done when the earthly 12 suffered Jesus' fateful act of commissioning Judas' 'betrayal'. The lord of the zodiac is going to try to put his constellations back in order. That order has been ruptured, even punctured.

The curtain had been torn by the vain attack on the living Jesus; spiritual radiation was able to pour through, like citizens of the old Eastern Bloc suddenly able to pick up news from the world beyond the 'iron curtain'. The breach in the wall would have to be mended, the '12' would have to be 'completed' by their god. The break in transmission of the Lie would have to be restored. Consciousness is just too dangerous for the powers-that-be.

I can understand if this is not entirely clear to everyone. It is quite a difficult picture to get over, especially if this material and story is new to you. But the conception is luminously simple.

Try thinking of it like *this* – because this is how Christian Gnostics saw it:

Jesus was about to 'pull off' the greatest cosmic heist in the history of the universe. He was about to release from bondage the scattered sparks of divine light that had got trapped in the physical universe. He has got to break into the bank, turn the code on the safe door, crack it open, find the treasure, and get out again without the cops discovering who he is and even, what precisely he has done.

This act is, from the point of view of the Head of Cosmic Police (the chief *archon* or 'demiurge') completely criminal. It is going to spoil everything he has been doing for thousands of years. This Chief has 'bought off' the mayor, drugged the people, and been living off the proceeds for as long as he cares to remember. He is the Law, and he is not going to let anyone take over the territory.

It is not as though everything has always been peaceful. Occasionally, someone begins to wake up a bit as the world-drug wears thin and starts causing trouble. Still, the Chief's been able to deal with that.

When simply killing the troublemaker fails to stop the disease in the cosmic body politic, the Chief has been able to take the *words* of the troublemaker, build a religion around them, and persuade most people to worship the 'new deity'. What they have not realized is that all these 'gods' point to *him*. He is worshipped. That is what matters. He is respected. Whatever fancy name people might have given their idea of the highest god, he is running the show. People are even prepared to die for him; *killing* for him was never a problem.

The Ruler has done something incredible. He has taken the most amazing, divine being – Man – and turned him into a complete idiot, blind to who he really is, and totally unconscious of where he came from. Instead of taking his place as lord of the universe, he stumbles about like an old drunk with a broken bottle.

Well, in order to outwit the Ruler, and out of love for the lost souls, Jesus has come down through the cosmic spheres and appeared to men and women – and to the chief *archon* – as a man: a manipulable being, someone the lord of this world thinks he can deal with.

Now that Jesus has delivered the keys to the kingdom – the *gnosis* – he has got to get away. It is like the extraordinary image of the young man who runs from the Garden of Gethsemane, leaving his garment (Mark 14,vv 51-2) behind him, after Judas hands Jesus over. Gnostics would understand the image of the 'garment' to be the body, the veil of the spirit. It is quite possible that the reference to the young man fleeing the garden unable to be stopped – and leaving his garment behind in the hands of others – was an original, gnostic element of the story. Perhaps it was 'left in' the narrative because it looked like a mere observed detail, just a part of the story.

Here is a possible case where the reading of a Gnostic (albeit later) gospel actually illuminates the submerged meaning of the canonical Gospel. Maybe we can benefit from the interpretative power of some of the Gnostic writings.

Their interpretation runs along the following lines. The real Jesus must get away. He has got to trick his enemies. The thing about the 'lord of this world' is that he is an out-and-out material-ist. His vision is limited to appearances, that is, he is blind. So he has not quite realized what he is dealing with. However, he has heard enough to know that this being had best be removed from the scene, once the lord's stooges can get their hands on him, without the crowd waking up to what they are trying to do. The real Jesus is a kind of 'antibody' whose presence has alerted the lord of this world's cosmic immunity system. (Jesus, an *antibody*? I did not intend the pun, but it is rather appropriate.)

Jesus' plan is to make sure that at the very moment when the lord of this world thinks he has triumphed – 'whacking' Jesus and 'putting him away' forever – at that very moment, the archons are going to be left holding the garment. What fools! Jesus has given them the slip. Free from the material dimension, he can rise up back to where he came from.

The Gnostics knew this story was hidden within the mainstream Gospel account, but being deprived of the eyes to see, the mainstream could not read it, even when the truth was right before their eyes: 'They parted my raiment among them, and for my vesture they did cast lots.' (John 19, v24)

In turning aside the attention of the cosmic guardians, the archons, Jesus' true and mighty being will surge out of the grip of the false god to forge a new path through the enveloping spheres of the cosmos. In establishing this new 'stairway to heaven', the pattern of the stars will be disrupted, as the very cosmos shakes in the echo of this transcendental act of liberation. 'And the sun was darkened, and the veil of the temple was rent in the midst.' (Luke 23,v45) The veil of the temple, like the garment of the body, was understood as that which hides the spiritual truth. The truth beyond the material dimension has been revealed, at last!

But the author of The Gospel of Judas knows that while a new path has been opened for those who seize this triumphant, incredible 'good news', this does not mean that for those still in this world, the false god has no power of compulsion. He is like a prison warder after a big break-out. He has got to look at the security; try and make sure nothing like this happens again. He has got his reputation to think of! He has got to fix those broken bolts, try to fill in those gaping holes; tell the prisoners remaining that it is business as usual – distract them from taking it too seriously. Maybe it was all just a dream.

And so, we are told, Judas will be replaced – as if nothing has happened – so that the '12' can 'again come to completion with their god'. Their god is going to repair the cosmic ceiling. It is going to be business as usual; even the Church can be brought to heel. Soon its priests will be indistinguishable from those unenlightened rulers of religion who preceded them. Thus, Jesus gives Judas an unappetizing taste of what is to come. Is he still willing? Having been asked to step away from the eleven, Judas then asks when Jesus is going to tell him the 'mysteries of the kingdom'. He also wants to know when 'the great day of light' will dawn for 'the generation'.

'But when he said this, Jesus left him.'

The Holy Generation

Jesus left him. It seems Judas' contact with this exalted Jesus failed. That is to say, he seems to have switched to the wrong 'frequency', a lower frequency. Jesus can only speak to Judas when he shows signs of the right level, or frequency, of comprehension. So perhaps it is not so much a question of Jesus 'walking away from him', rather that the Jesus who speaks the mysteries is impossible to perceive, unless one's consciousness is 'up to it'.

This is a bit like a poet writing a masterpiece from the mysterious well of inspiration, only to be distracted by a knock at the door. The poet comes back to his notebook, only to find, however hard he tries, that the end of the poem has 'left him'.

It is not surprising Judas' perception fails, as the next passage in the gospel makes clear. What seems to have cut off the communication is a failure of Judas to perceive a spiritual truth. It turns out that the breakdown concerns his choosing to ask about when the great day of light will dawn for the generation. Many religious groups today round the world are continually focused on the question of when the world will end – and, specifically – when they will themselves (and their families) be having a better time of it! They always imagine they are going to be the lucky winners in the hoped-for 'Last Judgement'.

Anyhow, all this talk about the light that will dawn for the generation sounds less like the usual apocalyptic warnings than the more optimistic idea about a fantastic new world order or New Age, or age of enlightenment. In fact, it sounds a bit reminiscent of some very far-out hopes voiced at the end of the 1960s!

John Lennon was interviewed about the future in 1969, for example, and with great, and genuinely touching, hope said the Sixties were just the *start*, 'Like getting up in the morning – and we haven't even got to dinner time yet!' As for the new decade (the 1970s), he continued: 'Everything's gonna be great, you know! It's just gonna be great!' He was certainly more optimistic than the miserable or shady politicians interviewed in the same TV series (*Man of the Decade*), but John was somewhat over-optimistic, all the same. But that's youth – ever ready to greet the dawn, as long as it does not mean getting out of bed!

From Jesus' point of view in The Gospel of Judas, Judas' hopes are still too tied to the ordinary plane of things, of dates and times. He is waiting to be *told*, the implication being that he *knows something already*; a knowledge he has demonstrated by his bold recognition of Jesus' transcendent identity. Yet he is still looking *outside of himself*. He is thinking in terms of space and time, with the same hopes of those around him. Like so many, he is waiting upon the dawn of the new era – the 'age of Aquarius' and suchlike.

The idea of dawn is evoked again in the next scene, which takes place at dawn the following day. (There is even perhaps a little hint of the Resurrection-morning scene, when the women come to the grave and find Jesus gone.) Dawn is a time of growing enlightenment. Jesus appears to his disciples again, whether as a child or not, is not said. They are eager to know where he has been in the meantime, what he has been doing.

Jesus picks up again on the 'generation' idea: 'I went to another great and holy generation', is his response to the disciples' curiosity. So Jesus is not referring to the generation Judas was thinking of, but *another*, described as 'great and holy'. This is where the light has dawned. The disciples seem, yet again, to be fairly contemptuous of the implications that Jesus has to go elsewhere to find the right generation. Aren't they, the disciples, the 'main men' in Jesus' operation? They wanted him to talk about 'their generation'.

Echoing phrases uttered in the orthodox Gospels, the disciples are eager to place themselves as winners in the messianic kingdom. 'Lord, what is the great generation that is superior to us and holier than us, that is not now in these realms?' If they think they are going to get a simple answer to this, they have got another thing coming!

Jesus laughs when he hears them jockeying for position. They can hardly conceive of something bigger than their own egos. He correctly perceives that they are thinking that if there is going to be any 'strong and holy generation' it is going to be *them*. But they are in for a rude shock. He tells the disciples, in no uncertain terms, that no one from 'this aeon' – the physical cosmos – will ever see the generation he is talking about. Furthermore – and this ties in with what we have been seeing about the lord of the zodiacal and stellar powers – 'no host of angels of the stars will rule over that generation, and no person of mortal birth can associate with it.' That's telling them! They don't stand a chance. Again, the 'angels of the stars', who will not govern the holy generation, are clearly meant as the '12'. The characters of the fixed stars are reflected in the disciples – and their lust for dominance.

Apocalypse Judas

As we shall see, all this talk of 'stars', which is such a powerful and to some extent unique feature of The Gospel of Judas (in the context of Gnostic writings), derives from a body of tradition very important in the formulation of Gnostic images. That body of tradition is called *apocalyptic*.

The Greek word refers to that which has been brought out of hiding: unveiled or revealed. We have then the twin ideas of secrets, and of revelation. It would not be an error to call The Gospel of Judas an 'Apocalypse of Judas'.

A number of other kindred Gnostic writings are called apocalypses. We tend to think of the 'apocalypse' as the end of the world, but the early apocalypses were very optimistic works.

Elements of apocalyptic thought go back to prophetic traditions written down in approximately the 5th and 6th centuries BC. But the enthusiasm for producing apocalyptic books (revelations of God's plans for the future) really 'took off' after the middle of the 2nd century BC. By the time of Jesus of Nazareth, ideas generated in apocalyptic books were very much in the air of Jewish religious discourse, especially in the north of their country.

One of the works read before and around the time of Jesus was called the Book of Enoch. Another, one with which Jesus was extremely familiar, was the Book of Daniel. It is very interesting that elements and images from both these works appear to have found their way into the imagery of The Gospel of Judas.

The emphasis on the stars in The Gospel of Judas seems to derive from the apocryphal Book of Enoch (actually a collection of apocalyptic works). You will not find this book in the New Testament. Nevertheless, it was very influential, at the time of Jesus and beyond. In fact, it was influential in select circles right up to the time of the Renaissance and even beyond then.

As we shall also see, the great and holy generation among whom Jesus has been spending his absences from the disciples, is the 'immovable generation': the generation of Seth. Seth is also Jesus in his transcendent, beyond-this-world aspect.

Seth

What is meant by this figure of Seth?

The significance of Seth derives, in part, from the account in the Book of Genesis of the first human family. After the horror of Abel's murder at the hands of his brother Cain, Adam and Eve have a new child. This child is Seth, and in the Sethian tradition, Seth stands as 'another seed', a new seed: a new beginning.

Allogenes is the Greek for 'another seed' or 'race', and a fragment of a Gnostic work about Allogenes was discovered with The Gospel of Judas. The word 'allogenes' can also mean 'alien' or 'stranger', which is how Gnostics saw themselves. So Seth is, in the Gnostic reading of Genesis, the progenitor of a new race of humanity, described as 'sons of God'. Yes, *sons of God*. In Genesis 6, the children of Seth ('sons of God') appear to be contrasted with the fair 'daughters of men'. When the 'sons of God' and the fair 'daughters of men' got together, their offspring were, we are told, giants, 'men of renown'. The seed of heroism is a Sethian seed.

The appearance of the Sethian line in Genesis coincides both with the time when the Lord was first called upon by his name (Genesis 4, v26), and with the degeneration of those not of Seth's seed. This coincidence was significant to 'Sethian Gnostics'. By the way, it is extremely doubtful that the people who valued the Sethian tradition called themselves 'Sethian Gnostics', any more than they called themselves 'Cainites'. 'Cainites' is really a nickname thought up by those who disapproved of them, while 'Sethian Gnostics' is just a way of identifying an unnamed community or communities with enthusiasm for the Sethian message.

Members of these communities were convinced that the Sethian line had been the preserved receptacle of the 'perfect man', somehow – even miraculously – preserved from the degeneracy of the lower world.

The 'seed' of Seth was understood not as DNA material (though I am sure they would have been fascinated by the insights of microbiology), but as an image for the divine spirit. Gnostic writings refer to the 'soul-seed'.

They saw the Sethian line appearing occasionally in history, throwing up great and inspired men who were somehow 'not of this world'. It is not surprising then that they saw in the prophetic character and otherworldly distinction of Jesus an incarnation of 'the Great Seth'. Seth was the fruit of humanity as a divine idea, made in the image of the highest God: man's secret identity lost in matter.

Seth was also powerfully associated with divine knowledge, wisdom and science. In Gnostic lore, Seth's work in the scientific sphere is linked to that body of knowledge and wisdom which also went under the name of Hermes, the divine messenger from ancient Greek mythology, known to Gnostics as the Thrice Greatest Hermes. Thrice Greatest Hermes (Hermes Trisemegistus) was patron both of medieval freemasons, and of the Platonic Renaissance that found a home in the palaces of Cosimo and Lorenzo de' Medici.

In The Gospel of Judas, Jesus looks at the disciples for signs of the Sethian identity. That special identity appears – *hiding under a bushel*, as it were – only in Judas.

Jesus has plans for Judas. That is all right for Judas, but what about the disciples? Does he have plans for them? It does not look like it. When the disciples hear Jesus' speech about the great and holy generation, they are 'troubled in spirit'. Completely deflated, 'They could not say a word.' The reader is inclined to sympathize with them!

A Dream Temple

The next scene takes place on 'another day'. The disciples have been dreaming. They take their dreaming to be a meaningful (collective) vision and they ask Jesus what it means. It is a dream about a 'large house' with an altar in it. It must be either the Temple (of Jerusalem) or a symbolic temple. They describe the priests who keep the disciples waiting. The priests are not a pretty sight.

Some sacrifice their own children at the altar, others their wives, 'in praise and humility with each other' – clearly some kind of blind hypocrisy. Some are involved in illicit sexual relations; some are criminals.

And in all this, at the altar, Jesus' name is invoked. That clinches it. This is not a vision of the Herodian Temple in Jerusalem, it is almost certainly the new 'temple' of the Christian Church. The priests are hypocrites and sinners.

Jesus says they 'have planted fruitless trees, in my name, in a shameless manner'. This reminds one of another Gnostic text where the priests and bishops of the mainstream Church are accused of worshiping the name of a dead man, and of being false leaders and 'dry canals'. It reflects the struggle between the Gnostic communities and the orthodox system.

Jesus sees no difference between the disciples and the priests they have described in their dream. They are not serving the name they claim. 'That is the god you serve,' he tells them bluntly. The cattle they have envisioned being brought for sacrifice are an image for all the people they and their followers will lead astray 'before that altar'. This is a savage indictment of the orthodox position. The people are herded like dumb animals, in innocence brought to slaughter – or sacrifice. Is there even a hint here of the terrible martyrdoms suffered by Christians? Is the writer trying to say they are both living and dying in a vain cause? It is a disturbing thought.

These false teachers, Jesus says, will 'make use of my name in this way, and generations of the pious will remain loyal to him. ... For to the human generations it has been said, "Look, God has received your sacrifice from the hands of a priest" – that is, a minister of error.' For their actions, Jesus says the Lord of the All will eventually put them to shame.

Then comes the command, 'Stop sacrificing,' after which some words suggest the archons are supporting the priestly imposture, but then about 15 lines of the text are lost – probably part of the damage done to the papyrus during the last 28 years.

The text picks up again with an interesting idea. 'Stop struggling with me,' says Jesus. 'Each of you has his own star.' It sounds like it is going to get even more interesting, but then some 17 more lines have been lost, apparently on the theme of the generation 'that will last': the one we have been hearing about – the Sethian generation.

Each of You Has His Own Star

This poignant statement about a link between the soul and a star is one of the most striking things about The Gospel of Judas. There is nothing quite like it in any of the Nag Hamamdi Gnostic writings, whose contents are, in other respects, so close in spirit and letter to the world of The Gospel of Judas.

Each of you has his own star. It sounds quite magical. One immediately thinks of the famous words propounded by 20th-century magician and poet, Edward Alexander Crowley: 'Every man and every woman is a star.'

And we should not forget that the root of Gnostic religion is magic. It is the 'occult' or hidden dimension of the primal Man that *gnosis* is concerned with. It is about power and mastery – as well as despair – over the things of nature. It is about supernatural awareness and hidden knowledge.

The idea of souls linked to stars was current in Platonist philosophy at the time Gnostic Christianity developed. In the *Timaeus*, Plato wrote of how good souls returned to their allotted star, but I do not think the source of Gnostic speculation on this secret stellar identity was Greek philosophy.

The link between stars and messianic righteousness will be familiar to anyone who thinks of Christmas – with the messiah's arrival heralded by a new star, whose meaning is grasped by magi from the east. 'We have seen his star,' they say.

The Jewish warrior who would lead the last Zealot rebellion against the Romans in Judaea called himself *Bar Kochba* (d135), which means 'Son of the Star'. The Star had become inextricably linked with the executors of God's righteousness, as the Zealots saw themselves. This idea of stars and the holy finds its most detailed expression in the Book of Enoch, copies of which were found at the Qumran caves (among the 'Dead Sea Scrolls'). The book's varied contents go back to some time in the centuries before Christ. Jesus was probably familiar with them.

It would seem likely that the Gnostics got a lot of their ideas and images – especially concerning the hierarchies of angels – from the pages of the Book of Enoch, and apocalyptic works of a similar nature. These works purported to reveal the hidden mysteries of the universe and how nature occasionally manifested messages from God: messages that required interpreting.

In chapters 43 and 44 of the Book of Enoch, Enoch (who is described as a 'son of Seth, son of Adam'), is given a vision of the righteous stars:

And I saw other lightnings and the stars of heaven, and I saw how He [the 'Father of Lights'] called them all by their names and they hearkened unto Him. And I saw how they are weighed in a righteous balance according to their proportions of light: I saw the width of their spaces and the day of their appearing, and how their revolution produces lightning: and I saw their revolution according to the number of the angels, and how they keep faith with each other. And I asked the angel who went with me who showed me what was hidden: 'What are these?' And he said to me: 'The Lord of Spirits hath showed thee their parable: these are the names of the holy who dwell on the earth and believe in the name of the Lord of Spirits for ever and ever.

The background to this Jewish interest in the secrets of the stars belongs to their longstanding relationship with the wisdom, science and magic of ancient Mesopotamia (especially in what is now northern Iraq). This cultural interchange is explicit in the Book of Daniel. Daniel was trained, we are told, by Chaldaean wise men, who taught him to interpret dreams and visions – as Jesus does in the pages of The Gospel of Judas. The Chaldaeans came from 'Kurdistan', bordering modern Turkey, Iran and Iraq: the biblical 'Urartu' ('Ur of the Chaldees' or 'Ararat').

The Daimon

In the next scene, the disciples enquire about the destiny of those belonging to the two 'generations': the holy and great generation, and the rest. The message is stark.

As to the Sethian generation, when these people 'have completed the time of the kingdom and the breath of life leaves them, their bodies will die but their souls will be alive, and they will be taken up.'

As for *the rest*, a curious Gnostic twist of the well-known Parable of the Sower says, 'It is impossible to sow seed on rock and harvest its fruit.' Having no root in the eternal generation, such beings can never flower spiritually and be harvested. It does not look good for them but, the speech implies, since they are totally insensitive to the life of the soul, they will not suffer from its absence. Gnostics have been accused of spiritual élitism: salvation for the elect only. Now you can see why.

In the next scene, having heard the dreams of the other disciples, Judas tells Jesus about his own vision, 'a great vision'. Jesus' response to Judas' announcement is itself amusing: 'You thirteenth *daimon*, why do you try so hard? But speak up, and I shall bear with you.' Jesus has already marked Judas out; the disciple does not need to 'push it'. The nickname 'thirteenth daimon' may refer to Judas being outside of the 12 – he has broken the circle, or the number 13 may have some other significance. The 'daimon' (a Greek word) is the hidden, essential being of a person. It does not find its root in this world. It belongs to a spiritual world beyond. Its projection into time and space is the visible person ('the body is that part of the soul perceived by the five senses'). The daimon is much deeper than the 'personality'. According to Plato's *Symposium*, it is the spiritual and therefore essential identity, the 'genius', if you like. To be truly inspired is to be a conduit for this extra-dimensional 'self' or even Angel.

Putting the conscious mind in contact with the unconscious being has long been a feature of arduous magical training. From the beginning of the Christian movement, there developed an increasingly bitter conflict with Magic. It persists to this day, though many people have come to think that both experiences are delusions. Magic was very real for everyone at the time of The Gospel of Judas, and the idea that Jesus was himself a magician was held in many places. If it was a Gnostic type of Christianity being observed, this conclusion is hardly surprising.

The first major critic of Gnostic communities, Bishop Irenaeus of Lyon (who knew of The Gospel of Judas) was convinced that the 'gnosis falsely so-called' began with a magician, Simon Magus.

We find Simon Magus in contest with the apostle Peter in the Acts of the Apostles. Peter rebukes Simon the Magus for trying to buy the secret (magic) of the Holy Spirit.

The view that Gnostic ideas may have grown up in Phoenicia, Samaria (where Simon Magus came from), northern Syria and what is now northern Iraq, makes a lot of sense, so Irenaeus may have been on the right lines, at least geographically speaking.

Judas the Victim

So, the thirteenth *daimon* dreams a dream. Judas speaks of 'the 12 disciples' (we had thought he was one of them) stoning and persecuting him. Judas then comes to a great house with a 'roof of greenery'. There are people within it. He begs to be taken 'along with these people'.

Jesus says he has got the wrong idea: 'your star has led you astray', he tells Judas. Is this 'star' a euphemism for Judas' inner energy, his sense of self? Up to a point, but Jesus will soon say that he has taught Judas about 'the error of the stars'. This 'error of the stars' seems to refer to an old apocalyptic myth of the rebellion of the stellar angels; fallen stars caught (in Gnostic lore) in the lower-worldly *matrix* of the chief *archon*.

Remember the quotation above about the righteous stars in the Book of Enoch. They 'keep faith with each other'. That means they abide by their proper, ordained course. That course is in tune with the will of the 'Father of Lights' or 'Lord of spirits'.

But there are rebel stars. There is a disorder in the universe that stems from the ignorance of the chief *archon*, whom we (and Judas) will soon hear about in vivid terms. Mankind's inability to perceive spiritual truth may be the result of this stellar disorder, reflected on earth according to the principle, 'as above, so below.' Something has gone wrong in the attic, so to speak, and the house of earth below is in a mess.

Judas has been led astray by his wilful star which sees a place for him in the dream house – the house above. 'No person of mortal birth', says Jesus, 'is worthy to enter the house you have seen, for that place is reserved for the holy. Neither the sun nor the moon will rule there, nor the day, but the holy will abide there always, in the eternal realm with the holy angels.' This passage could have come straight out of the Book of Enoch.

Judas is troubled by what Jesus has told him. Maybe there is something profoundly wrong with Judas: 'Master,' he asks, 'could it be that my seed is under the control of the archons?' Two lines are then missing.

Coming out of the lacuna in the manuscript, there is another reference to Judas' grief. He has earlier been told that he can 'make it' to the kingdom but he will grieve much. Now, again, Judas 'will grieve much when you see the kingdom and all its generation'.

This is a kind of tease. Judas is going to grieve because he has now got a taste for the holy generation. Where they are going is looking very attractive to him. But it seems for all that, that he is going to be denied fulfilment of his dream wish – to escape from the attacks of the disciples and to enter the great house.

'What good is it that I have received it? For you have set me apart from that generation,' he cries. Poor Judas! He is outside the familiar 12; now he is outside the holy generation as well.

Now Jesus reassures him: 'You will become the thirteenth, and you will be cursed by the other generations – and you will come to rule over them. In the last days they will curse your rising to the holy generation.'

But rise he will. Judas will make it in the end.

The Hidden Cosmos

The Gospel of Judas now launches into a description very common to Gnostic literature. Understanding what was going on in the universe, and how things had come to be what they were, seems to have been very important to Gnostics. Indeed, when Irenaeus attacks 'the *gnosis* falsely so-called', most of his energy is spent delineating the cosmologies and beliefs of a 'fall' in the divine being, that character-ized the *gnosis*, or liberating knowledge, of the Gnostic communities.

Jesus invites Judas to hear about 'what no eye of an angel has ever seen, no thought of heart has ever comprehended, and it was never called by any name'. Who could resist? Well, we can. Whatever else people gain nowadays from Gnostic scriptures, one thing is clear. There is very little real interest in the way Gnostics described the creation of the universe and the angels they would have to pass when returning to the *Pleroma*, or 'Fullness of the Godhead', either in vision or at death.

There must be a reason for this. I think it is because we do not believe in this sort of itinerary any more. Science has presented us with a very different picture of the apparently infinite universe. For a start, we do not see it as a series of spheres going concentrically around our world. In fact, as science emits greater quantities of often startling visual and mathematical information, we do not really know what to think of the universe.

One idea we might share with some Gnostics' ideas of the cosmos is that it came from a primal catastrophic event, with space and time coming into being simultaneously with a kind of 'Big Bang'. The Gnostics would find this quite comprehensible. They saw the universe as emerging through a kind of divine error that broke an incomprehensible existence of a primal *Silence*. But apart from this idea – and it is significant – we do not feel the *presence* of the universe in the same way as our ancestors.

Only poets and lovers suggest stars are windows into heaven. We know that if we started to ascend 'into heaven' without breathing equipment, we would soon die of suffocation. But the poetic, or mystical, idea of an *inner ascension* (which is also Gnostic) – this we can appreciate, up to a point. The problem we might face would be the abundance of technical names (mostly for angels), based chiefly on Jewish and Chaldaean traditions, that are repeated in Gnostic ascension accounts, often to a tedious degree.

However, these stellar beings were very important to Gnostics. It was widely held that the soul on rising to the higher reality would have to know certain passwords and signs that would prevent the archons from inhibiting the soul's return. Jesus had shown the Way and in his Name, and armed with his Knowledge, the soul could eventually follow.

These Gnostics were not materialistic. They believed the world they saw with their eyes and touched with their hands was, on reaching *gnosis*, revealed to be only a thin canvas stretched over vast spiritual realities (the *aeons*). The spiritual realities governing the visible world were held to be in rebellion against, or ignorant of, their source (just as the soul is in rebellion against its bodily casing). These spiritual rulers (archons) generated the illusion of absoluteness and permanence that we perceive to be the character of matter.

You could not wake the archons up – but *you* could be awoken – and what a world, the Gnostic writings suggest, you would see! And, by the way, it is not all that different to the kind of way our medieval (orthodox) Christian ancestors saw the universe, with its governing angels and distant Father enthroned in Heaven.

One important difference perhaps was that where the medieval Church saw benign angels, the Gnostics were often haunted by the idea that these controlling entities could be malevolent, hostile to salvation. You had better get your passwords right!

The medieval Church knew about rebel angels of course, but it mostly transferred the idea of wicked spiritual entities to the world of devils and evil fairies, with all their nasty concoctions for deceiving humankind.

A Luminous Cloud

Judas' 'trip' begins with the appearance of 'a luminous cloud'. Jesus says: 'Let an angel come into being as my attendant.' There emerges from the cloud, 'the enlightened divine Self-Generated', who is called 'a great angel'. This idea of a guiding angel is very characteristic of Gnostic journeys to the inner worlds or worlds beyond.

This divine Self-Generated brings forth four other angels from another cloud. 'And he created the first light-being to reign over him.' Just who is this light-being is unclear because of the fragmented text. Angels are called to serve 'him'.

There then follows the creation of an enlightened aeon, a second light-being to reign over 'him', more angels (myriads), and more enlightened aeons, and still more myriads of angels to assist. It's like a great, silent, slow-motion explosion – completely pacific – and not in any way a 'Bang'. That is because we are in the higher, spiritual realm.

The creation of the Idea of Man, who is divine, is referred to next: 'Adamas was in the first luminous cloud that no angel has ever seen among all those called "God".' Adamas 'made the incorruptible generation of Seth appear'. To accord with 'the will of the Spirit' 72 luminaries (or light beings) 'appear in the incorruptible generation'. Then 360 luminaries appear in that same holy generation, 'in accordance with the will of the Spirit, that their number should be five for each' (that is, five of this second batch of luminaries relate to each one of the first batch of luminaries).

And in this way the aeons and the heavens and the firmaments come into being. Judas' attention is next directed to the cosmos in which the first human appeared 'with his incorruptible powers'. The original man is not the product of biological evolution. His identity begins as a spiritual being, a reflection of the divine.

An angel called El (the ancient Semitic word for god or God) gets 12 angels to rule over chaos and the underworld. A face appears from a cloud, 'flashed with fire' and covered with blood. 'His name was Nebro, which means "rebel"; others call him Yaldabaoth [translation uncertain].'

This terrifying visage is the chief *archon*, the 'lord of this world', the 'jealous god', the real villain of Gnostic mythology. This being, intended to run the underworld, gets right above his station and impersonates the 'highest God'. He has got mankind to share his self-delusions of grandeur, as we have seen earlier.

Nebro creates six angels. One is called *Saklas*. In other Gnostic texts, Saklas (meaning 'Fool'), is another name for the creator of the lower world. The six angels produce 12 angels in the heavens, 'with each one receiving a portion in the heavens' (possibly the zodiacal signs).

Unfortunately, the next movement is obscure as the text has been damaged. It returns with the creation of five angels 'who ruled over the underworld, and first of all over chaos': 'The first is Seth, who is called Christ', followed by Harmathoth, Galila, Yobel, and Adonaios.

The Creation of Adam

Taking a phrase from the Book of Genesis, where God is called *Elohim* (*plural*), Saklas parodies the great creation statement: 'Let us make man in our own image, after our likeness.' (Genesis 1, v26). Saklas says to his angels, terrifyingly: 'Let us create a human being after the likeness and after the image.' They fashion Adam and Eve. Adam is based on a copy of the celestial *Adamas*, the spiritual archetype of Man, sometimes called *Anthropos*.

Saklas appears kindly to wish Adam long life and children. Though at first sight it looks like kindness, it is not. There is not only the hint of cold indifference, but a profound and quite disturbing sarcasm in this injunction to procreate. The source for this nasty joke is the speech made to Adam and Eve when they are ejected from the Paradise of Eden in Genesis. Woman will suffer hard; man will have to earn his bread by the sweat of his brow. The gates of the Garden are closed. Man has fallen.

Judas, touchingly perhaps, asks Jesus, 'What is the long duration of time that the human being will live?' This may not simply mean, 'what's the longest time a man can live?' Rather it seems to imply the desperate question: 'How long can human beings carry on for?'

Judas has already shown he is nervous about the destiny of human beings. Jesus says something to suggest he is interested to know why Judas finds there's something not quite right about the picture of Adam living a long life, having 'received his kingdom' (meaning possibly 'his lot or inheritance'), 'with longevity with his ruler'.

One thinks of the ancient adage, 'What is man that Thou should be mindful of him?' Jesus is leading Judas on. Then Judas asks, 'Does the human spirit die?' *Good*, thinks Jesus. Good question. Judas is getting the idea that Adam's problem has to do with his 'ruler'. We know this ruler is the one worshipped by the other disciples. The ruler rules 'the 12'.

Jesus answers that God ordered Michael (the archangel) to give the spirits (the breath of life) to people as a loan, 'so that they might offer service' (to God), but 'the Great One ordered Gabriel to grant spirits to the great generation with no ruler over it – that is, the spirit and the soul.'

Tantalizingly, the next sentence beginning, 'Therefore the rest of the souls...' has, rather poignantly, gone.

Salvation and Destruction

Luckily for Adam, God saw to it that *gnosis* was given to him 'and those with him'. *Why?* 'So that the kings of chaos and the underworld might not lord it over them.'

Jesus then tells Judas that the angel Saklas' time will come, when 'the stars bring matters to completion', and Saklas thereby completes the span of time allotted to him.

Jesus then starts laughing, not at Judas, the thirteenth *daimon* is reassured, 'but at the error of the stars, because these six stars wander about with these *five combatants*, and they all will be destroyed along with their creatures.' The use of the word 'wandering' (planet means 'wanderer') might imply that the 'five combatants' are the angels of the five planets: Venus, Mercury, Jupiter, Saturn and Mars.

Judas then asks about the destiny of those who have been baptized in Jesus' name. The implication seems to be: what is going to happen to people who call themselves Christians, but who do not realize that they are ignorant of the highest deity? Unfortunately, 12 lines are missing from the text. The number is not significant. Whoever has been discussed in this missing section, Judas is compared to them. In doing so, Jesus defines Judas' role and, in a sentence that has now been printed in newspapers round the world, explains what needs to be done and why:

> But you [Judas] will exceed all of them. For you will sacrifice the man that clothes me.

Many readers of newspapers may be in some doubt about this, but we should know by now exactly what this neat phrase means. 'The man that clothes me' is Jesus' body, his 'garment', the thing that has made him visible to human eyes. Jesus' spiritual being will escape Saklas. The Fool will be left with the garment: a hollow victory indeed.

There then follows a fascinating (if incomplete) poem about Judas: 'Already your horn has been raised, your wrath has been kindled, your star has shone brightly...' Judas is being set on track with some curiously messianic overtones. What is all this about a horn being raised and wrath kindled?

Judas the Horn

As we have seen, some key features of Gnostic thought belong to, or are at least rooted in, the literary genre of apocalyptic. There is always a divine mystery, a secret that is revealed to the select few who are capable of receiving a divine, not a human, wisdom. In this case, it is Judas Iscariot.

He was bound to 'stand out' when you start reading biblical scriptures 'in the negative' (in photographic terms), where black becomes white. You can do this, because you think you have seen through the great conspiracy. The image of the significant horn – and the 'wrath' of the suggested ram goes back to passages in the Book of Daniel, in particular chapter eight:

> I considered the horns, and behold, there came up among them
> another little horn, before whom there were three of the first
> horns plucked up by the roots: and, behold, in this horn were
> eyes like the eyes of man, and a mouth speaking great things.

In verse 20 we hear that this horn that spoke great things had a special look. The horn's look 'was more stout than his fellows'. This sounds like Judas being able to stand before Jesus while the other disciples could not. The idea of Judas learning to stand tall may also be reflected in ideas in other apocalyptic writings. In the Book of Enoch, David and Solomon are presented as sheep, but on coming to the throne become rams. Also we are told in Daniel that the little horn 'made war with the saints, and prevailed against them'. The 'saints' in the context of The Gospel of Judas would be the other disciples.

It seems quite likely that these apocalyptic images were in the mind of the writer of The Gospel of Judas. More weight is added to this insight when we look at Daniel 8 (v 9), for example. There we have another suggestive reference to a wrathful little horn. This reference brings us back to the vision of the disciples of the sinful sacrifices in the Temple, as well as Jesus' promises that the stars are going to suffer for it:

> And it [the horn] waxed great, even to the host of heaven; and
> it cast down some of the host and of the stars to the ground,
> and stamped upon them.
>
> Yea, he magnified himself even to the prince of the host, and
> by him the daily sacrifice was taken away, and the place of his
> sanctuary was cast down.

The ceasing of Temple sacrifices is seen as a sign of the impending end of the reign of wickedness. We have already heard of the disciples' dream of the false priests making false sacrifices in the Temple. These will cease.

Judas, the so-called betrayer – it is he who is going to be

vindicated in the final days. He is part of the plan. Thanks to him, the wicked stars will fall and the archetype of 'the great generation of Adam', the generation 'which is from the eternal realms' will be exalted.

Having made all that perfectly clear to Judas, Jesus tells him to lift up his eyes 'and look at the cloud and the light within it and the stars surrounding it. The star that leads the way is your star.'

This rather beautiful exaltation of Judas' consciousness is followed by a brief (but incomplete) transfiguration scene, reminiscent of that familiar to readers of the canonical Gospels. Jesus lifts up his eyes and sees a luminous cloud. He enters it, and those on the ground hear a voice saying something that appears to be another hymn of praise to the generation of the Great Seth.

The End

A brief account wraps up the gospel. It has elements familiar from the well-known Gospel story, the Last Supper, bargaining between Judas and the high priests, and the arrest, but it is heavily muted. The writer appears to be uninterested in the details, as if he had contempt for mere history.

Jesus goes into the 'guest room' to pray. Some scribes are there, watching him so they might arrest him during the prayer. We are told they were 'afraid of the people, since he was regarded by all as a prophet'. The reader of the gospel, of course, now 'knows better'. The People could not see him at all. No democracy here; the masses are as blind as their so-called 'leaders'. The archons rule the earth – and that is all they are ever going to get: nothing.

The scribes then approach Judas and, bizarrely, ask him what he is doing there. 'You are Jesus' disciple,' they say. The meaning and origin of this poignant statement will be discussed in chapter four.

Judas answers them 'as they wished', which suggests either he knows the kind of thing they want to hear, or perhaps that there was some kind of verbal signal: the effect is one of deliberate, even vague, ambiguity. Any potential human drama has been utterly drained from this scene. It is not emotional; it is simply necessary, logical. The interest is not in the handing over, but in the reason for it, now established. 'And he [Judas] received some money and handed him over to them.'

And there it ends.

On the original manuscript, this blunt, if perhaps mysterious, ending is followed by the title of the work – the one that Stephen Emmel sadly did not see in that hotel in Geneva in 1983: The Gospel of Judas. Not the gospel *according to* Judas, no – *Judas'* gospel: *his* good news and the good news about him. After all, until now we had only ever heard the *bad*, hadn't we?

Works Found with The Gospel of Judas

Whoever first possessed The Gospel of Judas held it within a codex, or book. That book contained three other works. One of them is very badly damaged (Allogenes), but the two others leave us in no doubt that The Gospel of Judas was a work held by people who regarded the warnings of Bishop Irenaeus and his theological companions as misplaced.

The two works with The Gospel of Judas in the original codex are an 'apocalypse' or 'revelation' of James, and The Letter of Peter to Philip. The former work is indicated by the title, James (Jacob), placed at the end of the work. This work is a version of a text known from the Nag Hammadi Library as The [first] Apocalypse of James (there is a second work with the same title). The Letter of Peter to Philip is also known in a Nag Hammadi Coptic version.

These two works support the philosophical structure and spiritual emphases of The Gospel of Judas, but they also hold interesting differences. The so-called Gnostics held many different views or ways of seeing. Gnostic communities took a dim view of people dictating dogma to others. Spiritual revelation could only exist in accordance with the capacity of the perceiver. The 'Gnostic' writings represent the visions of the writers within a broadly shared tradition.

Not everyone who valued *gnosis* shared Judas' experience that the 11 other disciples were 'beyond the pale'. In The Letter of Peter to Philip, Peter is regarded as one who has received the *gnosis*. In James, as in the Didymos Judas Thomas literature, James the Righteous, brother of the Lord, is an authority for the 12 to look towards, after Jesus has returned to his proper world. The authority given to James reflects the history of the primitive Church, as far as we can call our fragments of knowledge from that period 'history'.

In the Apocalypse of James, the sufferings and martyrdom of the brother reflect the treatment of Jesus' body:

> James said, 'Rabbi, you have said, "They will seize me." [no mention of Judas Iscariot, note] But I, what can I do?' He said to me, 'Fear not, James. You too will they seize. But leave Jerusalem. For it is she who always gives the cup of bitterness to the sons of light. She is a dwelling place of a great number of archons. But your redemption will be preserved from them.'

The Apocalypse of James reveals that while Jesus suffered for others – meaning he had compassion – he did not suffer loss *in himself*. This was an important distinction for the 'Gnostics', but it has been used as a stick to beat them with. It has been said that 'their' Jesus was not fully human and therefore humanity in its full terrestrial identity cannot be saved through him.

This is an interpretation that is not entirely borne out by the written evidence of the 'Gnostics' themselves. They were not interested in 'saving' the full terrestrial identity. Death meant a grateful 'goodbye' to aching flesh and bones forever. For them, the true 'humanity' is the spiritual being created of God that has become, through attachment to the body, distorted by the laws and constraints of a lower world:

And the Lord appeared to him [James]. Then he stopped (his) prayer and embraced him. He kissed him, saying, 'Rabbi, I have found you! I have heard of your sufferings, which you endured. And I have been much distressed. My compassion you know. Therefore, on reflection, I was wishing that I would not see this people [those who seized Jesus]. They must be judged for these things that they have done. For these things that they have done are contrary to what is fitting.' The Lord said, 'James, do not be concerned for me or for this people. I am he who was within me. Never have I suffered in any way, nor have I been distressed. And this people has done me no harm. But this (people) existed [as] a type of the Archons...'

I am he who was within me. This is the key statement; this is the good news for the Gnostic Christian. The spiritual being of the spiritual man is not damaged by the painful experiences of the world. The spirit gives strength and hope to the body's trials, but is not subjected to it. The essential being of Jesus was divine. The difference between him and us is that he *knew* it. He calls on those who see this to know it too.

The true views of the so-called Gnostics have, throughout history, been grossly parodied by their enemies. This point has been made time and time again by many scholars who have studied their works and the things their enemies have said about them.

In every organization, there are bound to be excesses and scandalous goings-on from time to time. People misunderstand or are driven by their personal conflicts to distort what has been inherited and attempt to mislead others. This sort of thing doubtless took place in the ancient Christian communities on many levels.

Christianity was meant, after all, to be a spiritual liberation from 'the prince of this world'. Christians had an excuse 'to party'. Liberation doubtless leads to excess in some. We can all learn from an occasional 'sore head'.

The opponents of the teachers of Christian *gnosis* did what some journalists and politicians do today: condemn the whole for the behaviour of the few. 'None is righteous; no, not one' says the psalmist in response to our tendency to self-righteousness – which, according to the canonical Gospels, is a, if not *the,* cardinal sin.

Returning to The Letter of Peter to Philip, the essential and allegedly heretical doctrines of *gnosis* present in The Gospel of Judas are also present in this letter. The letter describes how the apostles were terrified after all that had happened in Jersualem. Peter calls Philip to an apostolic prayer meeting on the Mount of Olives to beg the risen Lord to explain why the archons are determined to destroy them. They pray to the Father and, interestingly, to 'thy holy child Jesus Christ. For he became for us an illuminator in the [darkness].'

There is the hint here that Jesus may manifest as a child – as in The Gospel of Judas. Suddenly a great light glows around the top of the mountain and they hear a voice. 'Why are you asking me?' says the voice, 'I am Jesus Christ who is with you forever.' The voice goes on to explain how the material universe emerged as a result of a female divine power – 'the mother' – desiring to create *aeons* like the Father did. In giving form to this desire, she simultaneously invoked the 'Arrogance'. She arrogated powers to herself that were properly not hers to work with alone. The result was what Gnostic writings call 'the Deficiency'.

The deficient aeons (the lowest aspects of which include our universe) were spiritually dead, but in the creation process, a divine seed (a gnostic image for the spirit or soul), was entrapped. The 'seed' came from the 'Mother'. The 'Mother' corresponds to 'Barbelo' in The Gospel of Judas.

Human bodies were based on a divine archetype, but the flesh could only live by virtue of the spirit entrapped within it. The spirit cried for home. When unconscious, the human experience answers to the 'first noble truth' of Buddhism, that 'everything is sorrow.' Melancholy characterizes the lonely soul.

When the seed or spirit is awoken, it yearns to return to its real home beyond the stars. This yearning is heard above, and so Jesus comes down:

> I was sent down in the body because of the seed which had fallen away. And I came down to their dead product. But they did not recognize me; they were thinking of me that I was a mortal man. And I spoke with him who belongs to me. And he hearkened to me, just as you too who hearkened today. And I gave him authority in order that he might enter into the inheritance of his fatherhood.

Thus 'Jesus the man' awakens to his true Self. This awakening is also urged upon the apostles. It is the only thing that will calm their fears and bring them to understanding: 'When you strip off from yourselves what is corrupted, then you will become illuminators in the midst of dead men.'

The apostles ask how they are to cope with the archons. Jesus says: 'Now you will fight with them in this way, for the archons are fighting with the inner man. And you are to fight with them in this way: come together and teach in the world the salvation with a promise. And you, gird yourselves with the power of my Father, and let your prayer be known.'

The whole scene is clearly an interpretation of events recorded in the Acts of the Apostles. The disciples are frightened. They are in 'an upper room' (taken symbolically perhaps; they are 'in the head' or on a spiritual level). They pray for help because they are afraid. Jesus comes to them. He commissions them to preach. They will suffer and be brought before powers, synagogues and authorities. He suffered 'because of us'. They will suffer too, so long as they are distant from their true being, but they will remember their true life is with Jesus, beyond harm. They then gain the courage to go out, preach and heal 'a multitude'.

Peter is 'filled with a holy spirit' and speaks thus:

Our illuminator, Jesus, [came] down and was crucified. And he bore a crown of thorns. And he put on a purple garment. And he was [crucified] on a tree and he was buried in a tomb. And he rose from the dead. My brothers, Jesus is a stranger to this suffering. But we are the ones who have suffered at the transgression of the mother.

It is significant that the word *gnosis* does not appear in The Letter of Peter to Philip. Those who heard or read it might not have appreciated the nickname 'Gnostics'. They would have said, as the letter plainly says: 'For the Lord Jesus, the Son of the immeasurable glory of the Father, he is the author of our life.'

These were Christians, and they were prepared to suffer in this world. Just as well they were, you could say, for those typified or ridiculed as 'Gnostics' have been persecuted ever afterwards by those set in authority over them.

The reaction to the publication of The Gospel of Judas shows the game is by no means over. According to Church leaders, Gnostics were – and are – alien to the Christian family. They stand *excommunicate*: wilfully beyond God's care.

But is Judas still standing?

Chapter Three

JUDAS – THE REACTION

The symbols of the divine show up in

our world initially at the trash stratum.

(Philip K Dick)

To judge from the scale of reaction to the publication of The Gospel of Judas at Easter 2006, you might think reviewers and commentators had already intuited the conclusion of the gospel before they had had a chance to read it.

That is to say, the final elevation of Judas, his spiritual rising to the Holy Generation of Seth, is reserved in his gospel for the time of the end of this world – and the end of this world has been a long time coming. People have been expecting it for over 2,000 years – rather a waste of time, one might think.

Nevertheless, Judas' final vindication must, according to his gospel, wait for the End Time. Before then, he would have to suffer a seemingly endless litany of calumny, blame, slander and total rejection from the bosom of Christian love.

Judas Iscariot? Didn't you know? He's the *fall guy*. Following this logic, if Judas is vindicated now or in the near future (as a result perhaps of the appearance of his gospel), then the final Apocalypse cannot be far off.

For those of a romantic or apocalyptic frame of mind, the

coincidence of the reappearance of The Gospel of Judas, with the widespread concerns of the world for its long-term future (war, climate change, asteroids, viruses, poverty, fundamentalism) may look profoundly, and disturbingly, suggestive.

Is Judas the herald of the End? Why has his gospel lain secret for so long? Is there something in the timing to suggest an unseen hand of providence?

Let's calm down a bit. Before we start praying to be preserved from any impending cataclysm, we should straightaway recall from chapter one that a part of that remarkable timing is due to the deliberate media strategy pursued by National Geographic and the Maecenas Foundation (Mario Roberty, lawyer to Frieda Tchacos Nussberger). Effective marketing is no mystery.

Furthermore, not only the Easter timing was deliberate and pre-planned, but the *way* it appeared was planned for maximum commercial effect. The Gospel of Judas was plugged directly into the main arteries of popular culture – satellite TV, the internet, DVD sales, bestseller lists, advertising, magazines and newspapers around the world. In the media, nothing succeeds quite as well as Disaster. Coming a close second to Disaster in public interest is the revelation of secrets. The mass media was born for apocalyptic; arguably, it was born *of* it! Come the 'last trumpet', tabloid sales will rocket.

Editors seem to love taking viewers and readers to the brink of apocalypse, only to bring them safely home for tea, sex and football. Many people like to be frightened a bit, under controlled conditions. The modern world provides many photo-opportunities for this guilty indulgence. The worse the news, the more we find it difficult not to enjoy reading it. Like many other indulgences, it might make us depressed from time to time, but we need our fix. We have got used to it. We are addicted. And we are prepared to pay for it.

We all think there should be more 'good news', but you can be sure that when it is printed, someone else thinks your good news is really bad (for them). If one country wins the World Cup, another loses. The vindication of the righteous is the judgement of the wicked.

The Gospel of Judas seems tailor-made for an era of mass communications and transgressive cultural obsessions. Sin is interesting. We have grown used to the idea that there is 'always another side of the story'. Royal figures, for example, turn out to be very human beings; heroes of the past have 'pasts' they would wish you had never known about. The good guys seem to do things as bad as the alleged bad guys. Sinners turn into saints; saints into sinners. We must forgive, as we have been forgiven.

So maybe we are not dealing here with some metaphysical revelation and cosmic catastrophe. Maybe it is just a question of pure coincidence, combined with the public's appetite for a good story. The Gospel of Judas means Judas' good news. He may look like the all-time loser, but *he's going to make it!* Furthermore, as we shall see, there are many who think Judas's good news is very bad news.

You, the reader, seeing the different sides to the argument, may make up your own minds.

The Time Bomb Explodes

For all the media hype and consumer manipulation, The Gospel of Judas may still be described as a 'time bomb': something highly charged, just waiting beneath the rubble of time (and an old safety deposit box) to 'go off'. It will not be the first case of an intriguing literary 'time bomb'.

Between 1493 and 1541 there lived in Europe an extraordinary Swiss doctor-genius called Paracelsus. He is famous for many things, not least of which was the discovery of *laudanum*, the first really effective painkiller. Imagine a world *without* painkillers. *Laudanum* (an opiate) appeared as a gift from God.

Paracelsus overturned many of the assumptions of his time

about medicine. For example, before Paracelsus, doctors used to stand by a patient's bed reading from an ancient text on medicine while a grubby assistant followed instructions in the old book, or did nothing at all. Little surprise then that the doctor's visit was, more often than not, a prelude to the priest's. The old methods, justified by centuries of tradition, frequently failed to make the patients better. But they did make doctors richer – and they were loath to welcome the new.

After Paracelsus' death in 1541, doctors slowly, very slowly, realized that the eccentric Swiss might have had his brain as well as his finger on the pulse after all. Doctors of the future really had to get to grips with the patient and actually try to cure them, by any means possible – whether approved by the ancestral tradition or not.

Paracelsus introduced chemistry into medicine. He was more interested in practice than in theory. Besides, he had theories of his own – lots of them. And they *changed* as he learned more about the real way nature actually worked. His rule of thumb was if magic made people better, then use magic. After all, magic is just bits of nature we do not yet understand. So if magic consists in what lies beyond the powers of nature, the way forward was simple: expand your knowledge of nature. Paracelsus believed the wisdom of God was hidden in nature; miracles would come from understanding it. One just had to bring it out and learn to work with it.

Mother's peaches were ripe for the picking, if you could see them.

As for Paracelsus' many bitter enemies, they were rather like the disciples in The Gospel of Judas, they had a 'god' within them which prevented the real insight from appearing. Paracelsus' medical ideas were all dangerously revolutionary in his day. Today, many of his insights are regarded as common knowledge – and human lives continue to be saved.

Apart from curing people (a rare thing for a doctor in those days), one other achievement of Paracelsus was writing volumes on the subject of religion. His thoughts were influenced not only by the

Gnostic tradition but, above all, by common sense and observation. He believed that the church of wood and stone was a dark doll's house full of fakery and mentally sclerotic quacks who had imprisoned the souls of believers and damaged their bodies.

The Church of Stone

Paracelsus advocated the complete freedom of the spirit to pursue the truth, without the heavy judgement of bishops, priests, popes and other self-professed religious authorities.

As a result of the power of the Church in his day to annihilate her errant believers, Paracelsus chose not to publish his plain-speaking religious works in his own lifetime. Had he published them, his primary duty to bring healing knowledge to the world would have ended very quickly. He left his theological manuscripts with friends, in the hope that after his death in 1541, they would be released from their hiding place. When followers of Paracelsus did release them, they soon caused a storm.

By the end of the 16th century, Paracelsus' hidden books had begun a movement for liberation of the spirit and of knowledge. All the religious authorities of the time – Catholic, Lutheran and Calvinist – persecuted the movement's supporters. Those inspired by Paracelsus' religious writings were given nicknames and condemned as dangerous heretics.

As he had hoped, Paracelsus' religious writings turned out to be time bombs. There is no doubt that the works helped to initiate movements of thought that encouraged the development of experimental science, freedom of conscience and of thought in general – benefits we may all enjoy today.

Paracelsus' religious works, however, cannot be said to have aided the work of most Roman Catholic or Protestant theologians of the time. Theology, like the old doctors, looked backwards, not forwards. It is unlikely that this healer of hundreds in his lifetime, using only the miracle of Nature to guide him, will be made a Saint.

While greeted in his time as good news by those who, often in secret, welcomed his challenging messages, Paracelsus was certainly seen as a betrayer of the truth and a dangerous madman by many others. For those who valued the Church's authority in religious matters, Paracelsus was deemed a kind of Judas: a self-appointed charlatan who thought he knew better.

However, it would be odd to find someone in the Vatican today attacking the gospel according to Paracelsus, while Pope Benedict's venerable predecessor was comforted in hospital by a medical system that may have been considerably less accomplished had Paracelsus not been born. Everybody loves their doctor - on the day they are cured.

Now, if we jump ahead 400 years or so, it may be that The Gospel of Judas will also prove to have been a beneficial time bomb, leading human beings on - after proper consideration - to greater awareness and, perhaps, spiritual and moral progress. Or, it may be that this and other kindred time bombs, while doubtless of interest to scholars of religion, are nothing but fireworks, decorating the night-sky for a few moments, only to fade quickly away in a puff of smoke, irrelevant to the world at large.

It is also possible that The Gospel of Judas will come to be seen as a dangerous firebrand that lit a hostile conflagration beneath the foundations of traditional faith and religious certainty: a wicked harbinger of the end of great and vital institutions of truth, charity and spiritual support.

Perhaps, as has been asserted by some believers, our interest in The Gospel of Judas is simply a sign that the end of the world is nigh and we are being seduced by a fatal curiosity as Satan makes his last stand against the true faith. Emerging at almost exactly the same time as the movie of Dan Brown's *Da Vinci Code* (May 2006), some commentators believe they can see an underlying pattern of threatening behaviour towards the sanctities of traditional religion.

Perhaps only time will tell the true significance of The Gospel of Judas and the enormous global interest that has been aroused by its appearance. Nevertheless, the modern world waits for no one, and most people – for or against The Gospel of Judas – have been quick to pass judgement on this surprising work of late antique literature. An objective observer might even be surprised to find that men and women of learning – men and women to whom deep study is thought to be habitual – have pronounced judgement after only superficial acquaintance with its contents.

While we may hear voices we agree with and support, the hardest thing is to hear what we do not agree with, and do not think we could ever support.

The Launch

For good or ill – or both – the bomb exploded on 6 April 2006, at a news conference called by the National Geographic Society in Washington DC. It was announced that the restoration and translation of The Gospel of Judas was complete. The manuscript itself was then unveiled at the National Geographic Society headquarters. Few remarked on the beauty of the papyrus, where it survived intact, that is.

The launch was accompanied three days later by a TV special, broadcast on the National Geographic Channel, entitled The Gospel of Judas. Terry Garcia, an executive vice-president of the National Geographic Society, announced that scholars considered the codex to be the most significant ancient, non-biblical text discovery since the 1940s. The press conference response to this news was not ecstatic.

There were doubts. Some of these doubts may derive from the fact that the launch had deliberate sensationalist characteristics, and the press are continually expected to echo marketing hype; occasionally they dig their feet in, especially when the sensation is neither political nor sexual.

Benny Ziffer in the Israeli newspaper *Haaretz* found himself disgusted at the style of the presentation and blamed the overblown character of American sales hype. As he put it, it was 'a kind of simple-mindedness verging on stupidity that makes a documentary television programme about Christian theology sound identical in tone to a stewardess explaining to airplane passengers how to fasten their seat belts.'

Besides, there had already been dissenting voices. Reactionary commentators were already challenging those who would have us believe that The Gospel of Judas could turn the Christian religion 'on its head', or that its contents were so potent that people might suffer crises of faith if they read it.

Dan Brown's hugely popular novel, *The Da Vinci Code*, was in many minds. People were accustomed to a narrative centring on 'secrets the Church had hidden for centuries', now revealed in our *reveal-all* 'post-Christian' culture. First Mary Magdalene had been misjudged and marginalized by Christian authorities – now it was Judas Iscariot! How long before a novelist came up with *The Judas Code*?

Furthermore, the presentation of the gospel suggested that this might actually be an historical gospel: a true record of events that happened nearly 2,000 years ago. That is to say, by use of hints and direct suggestion, readers were encouraged to see The Gospel of Judas in terms similar to those found in the more familiar Gospels.

'This scriptural text could shatter some of the interpretations, even the foundations, of faith throughout the Christian world,' wrote Herbert Krosney in *The Lost Gospel*. [1] 'It was not a novel,' Krosney continued, 'It was a real gospel straight from the world of early Christianity.'

The fact is that traditional faith has *already* been shattered throughout the Christian world. That is not to say that faith is necessarily weak or that the need for it has lessened, but the support system of faith is failing. Many reasons have been offered for this religious crisis. One reason with great relevance for The Gospel of Judas phenomenon is a perceived, if gradual, *pushing out* of people's minds of ideas and images of supernaturalism and personal experiences of the sacred.

The outside world seems a little flatter perhaps than it used to. Even TV sets boast of flat screens! We can have the world on a plate. Perhaps TV manufacturers are putting great effort into marketing 'high-definition' television images and sounds as compensation for a lack of immediacy and spiritual content in the outside world.

Meanwhile, by contrast, modern cinema films that try to give a realistic feeling to a story tend to diminish colour content (with 'washed out' images) or try to look as if scenes were shot with low-definition film or video. What does this suggest?

Reality is low definition; fantasy is high definition, super-enhanced with computer-generated effects. It may be that people are seeking religious experiences in the 'high-definition' range.

Furthermore, people have got used to the idea that it is science that explains things. But people still feel a need for mystery and spiritual meaning. Something is not being adequately explained. *What are we? Where do we come from? Where are we going?*

Oddly enough, it was these very questions that a 2nd-century heresy-hunter, Tertullian, said were the questions that made people heretics! Tertullian believed that once you became a faithful Christian, you should never need to ask any more questions. For him, the coming of Christianity meant that philosophy was redundant. You were either saved, or not saved; that was all that mattered.

Maybe many of us just don't feel 'saved' any more, or even want to feel saved, if it means that the joy in thinking for ourselves should cease. We like asking questions. We want our children to go to places where they can ask lots of questions, and find answers and, yes, more questions. We believe that our progress as a species relies on us asking more and more questions. We are *thinking*, and neither the Church nor the State can prevent it any longer.

And why are we asking more questions? Because our body of knowledge is increasing, exponentially. As we learn more, we want to know more. We are not perhaps looking any more for *final* answers, but are learning slowly to enjoy an on-going quest. Life is a trip, not just an accommodation with the forces around us. In our fascination with spiritual thrillers – or even quasi-spiritual stories – both the scientific attitude and the latent supernaturalism of the human imagination combine in powerful unison.

Because people are prepared to ask questions and seek solutions, if the Church is not asking the same questions or offering solutions, people will seek their own. A hungry person will not find satisfaction until he or she is fed.

So all the following questions, raised by the appearance of The Gospel of Judas, are really only the tip of a global iceberg of questioning. Within that iceberg lives the psychological and spiritual desire for personal self-validation and cosmic meaning. The immediate questions are:

Had The Gospel of Judas been 'dropped' from the Bible at some distant time?

Were the words recorded in the gospel the actual words of Judas?

Did Judas Iscariot write the gospel?

Was the New Testament wrong to see Judas as a traitor?

Was this book older than the Gospels?

Was this version of events at the time of Jesus' Crucifixion one that the Church suppressed – not because it was untrue, but because its truth was too threatening to the religious *status quo*?

Did The Gospel of Judas have the authentic tradition?

Not everyone, of course, is fascinated by such questions. Even people with little care for religion often show themselves to be remarkably conservative when it comes to questioning religious traditions. Perhaps this is because they prefer religion to be quiet, pacific, and *removed*. It is all right to bring religion out for christenings, marriages and funerals – and even charity calls – but after that, it is bad taste to give it much time. This conservatism is as prevalent among some journalists as it is anywhere else.

Perhaps there exists a secret fear that religion might turn out to be nothing other than wishful thinking; atheism is not as common as was supposed a few decades ago. In the mainstream of European culture, a fairly respectful agnosticism strikes the dominant note.

If religion is a 'crutch', an occasional comfort, as many 'liberals' suspect, no one wants the crutch to break the moment you lean on it! People who share this anxiety do not want to have to think about religious questions. Leave it to 'faith'. Leave it to the experts! And this is pretty much what most broadsheet newspapers did when The Gospel of Judas was published. The trouble in this case was that the 'experts' seemed to share no common mind on this remarkable discovery. This conflict of interpretation could have been a good story in itself, but was too involved for many newspaper editors. The editor wants to know in simple terms *What is the Story?*

The Story

Was the *story* about the *discovery* of the manuscripts? *Yes, but...* it happened a long time ago.

Was the story about the strange tale of how the manuscripts disappeared for such a long time – the conflicts between competing antiquities dealers? *Yes, but...* that was all over now. Now there was one unified front: the Maecenas Foundation and the National Geographic Society – unimpeachable respectability!

Was the story about the true content of the texts? *Yes, but...* this was a *Gnostic* gospel and a bit too deep perhaps for mainstream readership, and even beyond the scope of most journalists, concerned perhaps about offending religious sensibilities.

Professional editors were thus compelled either to tell the sensationalist version of events (a good story) or to deny that there was really an important story here at all. This latter approach did provide a *story*, in journalistic terms, though not as good in terms of 'copy' as the other, sensational, alternative. The more prestigious the newspaper, the greater was the reliance on (conservative) theological expertise.

National Geographic's presentation had to be ready for a high-calibre theological onslaught on The Gospel of Judas. The organization chose Bart D Ehrman (Chair of Religious Studies at the University of North Carolina) to introduce the work of the translators and restorers. He was photogenic, tanned and fit, and spoke with the kind of warm enthusiasm that comes over well on television. He had academic credentials and understood the theological background to the text. In his contributions to this National Geographic flagship, and on the dramatic TV presentation and DVD release, Ehrman made convincing efforts to persuade non-specialist readers and viewers that The Gospel of Judas had importance to anyone concerned with the Christian religion.

Bart Ehrman was not among the most well-known scholars of Gnostic material. His expertise lay in religious studies in general. On the other hand, this general expertise could suggest that he had no particular axe to grind on the subject of Gnostic gospels. While being positive about the discovery, he could appear objective.

Ehrman was an interested professional who could speak in ordinary, not technical, language. That was his advantage, and his usefulness to the promotion strategy. In his foreword to Krosney's *The Lost Gospel* (published to coincide with the official English translation of The Gospel of Judas), Ehrman spoke warmly of the Gnostic gospel as 'an alternative vision of what it means to follow Christ and to be faithful to his teachings'.

Professor James Robinson, having a much longer and closer acquaintance with Gnostic writings, was considerably more cautious. He did not see the text as seriously relevant to living out Christian doctrine today. Judas' gospel would not offer any insights into the disciple who betrayed Jesus. This was because the document, though old, was 'not old enough'. The gospel was a revisionist document, he argued. The earlier accounts (the four Gospels) must have first call on our attention, just as they did, so

Robinson believed, for whoever wrote The Gospel of Judas in the first place.

Robinson did not underestimate the gospel's importance for scholars studying the Gnostic movement in the 2nd century and afterwards; for them it would be an important source text, a marvellous addition to their source base. Students of theology and Church history would find it a stimulating source. After all the hype, The Gospel of Judas would settle down comfortably into university and college reading lists, no more significant than many another ancient text.

Basically, Robinson was saying that the only people who should be truly excited about the discovery were scholars, and those who enjoyed following the work of scholarship. This would be a widely held position, as we shall see.

Readers may ask themselves whether there might be something just a little bit patronizing in this approach – however much such an impression might be unintended.

In short, The Gospel of Judas would not contribute to the mainstream Christian's understanding of the Bible. In Robinson's view, it was simply regrettable that the process of selling the original had led to it being re-presented in a sensationalist light. Popular culture is one thing; serious culture is something else.

Robinson believed that scholars should not allow themselves to be co-opted into commercially driven enterprises. If they were to participate in non-academic enterprises, they should take serious care that the results would be genuinely educational. Contributions should conform to the pure, emotionally disinterested disciplines of science, accountability and due academic checks and balances.

Apart from the fact that the greater number of theologians and historians of religion do have deep personal relationships with the subject about which they are supposed to be objective, National Geographic had its own response to what they took as Robinson's criticism of their approach.

National Geographic found it 'ironic' that Robinson had raised doubts over the religious status of The Gospel of Judas since he had 'for years, tried unsuccessfully to acquire the codex himself, and is publishing his own book in April 2006, despite having no direct access to the materials'.

Readers may judge for themselves whether this was a valid, or even mature, response to Robinson's point of view. He could be cheeky, of course. He had drawn attention to the fact that The Gospel of Judas could not necessarily be seen as a culturally unique revelation. He mentioned a novel by Simon Mawer, *The Gospel of Judas*,[2] revolving around the discovery of a gospel of Judas in a Dead Sea cave and its subsequent effect on a scholarly priest.

The underlying message that might emerge was that The Gospel of Judas should be treated as an ancient novel, a fantasy, a *jeu d'ésprit*. This was certainly a viewpoint voiced by representatives of the Roman Catholic Church in the period around the disclosure of the gospel.

Rome

As the media hype got under way at the beginning of 2006, the Vatican was reported to be taking the view that there was nothing to get excited about. There was nothing in all this 'newly discovered gospel' stuff that should upset or disturb Christians. Catholics were firmly rooted to the rock of truth. Any so-called gospel purporting to come from Judas Iscariot was, the Vatican claimed, a 'product of religious fantasy'.

This relaxed stance did not suffuse the media airwaves for long. The Vatican found it difficult to disentangle the appearance of The Gospel of Judas from the global success of *The Da Vinci Code*, excitement around which was increasing as Hollywood's finest found their way around the sacred sites of Europe in a costly quest for a box office hit.

The Vatican knew that the common thread linking the gospel discovery and the popular novel was the old heresy (as the Church sees it) of 'Gnosticism'. It had been hoped that Gnostic interpretations of Jesus' teaching had been definitively dumped before the Dark Ages. But Gnostic 'heresy' – like sinful practices in general – had a nasty habit of reappearing.

On the other hand, the Church did not wish to advertise the concept of an 'alternative' to the Catholic faith (however theologically questionable). It was also not in the Church's interest to open up a massive theological debate on the issue.

The issue was closed.

However, the question was not simply about an old heresy reappearing in popular culture. There was at stake the basic issue of whether Judas Iscariot had been completely misjudged. And even whether the love of Christ was ultimately extendable to the one who betrayed Jesus. This was for some Catholic theologians a thorny issue. Did the Church have an authoritative view on the subject?

A London report in *The Times* newspaper alleging the innocence of the man who paid 30 pieces of silver to identify Jesus to his enemies in the Garden of Gethsemane, was repeated as far away as Israel and India. According to these reports, Judas was not deliberately evil, but was just 'fulfilling his part in God's plan'. Salvation required the Crucifixion; crucifixion required a betrayal; the betrayal required a Judas. A 'makeover' by Vatican scholars was expected.

Monsignor Walter Brandmuller, head of the Pontifical Committee for Historical Science, was apparently heading a campaign aimed at a 're-reading' of the Judas story. Apparently, Brandmuller was supported by Vittorio Messori, a prominent Catholic writer close to both Pope Benedict XVI and the late John Paul II. Signor Messori said that the rehabilitation of Judas would 'resolve the problem of an apparent lack of mercy by Jesus towards one of his closest collaborators'. He told *La Stampa* there was a Christian tradition that held that Judas was forgiven by Jesus and was ordered to purify himself with 'spiritual exercises' in the desert.

Richard Owen, Rome correspondent of *The Times*, observed that the move to propose a redemption for Judas coincided with plans to publish the 'alleged' Gospel of Judas for the first time in English, German and French. The report suggested that a belief of early Christians – that Judas was fulfilling a divinely ordained mission necessary for salvation – was now gaining ground in the Vatican.

Judas Is Innocent, OK?

The result of this apparent coincidence was that the story grew, albeit perhaps as a journalistic concoction. To set the record straight, Monsignor Brandmuller was reported to have said that he expected 'no new historical evidence' from the supposed gospel, which had been excluded from the canon of accepted Scripture. In other words, there was no real connection between theological considerations about the possibility of Judas's ultimate redemption and The Gospel of Judas.

Nevertheless, Vatican scholars were soon expressing concern over an imminent reconsideration of Judas Iscariot. The Vatican theologian Monsignor Giovanni D'Ercole said it was 'dangerous to re-evaluate Judas and muddy the Gospel accounts by reference to apocryphal writings. This can only create confusion in believers.'

Richard Owen's article seemed to suggest that the Vatican was proposing its reassessment of Judas as part of a movement of theological progress. Owen noted that the New Testament gives different accounts of what happened to Judas. The canonical Gospels tell how Judas returned the 30 pieces of silver, his 'blood money', then hanged himself. In The Acts of the Apostles, on the other hand, Judas 'fell headlong and burst open so that all his entrails burst out'. They could not both be true, could they? And if one version was wrong, could the other also not be wrong? Who had the authority to judge in such a matter? Owen saw the developments as yet another reminder that we must not forget recent Catholic pronouncements that believers 'should not expect total accuracy from the Bible'.

The rehabilitation story was brought back to Britain where Father Allen Morris, Christian Life and Worship secretary for the Catholic Bishops of England and Wales, was asked to reflect on the story's implications. He was reported to have said: 'If Christ died for all – is it possible that Judas too was redeemed through the Master he betrayed?'

Jewish-Christian Relations

It would appear that the consideration of Judas' rescue from damnation has something to do with the Pope's drive to improve Christian-Jewish relations, a priority of his pontificate. This issue appears to be the genuine root of the story.

The figure of Judas Iscariot has been troubling for Jews, to say the least. The name 'Judas' means 'praised'. Since Jacob's son Judah had given his name to the place known to the Romans as Judaea, then 'Judas' (the same name as Judah) had practically come to be synonymous with the pride in being a Jewish man. Jesus had a brother called Judas. Judas was also the name of the great Jewish hero who had fought a Greek-Syrian army for possession of the Temple Mount in Jerusalem in the 2nd century BC. And it was a popular name for Jewish boys in the 1st century AD. The Jewish historian Josephus, a near contemporary of St Paul, refers to a Jewish warrior called Judas who founded a religious sect and who was defeated by Roman forces in AD 6.

The guilt of the betrayal by Judas Iscariot, who has sometimes been depicted with a pronounced hooked nose, has somehow been linked to an alleged guilt shared by all Jews who would not accept Jesus as the messiah.

Theologians have long realized that in spite of the fact that the Gospels state that Jesus was executed by order of a Roman Procurator and by a specifically Roman method, the narrative over-simplified the situation. The Christian Church wished to distance itself from rebellious Jewish patriots (Zealots) in order to appease the Roman authorities. The Zealots struggled violently against Roman rule throughout the 1st century AD, and Judas Iscariot might have been one of them. Christians in Rome and other parts of the Roman Empire did not wish to be blamed for anti-Roman hostilities taking place in Judaea (especially after AD 66 when the Jewish Revolt against Rome broke out). Some Jewish scholars have taken the view that Judas Iscariot's image was seriously blackened for the sake of anti-Zealot or anti-Jewish propaganda.

So the story of Jesus' trial could be reduced to the view that Jews crucified the messiah; a Jewish man betrayed him. The traditional Christian reading, which the Church has now repudiated, was that Jesus was betrayed by 'one of his own', and 'his own' (the Jews) were stained with the guilt. The guilt of the Crucifixion lay not with the Roman government but with Jews who refused to recognize Jesus.

The Roman Catholic Church, under the late Pope John Paul II, has now exonerated the Jewish people of this traditionally held accusation of guilt in the killing of God's messiah. By sheer coincidence, this story of tentative religious reconciliation on the part of the Vatican became involved with the hype surrounding the imminent publication of The Gospel of Judas.

There was no way the Vatican was going to offer support to the promulgation of Judas' alleged 'gospel'. In a further effort to set the record straight, Monsignor Brandmuller declared, 'There is no campaign, no movement for the rehabilitation of the traitor of Jesus.'

If that message was not clear and definitive enough, then on 15 April 2006 the *Guardian* newspaper in Britain reported that Pope Benedict XVI himself was determined to combat efforts to rehabilitate Christianity's most hated villain after 'a newly discovered gospel according to Judas' had been revealed. In the Pope's first Easter sermon at St Peter's Basilica, the man formerly known as Joseph Ratzinger, Prefect of the Congregation of the Doctrine of the Faith, declared to the world that the treacherous disciple known as Judas Iscariot was a greedy liar. According to His Holiness the Pope: 'He [Judas] evaluated Jesus in terms of power and success. For him, only power and success were real. Love didn't count.' He made Judas sound like a 'yuppie' in a socialist stereotype.

The task of the Congregation of the Doctrine of the Faith was to prevent unauthorized teaching or doctrine in the Catholic Church, so it would have been extraordinary in the extreme if the Pope had deviated from the traditional view of Judas' capital sin. It was not the sin of Judas' race – that was understood – but it was Judas' personal choice to sin. That God knew that was only to be expected; God knows everything.

Judas was guilty, and the guilt was entirely his own; it was not representative. But was there any love or forgiveness for Judas? The question has continued to hang in the air.

Meanwhile, The Gospel of Judas continued to be linked to the imminent release of *The Da Vinci Code*. The connection was fairly straightforward. *The Da Vinci Code* relied on interpretations of Gnostic writings for its story – that Jesus had a special relationship with Mary Magdalene of which the disciples did not approve. The Gospel of Judas was also hostile to the disciples, and therefore hostile to the orthodox teachings of the Church which the disciples allegedly founded. The power of both works to capture the imagination of millions was seen as threatening to traditional faith and Church order.

Judas Meets *The Da Vinci Code*

On 17 May 2006 the Catholic News Service reported – with barely suppressed delight – the lukewarm critical reception offered to the premiere of *The Da Vinci Code* movie in Cannes the day before. Towards the end of the movie, the main character, Robert Langdon, tells his sleuthing partner Sophie Neveu: 'You are the last living descendent of Jesus Christ.' The line, the climax to the story, elicited laughter from the critics. Catholics could apparently sigh with relief.

Catholic criticisms of the book were somehow being echoed in the reactions of secular critics. The Church's view was perceived as being vindicated – even by those outside its theological influence.

The director of the movie, Ron Howard, was quoted as giving kindly advice to those who might be offended: 'My advice is not to go see the movie if you think you're going to be upset. Wait. Talk to somebody who has seen it. Discuss it. And then arrive at an opinion.' Even the director seemed to be advising pious people to stay away! Howard then disclaimed any pretension to religious meaning in the film: 'But again, this is supposed to be entertainment. It's not theology and I don't think it should be misunderstood as such.'

It would not be so easy to say the same thing about The Gospel of Judas – nor the extracts from other Gnostic writings that underpinned the main axis of *The Da Vinci Code*'s narrative. Perhaps the Catholic News Service would like to have said the following about The Gospel of Judas: 'The film doesn't make any claim to accuracy of any kind – artistic, historical, religious or biblical.'

And neither could it. The Gospel of Judas does not claim to be historically accurate, but it does claim to state spiritual truth. Spiritual truth may not be what things *appear to be*. As St Paul himself wrote, 'Spiritual things are spiritually discerned.'

Radical dramatist Bertolt Brecht made an interesting, and analogous, plea for the significance of the theatrical experience when he said: 'Realism does not consist in reproducing reality, but in showing how things really are.' A fiction may have more 'truth' in it than a repetition of simple facts or external observations. That is to say, a fiction may contain meaning of a profound kind. Perhaps people should ask, 'What *meaning* do people gain from these works, *The Da Vinci Code*, or even The Gospel of Judas?'

The Catholic report on the Cannes gala opening of *The Da Vinci Code* tells of how Carmelite Sister Mary Michael, of Lincoln, England, knelt and prayed the rosary at the foot of the main entrance hours before the premiere. She is reported to have told journalists: 'I'm praying for all the movie stars and for Dan Brown and all of them,' adding, 'They're not bad people. I'm also praying to make reparation for what is really a bad story, an old heresy in the church that's just being used again.'

Canadian Father Bernard Heffernan stood nearby, handing out literature to oppose what he saw as the film's message: 'What bothers me most is that it reflects the lack of truth in the world today. It doesn't seem to matter anymore what's true and what's not.' From the Catholic point of view, 'heresies' just aren't true. How do we know what a heresy is? A heresy is what the Church believes is not true. What is truth? The truth is what the Church believes. The Gospel of Judas is the work of condemned heretics. Therefore, it is not true.

True or not, we now come to another issue raised in the wake of the publication of The Gospel of Judas. That is, whether the Catholic Church has deliberately suppressed a whole body of unacceptable literature, while retaining copies for its own records. Was it OK for Church authorities to read the condemned literature, but forbid other members of the Church to read it?

We now hear again from Vatican spokesperson Monsignor Walter Brandmuller, president of the Vatican's Committee for Historical Science. He maintains that the Church does not desire to suppress The Gospel of Judas. Rather, 'We welcome the [manuscript] like we welcome the critical study of any text of ancient literature.' But was The Gospel of Judas just 'any text of ancient literature'?

Brandmuller's statement was made with reference to an earlier one made by the president of the Maecenas Foundation, Mario Roberty. Roberty had suggested that the *Codex Tchacos* might not be the only copy of the gospel in existence. Roberty reckoned it was possible the Vatican might have had another copy locked away. This statement gave a strong whiff of conspiracy to the promotional proceedings. One can almost envision the scene, as Dan Brown's hero 'Robert Langdon' sneaks into the most secret Vatican archives with torch in hand, only to find pristine copies of Gnostic gospels – and who knows what else? All fiction, of course!

Roberty made the claim: 'In those days the Church decided for political reasons to include the Gospels of Matthew, Mark, Luke, and John in the Bible. The other gospels were banned. It is highly logical that the Catholic Church would have kept a copy of the forbidden gospels. Sadly, the Vatican does not want to clarify further. Their policy has been the same for years – "No further comment".'

In fact, at least one part of the Vatican library has been catalogued for the use of scholarship. On the other hand, the rest of the library has no catalogue available to the public. You can research there, if you wish, but only if you name the text you require. It is difficult to know what to ask for, if you do not know what is there. Perhaps Roberty should go and ask for The Gospel of Judas (original version of course) and see what happens.

Journalists have recently asked Father Thomas D Williams, Dean of Theology at the *Regina Apostolorum* university in Rome, if it is true that the Catholic Church has attempted to cover up The Gospel of Judas, and other texts. According to Father Williams, 'These are myths circulated by Dan Brown and other conspiracy theorists. You can go to any Catholic bookstore and pick up a copy of the Gnostic gospels. Christians may not believe them to be true, but there is no attempt to hide them.'

Be that as it may, how could the Church prevent publication of any book today, unless it was in breach of civil, not canon, law? The world has changed. The Congregation for the Doctrine of the Faith used to be better known in the old days as 'the Holy Inquisition'. However, it is true that apocryphal texts were subject to destruction orders on pain of excommunication in the 4th century AD, and later, when heresy became a crime also against the state, on pain of death.

There is another way that unwanted literature can be suppressed. It might even be more effective than banning works, which, as we know, tends to make the forbidden fruit look even more attractive. This other way involves introducing guilt. If reading an unwanted work bears the character of sin or spiritual disobedience, then, as a faithful Catholic, one might not wish to linger in its verbal precincts for long.

Guilty Pleasures

In a Good Friday sermon of 14 April 2006, delivered in St Peter's Basilica, Father Raniero Cantalamessa, preacher to the pontifical household since 1980, told Pope Benedict XVI and Vatican Curia officials that 'pseudo-historical literature' crassly manipulates the faith of millions.

Father Cantalamessa compared the selling of such works as *The Da Vinci Code* and The Gospel of Judas to the betrayal of Jesus, by Judas, for money. Is this not a serious spiritual accusation? Well, Father Cantalamessa thinks the sin is serious. He linked the two works as examples of 'the itching for anything new,' which is 'being realized in a new and impressive way in our days.'

The 71-year-old Capucin said that the publication of the books was effectively a seduction. Clever writing promoted ancient legends for the purpose of denying the Saviour's passion and death. 'There is much talk about Judas' betrayal,' he said, 'without realizing that it is being repeated. Christ is being sold again, no longer to the leaders of the Sanhedrin for 30 *denarii*, but to editors and booksellers for billions of *denarii*'.

'We cannot allow the silence of believers to be mistaken for embarrassment and that the good faith of millions of people be crassly manipulated by the media, without raising a cry of protest, not only in the name of the faith, but also of common sense and healthy reason ... No one will succeed in halting this speculative wave, which instead will flare up with the imminent release of a certain film,' he said. 'The apocryphal gospels on which they lean are texts that have always been known, in whole or in part, but with which not even the most critical and hostile historians of Christianity even thought, before today, that history could be made.'

What did all this tell us? asked Father Cantalamessa. The explanation for the phenomenon of such works as The Gospel of Judas and *The Da Vinci Code* was that, 'We are in the age of the media and the media are more interested in novelty than in truth.' The media was guilty. The people who sell the works are guilty. The people who read them are...seduced. The Church cannot stop the media from being tuned in to novelty, but it can give a powerful sermon.

On Friday 5 May 2006, Archbishop Angelo Amato addressed a Catholic conference in Rome. He was secretary to the Vatican's Congregation for the Doctrine of the Faith, and as such had a duty to protect the Church from unsound doctrine. He called *The Da Vinci Code* (which has sold more than 40 million copies) 'stridently anti-Christian ... full of calumnies, offences and historical and theological errors regarding Jesus, the Gospels and the Church.' He added, 'I hope that you all will boycott the film.'

Amato attributed much of the book's success to 'the extreme cultural poverty on the part of a good number of the Christian faithful'. He said Christians should be more willing 'to reject lies and gratuitous defamation', adding that if 'such lies and errors had been directed at the Koran or the Holocaust they would have justly provoked a world uprising.'

Justly provoked a world uprising?

Amato continued, 'Instead, if they [the lies] are directed against the Church and Christians, they remain unpunished.'

Unpunished...? What did he have in mind? Amato seemed to be looking back at the old days with a degree of nostalgia. Admittedly, this tirade was aimed at a book and a movie that held up the Catholic organization *Opus Dei* as a source of intrigue and even psychopathy. But the novel has been linked in Catholic pronouncements to The Gospel of Judas. One wonders if this has been altogether a responsible line to take.

It is a relief to know there is still a less strident voice speaking for Catholics in the media. The Egyptian newspaper *Al-Ahram* reported how Father Senior, president of the Catholic Theological Union in Chicago, and a member of the Pontifical Biblical Commission, which advises the Pope, told *The New York Times* that the Vatican was unlikely to regard The Gospel of Judas as a threat.

He said that the Roman Catholic Church's response would

probably be to 'affirm the canonical texts' in the New Testament rather than seek to refute each new discovery. 'If The Gospel of Judas suddenly became something that hundreds of thousands of Christians were claiming as their revelation and scripture, perhaps the Church would come out with some kind of statement. But mostly I think it's just not even on the radar screen,' said Father Senior, adding, 'I'm just glad it wasn't found in a bank vault in the Vatican.'

On Wednesday 17 May 2006, Archbishop Angelo Amato, aged 67, was back on the theological barricades once more. Readers should bear in mind that when the Archbishop pronounces on issues of theology, that theology must, by definition, maintain the interests of the Church as an institution, since – by definition – the Church is the cup of truth from which believers may drink. The interests of the Church and the interests of the truth are the same. The Church receives its commission from Jesus alone, and from no earthly power whatsoever. That is the theory.

In the colleges, schools and universities of the world, theologians make efforts to explore theological issues in pursuance of the objective truth, whether it maintains any institution or not. Personal convictions should not prejudice outcomes where new evidence renders convictions questionable or even obsolete. This high standard of truthfulness is generally much easier to maintain from the point of view of agnosticism or atheism than it is from belief.

The policy of the Congregation of the Doctrine of the Faith is that a theologian who holds a position in a university supported by the Church must uphold the interests of the institution of the Church, regardless of personal conscience. If, that is, he or she wishes to remain in the position of a teacher of the Church.

The Church's doctrines of spiritual salvation uphold the precious sanctity of individual conscience. The conscience is respected as the place where God's will may be manifested for the individual. This protection of the soul, however, does not necessarily entitle the believer to earn a living as an official teacher of Christian theology. The Church's doctrinal authorities are also subject to the manifestation of God's will; such authority believers must accept as a matter of faith and order, and as a condition of employment.

This conception explains why some Catholic theologians have lost their chairs of theology, and why it is unlikely that a Catholic theologian will find anything positive to say about the contents of The Gospel of Judas.

The problem of this position to its critic is simply that it involves a belief that the Congregation for the Doctrine of the Faith holds infallible access to truth. This means effectively the Church's 'doctrinal conscience' makes its home only in the minds of a tiny fraction of its members. To a critic of the theory, this might seem to limit the freedom of God to make his will known to whomsoever he may wish. That is to say, how do we know if God respects the position of the Congregation of the Doctrine of the Faith?

As the Archbishop's comments make clear, the motive of the Catholic Church's position is the protection of the soul of the believer. The needs of the Church must inhabit the consciences of Catholic believers.

The secretary to the Congregation of the Doctrine of the Faith told Vatican Radio that works such as *The Da Vinci Code* and The Gospel of Judas were being used to slander the Church because the Church was the only institution that explicitly defends questions that are fundamental to man. Therefore, to support these works in any way is to act against God's will. If the conscience is subject to God's will, the reader or viewer who enjoys these works should feel guilty. This can only mean one thing: enjoyment of *The Da Vinci Code* and The Gospel of Judas is sinful.

'It is a fact', asserted the Archbishop, 'that today one can speak badly of the Pope with impunity, as is being done in Germany with some cartoons'. He further observed that: 'One can also falsify at will the history of Christianity without the least respect – I won't say, for religious people – but for elementary historical ethics.'

What was at stake was the Truth.

The works in question lacked 'real foundation', the Archbishop declared. They had only appeared at this time because 'the Church is today the only institution that clearly and explicitly protects human life from the beginning until death, that protects the family, that says a clear word on topics of sexual and bio-ethical ethics, that proposes the values of the Ten Commandments'.

He pointed out factual errors in Dan Brown's novel which, he said, was 'a wicked distortion of the truth'. When is fiction truth?

Amato asserted that Jesus' divinity was not invented by the Council of Nicaea in AD 325, as the novel said. It was asserted, Amato insisted, in a hymn contained in Paul's Letter to the Philippians, written 'around the AD 40s'.

He used the popular interest generated by these works to justify the ongoing activities of the Congregation of the Doctrine of the Faith, , whose task was to join with the *magisterium* of the Pope and the Bishops to defend the Truth, and 'to protect the Christian people also through the correction of mistaken theological theories'. It was, in the Archbishop's opinion, the duty of Christian communities to 'speak out strongly', to 'cry out the truth from the rooftops, as the Gospel says, to stop the lies that, unfortunately, use all the weapons of media persuasion to achieve this mass consensus.'

The impression given was that the modern world is a perilous place for Christians, but so long as we cling to the work of the Church and observe its pronouncements, the Church would do its best to defend us from the wicked world, from cradle to grave.

I think it is fair to conclude that the Roman Catholic Church's highest authorities do not care for The Gospel of Judas. It is also fair to conclude that the author or authors of The Gospel of Judas would not care for the highest authorities of the Roman Catholic Church. It seems the old conflict has been taken out of mothballs and is being played out again, this time with a different cast.

Meanwhile in Canterbury

Perhaps Dr Rowan Williams, Lord Archbishop of Canterbury and senior cleric of the Anglican Church (with 77 million members), had been listening to the clamour for Christians to cry from the rooftops against *The Da Vinci Code* and The Gospel of Judas. Curiously, the two works were linked in England, as they were in Rome. One might have thought they had emerged from the same publication programme.

The Archbishop of Canterbury used his Easter Sermon (16 April 2006) specifically to slam both the Judas gospel and *The Da Vinci Code*. He declared that public interest in conspiracy stories was weakening the public's hold on the truth. That the leader of the Anglican Church should choose this time to concentrate on an ancient manuscript and a film of fiction, when threats to religion and world peace were coming from violent religious fundamentalism, might have appeared strange to some observers.

One might conclude that either the Archbishop was avoiding the serious and thorny issues of his time, or these works really do represent a threat to Christian belief. If the latter is the case, then one might wish to know whether there is any truth in the works themselves.

According to Dr Williams, it was really an issue of seasonal hype. To begin with, he tried to make light of this outbreak of doctrinal deviance: 'One of the ways in which we now celebrate the great Christian festivals in our society is by a little flurry of newspaper articles and television programmes, raking over the coals of controversies about the historical basis of faith.'

If this was the case, why add to the allegedly misguided publicity? Williams was concerned with the effect of conspiracy theories on the minds of people – an issue that goes beyond the purely seasonal nature of the excitement. In fact, the belief in conspiracies is an issue also addressed by the US government in its attempts to convince people of the rightness of its policies in the Middle East. Williams said that 'saturation coverage of *The Da Vinci*

Code literature' and the recent rediscovery of the ancient Gospel of Judas were part of a widespread desire to trust conspiracy instead of authority.

Get that word: *authority*. Hadn't the Archbishop heard of the Enlightenment? A principle of enlightened debate is that authority must account for itself, rationally. Otherwise, we shall soon find ourselves living under dictatorship. Perhaps he was too young to remember the War!

'Anything that looks like the official version is automatically suspect,' Williams told worshippers at Canterbury Cathedral, as if he had discovered something new.

Jesus Was Not a Guru

The Archbishop of Canterbury also expounded his concerns about the Judas gospel in a conservative UK newspaper, *The Mail On Sunday*. He contrasted the radical person and message of Jesus with élitist 'mystery cults'. The leading cleric of global Anglicanism dismissed The Gospel of Judas. It came from the fringes of the Christian movement, he said. It was wrong to turn Jesus into 'a mystery man, a guru'.

Dr Williams reckoned the people who originally liked (and presumably, might still like) The Gospel of Judas were afraid 'to come down to earth and face what's wrong with us. Is it surprising that some people found this too direct, too in-your-face to cope with? No wonder they preferred to go on about the names of angels and the secrets of how the world began.'

Dr Williams, a respected biblical scholar himself, takes the view that the Gnostic Christians were not able to grasp the moral power of the mainstream Gospels: 'People who weren't satisfied with the sort of thing the New Testament had to say spent quite a lot of energy trying to produce something which suited them better.' According to Dr Williams, 'They [Gnostic Christians] wanted Christian teaching to be a matter of exotic and mystical information, shared only with an in-group. So a lot of these books imagine Jesus having long conversations with various people whose names are in the Bible but who we don't know much about. This they claim is the real thing – not the boring stuff in the official books. *Don't believe the official version*, they say. The truth has been concealed from you by sinister conspiracies of bishops and suchlike villains. But now it can be told.'

The Gospel of Judas was just going to be used to promote conspiracy stories: 'We're familiar with a world of cover-up stories; we're on safer ground with their cynicism and worldly wisdom; they are less challenging and don't force us to confront difficult realities. And, like any kind of cynicism, it actually stops us hearing anything genuinely new or surprising. We need to stop and ask ourselves from time to time just why the cynical version is the one that appeals to us, is it just because we can cope much more easily with the picture of a world that always works by manipulation and deceit? Don't we want to see anything more challenging? Are we just too lazy to recognize something really fresh, something that hints at a bigger and a better world?

'The people who wrote the Gospel of Judas were trying to persuade their readers that everyone before them had got Jesus wrong, and that the folk who ran the churches were only in it for their own profit (never mind that these leaders and their followers regularly faced death for what they believed, just as some believers still do now, as we've been reminded in recent weeks). This story in itself was an easy option, something that couldn't ever be completely disproved but would create a climate of mistrust.'

For Dr Williams, the true Jesus promoted an overwhelmingly moral religion, absolutely concerned with the moral defects of human beings in this world, and how to overcome them with forgiveness, self-sacrifice and love.

This world was not something to escape from, but somewhere where we encounter God through His love. 'When the Jesus of the Gospels comes back from the dead,' wrote Dr Williams, 'he doesn't go and crow over his enemies. He meets his friends and tells them to get out there and talk about him – about what his life and death have made possible, about forgiveness, making peace, being honest about yourself, checking the temptation to judge and condemn, tackling your selfishness at the root, praying simply and trustingly.

'This is flesh and blood. It's not about exotic mysteries. It is about how God makes it possible for us to live a life that isn't paralysed by guilt, aggression and pride.'

Clearly, the Archbishop found The Gospel of Judas destructive of the moral nature of Jesus' religion. He reckoned it was easier to cope with the idea of conspiracies because believing in them removed any responsibility we might ourselves have for the state of human relations in the world. This was a message of despair, not hope. There was no 'good news' in The Gospel of Judas.

Its challenge to us was as nothing compared with the challenge to face reality, according to Dr Williams. 'That's the question we ought to be asking at Easter,' asserted Dr Williams, 'What if this surprising character in the New Testament is not just another teacher, another guru, but someone who really could change the world? Everything truly can be different because of the real story of Jesus, the Son of God.'

'Well, that is the real front-page story, bigger than any story about the discovery of a lost document and ultimately more exciting than any number of conspiracy theories. And that's perhaps why the Bible story is still being told two thousand years on, by people who have discovered that the world and their lives really have changed.'

The Archbishop was indignant at a media that titillated the public with exotic conspiracy stories while playing down stories that should really matter to Christians. He gave the example of Abdul Rahman in Afghanistan who was threatened with the death penalty because he had converted to Christianity. The Church of fact – unlike the Church of fiction – was truly concerned with issues like that: real *this-world* issues, not in 'a cover-up for the sake of the powerful'.

Coming from 'the more eccentric fringes' of the ancient Church, Dr Williams implied that The Gospel of Judas would best be appreciated by fringe eccentrics today. The mainstream should resist being distracted by such exotica, and instead re-engage with the real world in which Christians are called to witness God's profound involvement within it. Contrary to the convictions of the heretics, the highest God is not distant from the world, but manifest in every truly Christian act. Cynicism must never be permitted to disable the Christian life and hope, he argued forcefully.

Dr Williams was mindful of reasons for the appeal of the conspiracy landscape. He recognized the influence of history, the mistakes of the past. 'We don't trust power', he said, 'and because the Church has historically been part of one or another sort of establishment, and has often stood very close to political power, perhaps we can hardly expect to be exempt from this general suspicion.'

Dr Williams maintained that the Anglican Church of today was aware of some of the disabling aspects of its history. Its face must now be fully turned to the facts of life, not the fictional illusions of power in the world. The Word of God was the power in the world that the Church existed to promote.

Since The Gospel of Judas denied God's involvement with the world as it is, it had no place in genuine Christian witness. Dismissed as heresy in its time, it was still useless to the Church of today.

The Archbishop of Canterbury's assessment of the value of The Gospel of Judas was echoed by Reverend Father Abraam Sleman of the Coptic Orthodox Church: 'The discovery of The Gospel of Judas was not a surprise to the scholars. It was known to be a heretical work in the second century. The Gospel of Judas is found as a trial to pervert the Gospel of Christ. St Paul warned of such kind of teachings and said, "Evidently some people are throwing you into confusion and are trying to pervert the Gospel of Christ. But even if we or an angel from heaven should preach a gospel other than the one we preached to you, let him be eternally condemned! As we have already said, so now I say again: If anybody is preaching to you a gospel other than what you accepted, let him be eternally condemned!" (Galatians 1, vv7-9).

'Such false teachers who introduce destructive heresies bring destruction on themselves and their followers. St Peter said, "But there were also false prophets among the people, just as there will be false teachers among you. They will secretly introduce destructive heresies, even denying the sovereign Lord who brought them – bringing swift destruction on themselves. Many will follow their shameful ways and will bring the way of truth into disrepute."' (2 Peter 2 vv 1-2).

Meanwhile, *Al-Ahram Weekly* in Egypt reported how the Coptic Orthodox Bishop Basanti of the Helwan and Massara told the paper that the New Testament Gospels of Mathew, Mark, Luke and John were the only Gospels accepted at the council of Nicaea in AD 325 and recognized by Eastern and Western Churches. 'Any other gospels ... are not authenticated or accepted', declared Bishop Basanti.

Believers and Non-believers

There was widespread reaction to The Gospel of Judas from many different churches. As one might expect, Christians whose traditions follow the Bible as the sole written guide of divine authority came out against The Gospel of Judas.

In the light of what the Archbishop of Canterbury had to say about the danger of getting hooked on conspiracy stories, it is remarkable how many Christians suspect that the appearance of The Gospel of Judas is itself part of an anti-Christian conspiracy.

Darrell Bock, research professor of New Testament Studies at Dallas Theological Seminary, maintained that 'Christians who came out of the original Christian movement would have naturally reacted against Gnosticism because of its view on creation.' Writing in the magazine *Christianity Today*, Bock gave voice to some Christian fears that the National Geographic Channel's documentary The

Gospel of Judas was part of a series of efforts to undermine the authority of the central tenets of Christianity. 'What's going on now – what you've had more recently – is sort of the rebirth of the Gnostics,' wrote Bock, adding, 'it's turned over to the new-age people, but the concepts are growing stronger.' Like the Anglican and Roman Catholic authorities, he linked the release of The Gospel of Judas to the Gnostic writings on which the central plot of *The Da Vinci Code* was based.

For those who wish to trawl the many Christian internet blogging sites, there is much more of this idea to be found. This is how one internet blogger summarizes – or prophesies – his concerns: '*The Da Vinci Code, Jesus Dynasty, The Jesus Papers* [a book by Michael Baigent], *the gospel of Judas* and probably more coming, prove that the Kingdom of Darkness is now launching an all out assault against Christ and his followers. So we know time is running out by the circumstances we see taking place.'

How representative these views are of the millions of Christians world-wide we have no way of knowing. But then, a view does not have to be representative of anyone other than the person who is saying it. Individual voices tell us something about some individuals, and therefore something about humanity.

The interesting thing about internet debates is the realization that for everyone who believes one thing, there is always someone else who believes the opposite, or who has more information. It all seems a very healthy way of opening subjects up. Like every form of debate, it has its limits, but there is real debate, and honest, direct expression of a kind rarely found in the mainstream broadcast media.

In many respects it could be argued that The Gospel of Judas belongs more to the internet generation than it does to the official organs of communication. It invites a freedom of thought and variety of interpretation.

One blogger, calling himself Joshua, writes: 'Over the past few days, everyone seems to have come to a clear consensus as to what import The Gospel of Judas has for orthodox Christians, that is, *nada*. Granted, this was an easy conclusion to reach given the clear Gnostic character of the text. I mean, how many people would immediately shut the book when Jesus starts talking about Nebro and the aeons and the like? That brings up something I appreciated about the National Geographic [TV] special: In the dramatizations of the canonical Judas and The Gospel of Judas, you get a clear impression of the character of the gnostic manuscript. The re-enactments of Mark, Matthew, and John are all recognizable and plausible – if different – accounts of the betrayal. Then you get to The Gospel of Judas, where Jesus appears as Haley Joel Osment, gives belly laughs the size of Paul Bunyan, and tells Judas to follow his star. And they didn't even get into the gospel's Cliff Notes version of the gnostic creation myth. Unlike some folks (see forthcoming post), I give your average orthodox follower credit and figure that they'll know right then and there that this is something completely foreign to their faith and something nearly completely unhistorical.'

Here is a commonly held reaction: 'When all the hype dies down, what we will be left with is further evidence of an interesting split off movement from early Christianity which began in the 2nd century AD and was tolerated for two centuries by the Church until the Church fathers and mothers had heard quite enough of these fairy tales. In short, it helps us understand post apostolic and Nicene Church history better; it tells us nothing about the origins of Christianity or the historical Jesus.'

And another: 'My greater concern is the revisionist history being touted by Elaine Pagels, Karen King, Bart Ehrman, Marvin Meyer and others, on the basis of such Gnostic documents, wanting to suggest that somehow, someway these documents reflect Christianity at its very point of origin – the 1st century AD.'

For some bloggers, 'perversions' (as they see them) of the Gospel are taken as signs to hold firm to the faith as the world approaches its end: 'There will always be perversions of the Gospel by those who would proclaim another gospel and another way to salvation except through the narrow door of Jesus' death and resurrection. That's why we have to be on our toes. Heresies are like viruses. They never really go away. They only go into remission, waiting for an opportune time to flare up again. In these grey and latter days, we can expect the gnostic virus to flare up with a vengeance, along with every other way people have invented to deny that Jesus is the Christ, the Son of God, and to scandalise the little ones of faith. Have no fear. Jesus has overcome the world and its religion. And that's no secret.'

Sometimes the blogger gives voice to a religious authority, such as this contribution from a Catholic in India: 'Archbishop Aguer noted that the contents of the "gospel of Judas" "have been known for at least 1800 years" and the text has always been considered part of the apocryphal writings of "a Gnostic sect where Christian truths, philosophical doctrines and, most especially, oriental mysteries were all mixed together, and the Church condemned it rapidly."'

Sometimes the contributor seeks enlightenment from scholarship and is quick to pass it on. One blogger found the following in an article in *The Times* attributed to Dead Sea Scrolls expert, Geza Vermes: 'In anti-Roman Judaea such an act was betrayal and its perpetrator was a despicable collaborator. When Luke (6, v16) refers to Judas as a *prodotês* or "traitor", instead of using the more subtle "he who handed him over" (Matthew 10, v4; Mark 3, v19), he simply calls a spade a spade. It is a red herring to maintain that "betraying" is a mistranslation. In the story of Judas "handing over" always carries a pejorative overtone.'

This correction by Professor Geza Vermes came in response to the expressed view that the canonical Gospels already contained some doubt as to the real guilt of Judas Iscariot. That is to say, a story originally about Judas 'handing over' Jesus (without the 'traitor' tag) became the far more damning '*betrayal*' of Jesus. This interpretation had been aired in some of the National Geographic publications on The Gospel of Judas.

The publication of The Gospel of Judas undoubtedly gave opportunities for widespread and often profound examination of Christian beliefs, as well as the evidential and experiential basis for those beliefs.

There has also been a great deal of learned commentary on the value of The Gospel of Judas. Pheme Perkins, a professor of New Testament studies at Boston College in Chestnut Hill, Massachusetts, and author of *Gnosticism and the New Testament*,[3] wrote a detailed account of the gospel for *America* magazine (20 May 2006). Entitled *Is 'Judas' gospel genuine and does it belong in the Bible?*, Professor Perkins makes the point that the publication of The Gospel of Judas ignored the other Gnostic writings in the codex. These writings (The Letter of Peter to Philip and the Apocalypse of James) would have given a fuller idea that the theology of the codex was hostile to the orthodox story of the Passion of Christ.

By launching at Easter, Professor Perkins felt that buyers of the translation might be misled into thinking they were obtaining a Passion narrative. Perkins writes of how 'the widespread publicity surrounding publication of The Gospel of Judas hinted that the Good Friday remembrance of Jesus' passion would be rewritten. We would find a more human face for Judas in a story to be told from his point of view. Not so.'

The Gospel of Judas does not, she argues, belong in the Bible: 'This work is a "hidden" teaching, not a text for public proclamation. As far as one can tell, neither The Gospel of Judas nor any other Gnostic revelation dialogue was intended to replace the canonical texts in the public worship and life of the Church.' The passionless Christ is regarded by Professor Perkins as a turn-off to the Christians she knows, and its ultimate importance to Christian faith and practice, contrary to the hype, 'remains marginal'.

Contrary to this view, journalist Nevine El-Aref, writing for an Egyptian paper about how the papyri will soon be returned to Cairo's Coptic Museum, quotes Professor Elaine Pagels of Princeton University, world-famous scholar of the Gnostic gospels: 'These discoveries are exploding the myth of a monolithic religion, and demonstrating how diverse – and fascinating – the early Christian movement really was.'

New York Post writer, Angela Montefinise, wrote an interesting account of a US debate in which Elaine Pagels took part.[4] Rev Jean-Pierre Ruiz, an associate professor of theology at St John's University, opened the debate by asserting that he did not think the hype challenging the traditional narratives about Jesus 'is much to be believed'. He was dismissive. Its religious significance was 'basically zero'.

This came as no surprise to Pagels. 'I think the Church is going to reject it. It rejected it in AD 180, and I don't think anything will change. But it should look at it and address it, I think.'

Dr Mary Callaway, chair of the theology department at Fordham University was doubtful about any ripple effect the publication of the gospel might have: 'We already have dozens of these gospels. This is not news in a way. We have a Gospel of Mary Magdalene, a Gospel of Pontius Pilate. These are already out there. This is just another one.'

Elaine Pagels perceived that the dismissal of The Gospel of Judas had much to do with the Gnostics' attitude to organized, hierarchical, dogmatic religion: 'Gnostics believe you don't need to go through the rituals and church officials to have access to God. That was seen by some as a threat to the institution.' She also believed that critics of the Gnostic writings sometimes failed to understand the place these writings had in the Christian under-standing of those who valued them. They were not meant to replace the traditional Gospels. They were intended as advanced interpretative tools. 'The traditional Gospels are written in a way that anyone can understand. That's why they're the basic founda-tion. That's why they're the canon. These other texts were a higher level of learning.'

Robert Neal, an instructor at the Association for Gnostic Anthropology in upstate New York and a practising gnostic, gave credence to The Gospel of Judas. He said that some people lacked the kind of awareness that made sense of the work: 'People have a very superficial understanding of good and evil. Duality always exists in the world. There are always two sides. A very superficial view of these characters [including Judas] as being totally evil doesn't allow one to enter deeply into the nature of the mysteries that these stories are trying to portray.'

Angela Montefinise reported how Neal had seen more and more people turn to Gnostic principles, not as acts of guilty sinfulness but as a heart-felt road to God. 'I think they're looking for an alternative to the Christian dogma, and this is it . . . We believe these gospels to be true, and we hope people read them just to see that there's more to Christianity than meets the eye.'

Writing in *The New Yorker*[5], Adam Gopnik found nothing in the publication of The Gospel of Judas to justify all the publicity. 'The finding of the new Gospel', he wrote, 'though obviously remarkable as a bit of textual history, no more challenges the basis of the Church's faith than the discovery of a document from the 19th century written in Ohio and defending King George would be a challenge to the basis of American democracy. There are no new beliefs, no new arguments, and certainly no new evidence in the papyrus that would cause anyone to doubt who did not doubt before.'

Straight-talking controversialist Christopher Hitchens took Gopnik to task for his low appraisal of the significance of The Gospel of Judas.[6] Hitchens sees its relevance in the effect it would have on the phenomenon of anti-Semitism: 'The Judas gospel would make one huge difference if it was accepted. It would dispel the centuries of anti-Semitic paranoia that were among the chief accompaniments of the Easter celebration until approximately 30 years after 1945, when the Vatican finally acquitted the Jews of the charge of Christ-killing. But if Jesus had been acting consistently and seeking a trusted companion who could facilitate his necessary martyrdom, then all the mental and moral garbage about the Jewish frame-up of the Redeemer goes straight over the side.'

An extremely well-researched and profound review of National Geographic's English translation of The Gospel of Judas appeared in the *New York Review of Books* under the title 'The Betrayer's Gospel',[7] written by Eduard Iricinschi, Lance Jenott and Philippa Townsend. The article examines in great detail both the thinking behind The Gospel of Judas and its historic significance. The reviewers are quite sure that, 'The Gospel of Judas, released to the public for the first time in April, is one of the most important contributions to our sources for early Christianity since the discovery of 13 papyrus codices near the Egyptian town of Nag Hammadi in 1945.'

Far from the material having no bearing on Christian faith and practice, the reviewers note that, 'Quite apart from their sensationalist appeal', recently published Gnostic writings 'have provided scholars with an unprecedented opportunity to expand our understanding of early Christian controversies over such issues as gender, heresy, and church leadership'. The reviewers recognize that since The Gospel of Judas was written 'decades after' the canonical Gospels (perhaps around AD 140) the gospel cannot offer an historical basis for re-evaluating Judas. They believe the gospel does not have new historical or biographical information about Judas Iscariot.

Unlike other responses to the gospel, however, the reviewers make this fact the basis of a fascinating question: why would a '2nd-century Christian ... be interested in rehabilitating Jesus' archenemy? What would inspire a writer to produce this particular response to the enigma of the betrayal, recasting the infamous traitor as Jesus' most loyal disciple and rewriting the Christian story in his name?'

The reviewers express the possibility that the community of Christians who valued the text felt themselves to be reviled and misunderstood as a result of their different perception, and therefore different interpretation, of the traditions surrounding Jesus' Crucifixion. Misunderstood, they identified with Judas, the loner who left the inner circle and therefore the protection of the brotherhood.

The reviewers also note how the early Church was not in one mind on many subjects – not least of which was martyrdom, whether or not to go 'to the lions' as a way of imitating Jesus' own willingness to die. Interestingly, the reviewers draw attention to the fact that some Gnostic Christians saw no value in sacrificing life. Commitment to the spiritual life did not require acts of extreme physical self-denial (*this poses the question: when is martyrdom suicide?*).

If, as has been stated of Gnostic Christians, they were only interested in leaving the body and this world, then surely martyrdom in the public arenas would have provided a perfect opportunity for a kind of virtual suicide.

These reviewers are not in a state of denial; they are prepared to examine the text, not simply accept or reject it. Their response to its appearance is rare; its rarity gives it value.

Contrary to what the Archbishop of Canterbury had to say about a world that is marred only by human beings' failure to do good works within it, the reviewers draw attention to a disconcerting fact. They make the point that, 'the theme that rebellious angelic powers rule the world is hardly unique to so-called Gnostic theology.'

'The Gospel of John, for example, describes the devil as "the Prince of this world"; and the Epistle to the Ephesians proclaims that "our struggle is not against enemies of blood and flesh, but against the rulers, against the authorities, against the cosmic powers of this present darkness" (6, v12). Like Satan, whom the Gospel of Luke tells us Jesus saw "fall from heaven like lightning" (10, v18), the figures of Nebro and Saklas give the author of the Judas gospel a way of explaining evil in the world as somehow both independent of, yet ultimately subject to, a perfect God.'

There is a strong suggestion here that official reaction to The Gospel of Judas has veered towards the dangerously superficial, leaving people who find value in the text open to officially sanctioned prejudice.

The reviewers note that at the end of The Gospel of Judas, the reader is left abruptly with the handing over of Judas and the latter taking 'some money'. They suggest that rather than being disinterested in the events of the Passion, as some critics have accused the gospel of being, the writer has no desire to add to or contradict familiar accounts. What the author of the gospel was interested in was the *meaning behind* the events. The work then can be seen as a pious meditation, not a careless, cynical or conspiracy-drenched assault on innocent Christian convictions.

The reviewers conclude by saying that no one who has deeply examined the condemned gospel is likely to read the traditional account in quite the same way again. While this is in no way the same as saying that Christianity has been turned on its head, as some of the promotional material has suggested, it is still a significant claim for a very old collection of Coptic papyri to make in the modern world.

Whilst the 'once-familiar landscape' will have changed, The Gospel of Judas is unlikely to overturn traditional accounts of the events of the Passion. Nevertheless, it does offer 'a sophisticated meditation on the relationship between God and evil – one that was perhaps inspired by personal experience as much as philosophical curiosity.'

Neither for nor against the gospel, the review demonstrates not only the virtue, but also the profit, of a detached thoughtfulness.

All Those in Favour, Please Stand Up

It might appear from what we have seen that the reaction to the publication of The Gospel of Judas has been almost uniformly hostile. While this is certainly true as a reflection of the views of organized religious bodies, it does not tell the whole truth.

A large number of people have been excited and stimulated by the many questions that have been raised since the appearance of the new gospel – even if its opponents think the word 'gospel' (good news) is a misnomer. In fact, it is clearly observable that where there has been the deepest thought and reflection about this ancient gospel's contents, the greatest level of approval has been found. That is not to say that the gospel's opponents have not thought deeply about why they object to its public broadcast, but that the objections raised are often fundamentally *reactionary*, relying on well established preconceptions, not fresh study in the light of a new work.

For example, the Archbishop of Canterbury is a learned man with a background in academic excellence. One might have supposed he would take a more detached, objective view of the phenomenon. He, of all people, one might think, would know that a work new to scholarship, such as The Gospel of Judas, requires careful, even specialist, study. Instead, he seemed to treat this extraordinary survivor of a bygone era as a kind of political pamphlet that had turned up on his doorstep, requiring a fairly cursory reading before summary dismissal.

It would appear from his comments that he already 'knew all about it'. He even said that the gospel was one of 'dozens' of works like it. As a matter of fact, The Gospel of Judas has very particular elements which make it unique in the surviving body of so-called Gnostic literature. Did he recognize these?

If the lonely gospel has nothing to say to Christians, then it cannot possibly be a Christian work. But the author or authors of the gospel believed themselves to be *completely* Christian, devoted to the spirit of Jesus. Not for a second did they ever consider that they were heretics. They observed the Church changing around them. They wrote about the changes; they suffered as a result of them.

Furthermore, the Archbishop of Canterbury joined the gospel up to a suspect (in his mind) public craving for conspiracy stories. He suggested that anyone interested in conspiracy stories was unlikely to be able to confront the real world. Here he has simply left all semblance of academic training behind him, an important element of which must be discrimination of genres. An ancient gospel writing cannot be equated with a modern commercial novel, even if you think the gospel is pure (or impure) fiction. If one wanted to talk of a conspiracy story at Easter, then one need look no further than the traditional Easter story itself!

Here you have a betrayer – a spy in fact – and one possessed by Satan, we are told, working for 'the other side'. Judas (possibly a terrorist or terrorist sympathizer) has gone out and conspired with the chief priests to take – in secret – a man from his fellows under cloak of night. There is a clandestine scene where money changes hands. There is a secret sign (a kiss) and a violent struggle in which one of the disciples attacks a guard with a sword and nearly kills him. The circumstances are plainly mysterious, the motives dark. And through all this, the one betrayed *already* knows the plot. He does not stop his betrayer even when he could prevent him from making a mess of his life; instead he encourages him: 'Do it quickly,' he tells the spy.

Even in the traditional story, the selling-out of Jesus by Judas Iscariot is a classic tale of conspiracy and revenge – one that leaves many avenues of enquiry open. There are secret motives at work; all is not what it seems (as we shall see in the next chapter). The simple truth is that no person in any Church anywhere can say with absolute, demonstrable and incontestable certainty what precisely was going on at the time. The jury of history, if not of faith, is out.

His Holiness the Pope has said that Judas was a 'greedy liar'. In a court of law, this statement would simply be regarded as one statement on behalf of the prosecution. It is unlikely that in a *post-mortem* trial in a civilized country, Judas would be convicted, given the limited, and contradictory, evidence against him. We know that the Church condemned him, but there may have been other reasons involved. There are reasons to doubt; honest doubt is legitimate, not sinful.

It is important to note that The Gospel of Judas was not the only work to have highlighted the presence of a question-begging conspiracy in all of this. Dr Williams knows very well that many books by respectable theologians and historians of religion have wondered what was really behind the trial of Jesus. Even the arch heresy-hunter himself, Bishop Irenaeus of Lyon, wrote of a 'mystery of betrayal', a mysterious phrase for sure.

The Archbishop seems to have a simplistic idea of the *events* surrounding the Crucifixion, hardly justified by the accounts themselves. His interpretation of those events is doubtless mighty and, for mainstream confessing Christians, mightily transforming. But here we come to the crux of the matter. What the Archbishop and his fellow mainstream Christian teachers object to in The Gospel of Judas is the *meaning* given to the Easter scenario. In their eyes, the meaning given to the events in The Gospel of Judas is *wrong*. Therefore, it can be dismissed. Members of the public who wish to investigate this condemned meaning are told that the root of their desire is not sanctioned by *real* Christianity. Conspiracy is hiding the truth!

This observation might lead one to suspect that some people are quickly going to come to the conclusion that the publication of The Gospel of Judas is *itself* a part of a conspiracy *against the truth*. The words of Dr Williams may in the long term be seen not as having doused the fires of conspiracy, but of having stimulated them.

In short, The Gospel of Judas has been condemned as unreal, and therefore unworthy of the attention of anyone but specialist scholars. The mainstream Churches, on the whole, do not want the public to be stirred by its contents because its contents are wrong. Wrong interpretation. Wrong meaning. Wrong text. Those that do not agree are wrong.

The Church *knows already*, and has nothing more to learn on the matter. This stance may not be in step with the mood of many serious people in the world today, wrong as they may be.

Exploding the Myth

One of those who advocate the value of giving consideration to the 'wrong' interpretation is the Gnostic specialist Professor Elaine Pagels. Her words on The Gospel of Judas have been quoted around the world: 'These discoveries are exploding the myth of a monolithic religion, and demonstrating how diverse – and fascinating – the early Christian movement really was.'

What does she mean by the 'myth of a monolithic religion'? What she means is the idea that there was a simple line of teaching from Jesus to his disciples, to the Jews, to Paul, then to the Gentiles – a kind of theological Golden Age. The myth demands that there was one body of doctrine taught by Jesus and carried on by Peter and by Paul to the world. Jesus gave Peter the 'keys to the kingdom', a fascinating phrase often taken to suggest Jesus had given Peter the front door keys to his one and only Church. Peter was to be, so to speak, Chief Bouncer at Club Jesus.

Along with this image of one, more or less harmonious, and sometimes miraculous, movement, goes the idea that almost from the beginning there were four Gospels. There were only four Gospels, plus The Acts of the Apostles, and sundry apostolic letters, and they all support one body of pure doctrine going back to the Master Himself. And these were not just an inspiring collection of writings, these were the 'Word of God', just as if Jesus had written them all himself. According to this theory, the apostles could not create anything; they could only *deliver*.

Anything that seemed manifestly different or contradictory to that once-and-for-all-time body of writing must be heresy. Heresy is wrong. Always.

But doesn't all this beg a question? If there was one divine movement of Church growth, one body of Christian doctrine, who were these heretics? Where had they come from? Who had taught them? We know, even from The Acts of the Apostles that Paul himself was regarded as a dangerous heretic by Jewish Christians who believed that Gentiles should accept the Jewish Law and be circumcised. What had been Jesus' teaching on this issue? According to the monolithic Church idea, both Peter and Paul should have known the answer and followed it.

The question then arises, why did not Jesus give precise instructions for how 'his Church' should develop? Did he expect the

Church? Was there a significant gap between the appearance of Jesus, his teaching, and the development of a Church? The traditional answer to this question is to say that Jesus promised the Holy Spirit would come after him and guide the apostles in the ways of truth.

After Jesus' departure from visible presence, the Holy Spirit would instruct the disciples. But we know Peter and Paul argued about it. Why didn't they get the same message from the guidance of the Holy Spirit? According to The Acts of the Apostles, Peter and Paul did eventually come to some agreement on the issue – and they agreed to part. Interestingly, the reason for Peter's change of mind is said to be because he had a visionary experience (visions were OK in the earliest Church). The vision gave him conviction and authority. However, in spite of this vision, and the harmonizing work of the Holy Spirit, it was suggested that Paul quit Judaea and go abroad.

Paul took this suggestion (or order) as a straightforward commission to preach his version of salvation (he always believed it was Christ's) to the Gentiles. Peter seems to have accepted the idea. However, many of the first followers of Jesus who had also 'received' the Holy Spirit did not trust Paul. Paul was not welcome. They saw him not as a 'deliverer' of Jesus' message but as an innovator, a dangerously creative spirit. They did not want creativity; they wanted law and order.

We also know from the letters of Paul that once the idea became dominant in early Christian meetings that the 'Holy Spirit' was the arbiter of right conduct, problems arose in personal discipline. These problems soon got out of hand. You can read about them in Paul's letters to the Corinthians. The Corinthians lived in a notoriously promiscuous seaport.

Had Jesus left instructions on how to deal with problems arising from the presence of the Holy Spirit? Or did Paul have to improvise as best he could? Paul was good at improvising. He was creative. And for a self-proclaimed apostle, he was even surprisingly flexible; he was able to *change his mind*. Amazing. He has been called 'the first

Christian theologian' (as well as the first Christian mystic) because he *interpreted* the traditions that came to him. And since he believed he did this in accordance with the Spirit of Christ that was, he believed, within him and those closest to him, then he was convinced that his writings were true.

This same justification would become the central justification of many of those people Church authorities would later condemn as heretics, including, of course, those responsible for The Gospel of Judas. Many so-called Gnostics looked to Paul as their chosen apostolic inspiration. Eventually, faith in the Holy Spirit as sole guide would come to be qualified by rules, and the Christian order controlled by authorized deacons, priests and bishops. What do we mean by 'authorized'? To have authority, you had to trace your teaching authority to an apostle.

It is simply fascinating that the people who found meaning in The Gospel of Judas chose Judas as their apostolic authority – he who had been in the circle, and who broke out of it. (Paul, of course, had never been in it.) Were these people just trouble-makers, anarchists, smart-alecks, automatic rebels, madmen? Do they have nothing to say to us?

The Spirit created unexpected developments, developments that were not to everybody's liking. The appearance of people who found meaning in the story of Judas may be described as one of those unexpected developments.

This is not the place to offer a history of the earliest Christian communities, much of which would have to be speculative or arguable, since so much of the evidence is disputed by responsible commentators. The point is, as Elaine Pagels asserts, that there was diversity of interpretation in the early Christian communities. The level of diversity depended on who the teacher was, and what the teacher knew, or thought he (or she) knew of the mind of Jesus.

There does not seem to have been much more charitable love, brotherhood and sisterhood among believers then than there is today. When a Roman commentator once famously remarked, 'See how these Christians love each other!', he had probably not attended a Synodical debate. 'Love one another', said Jesus, and his followers have been arguing about what he meant by it for nearly 2,000 years. When 'love and peace' became the cry of young social critics in the 1960s, the response from the Church was, to say the least, nervous.

The Church has had to disown many of its early enthusiasms in the name of a moral order. One of those early enthusiasms was what was called 'prophecy' , some aspects of which might today be called 'mysticism' – direct experience of divine mind. We know there used to be a lot of prophecy in the earliest Christian communities; there is not so much today, at least in Europe.

I was once told by the (then) Dean of Lichfield that the Church does not really like prophets; they have always been a problem. Experience has shown that it is difficult at the time to know whether one is in the presence of a good prophet, or a false one. It is much easier to put them all in the same bag and say, 'Look, we have got a prophet called Jesus. And we have got enough trouble trying to live as he commanded without listening to any more!'

If Jesus spoke for all time when he is reported to have said 'A prophet is not without honour – except in his own country,' then we may, by definition, expect a prophet to get a fairer hearing *outside* the Church than within it. This may or may not be the case with The Gospel of Judas – because it certainly speaks to some people. It is not, apparently, a dead letter, a mere sub-literary survival of a vanished antiquity. There are people out there who have found real meaning not only within its pages, but in the predictable effect it has had on religious authorities.

Here is a summary of some of the interesting points made by many different people who have *not* rejected The Gospel of Judas.

Some observers have recorded how the general reaction to Judas' gospel prompts the question of whether there has been any spiritual or psychological progress in the human being in the last 2,000 years. *Precious little* seems to be their conclusion.

While Judas' gospel brings light into the darkness of our under-standings, the Church, yet again, has striven to marginalize it. The authorities remain in a state of denial and intend to distract us from considering the work on its own terms. The usual gamut of condemnatory words are brought out: the work is called 'Gnostic' (as if that explains it all), 'Sethian', 'Cainite', 'oriental' – *exotic*. Its date of origin is apparently too late for us to take the work seriously. It was not liked by the 'holy fathers of the Church' who saved us from its sullying presence. Its author hates our real world and our real bodies. It supports the work of Satan (because Judas was full of Satan).

By lumping the gospel together with the 'Gnostic heresy', or with the scholars' term 'Gnosticism', the work is pre-judged and pre-framed. The implication is that it is not really to do with 'us'. We are too quick to judge it – we attach to it ideas which may not have been shared by its author or authors. The gospel has been judged, above all, by those who have been taught to hate anything like it.

It has not been allowed free and objective study. It has been presented as either sensational, or wicked, or both. If it is wicked, it is dismissed as being irrelevant. If it is sensational, it is dismissed as not being worth profound attention. If it is like *The Da Vinci Code*, then it is fiction. If it is not fiction, then it is fantasy.

In fact, it has been correctly observed that the whole history of biblical scholarship shows that one cherished idea after another has been dumped or been radically reappraised as time goes on. It is less than 200 years since many learned men believed the world was created in 4004 BC and that Adam and Eve were the names of the first members of the species, and that they lived as a couple in a 'garden'. Until fairly recently, the Gospels were regarded as biogra-phies or as 'automatic writing', their writers' fingers positively charged with God's will to self-express.

New knowledge brings changes that are for many – but especially for those in authority – discomfiting. Our picture of the early Christian movement is changing. Rather than seeing beliefs nicknamed 'Gnostic' or 'Gnosticism' as outside the Church, they appear to have been present in some form or other all the time. In what form and precisely where, are questions which will keep scholars occupied for many years to come. But they will find answers and better understanding if they do their job well enough; if they are *permitted* to do their job well enough. Freedom is not inevitable.

The mind of Jesus is still taxing our best minds for understanding. Jesus himself may have shared ideas that would later be seen as heretical. Would Jesus survive the investigation of the Holy Inquisition – or even the Congregation for the Doctrine of the Faith?

The description 'Gnostic' has been used to define the borders of the dominant power in the Church. The Church has defined itself by comparing itself to what it is not. Anyone who has said the Creed in church and knows a bit about Church history can virtually feel the presence of one Church council after another bitterly arguing over whether Jesus was God, or not, or if so, how so. What does it mean to be 'of one substance with the Father', for example? Does it mean he was 'made of God'? And why is Jesus said to be sitting down at God's 'right hand', when believers say he is active in the real world?

Anyone who looks deeply at some of the ideas in the rejected writings can see that some of them are compatible with the Gospels, and often illuminate their meaning. But that meaning is arrived at independently of Church authority. And it is this issue of Church authority, law, structure and power that emerges time and time again as the key factor both in understanding why the material was rejected (and is again) and whether the material has any spiritual, psychological or historical value for us today.

It should also be borne in mind that these writings, found in Egypt, may represent a developmental stage in the movement of Christian thought. We have them now, as it were, frozen in time. But had they been allowed to develop, these ideas may have found more refined means of expression as succeeding generations gained in experience as a result of dialogue and creative engagement with others.

Had those who loved the works not been threatened with excommunication, there may have been mutually beneficial interaction between the schools of thought. Some of the more difficult concepts may have had the edges rounded off and we could have seen a kind of 'college of mystics' for those who looked more deeply into their inherited traditions.

Nothing in this world is perfect, but couldn't people have made a better job of coping with their differences, many of which result from mere accidents of birth? Orthodox Christianity is not a God to be worshipped, any more than 'Holy Church' is a miraculous idol to cower before. Orthodox Christianity is an interpretation of remote events. Was there only one interpretation of events in the early Church? Who has the right to interpret those events?

One contributor to an internet blogging site has referred to the psychoanalyst Wilfred Bion's idea of what he calls the 'selected fact': 'The "selected fact" is the fact that can't be selected because it will result in catastrophic change for the psyche or group. The selected fact is the fact that cannot be integrated into the current defining hypothesis or basic belief system, because its integration will cause the destruction of the container, the current defining hypothesis maintained by mythical assumptions.

'The selected fact in the current belief system of biblical scholarship – and mainstream Christianity – is the probability that "Gnostic influences" reach into the pre-history of both orthodox Christianity and normative Judaism.'

The contributor draws attention to his perception that Jesus taught on many levels 'to reach the various levels of psycho-spiritual development of his audience'. Those with the ears to hear the 'mysteries of the kingdom of God' (a phrase from the New Testament) were given a higher level of insight which may have developed into a wide variety of *gnosis* teachings.

Why is this idea so hard for some people to bear? Is it because it is 'élitist'? Do we not have levels of education? Is everyone capable of being a professor of sub-atomic physics? Can everyone learn 12 languages? Why, then, is it suggested that everyone can understand all levels of spiritual truth? We advance – if we advance – step by step. Faith is a beginning, not an end in itself. Clerical office does not give you a head-start in spiritual understanding; Jesus reckoned children were closer to heaven than his disciples.

Is there not justice in the idea that you 'reap what you sow'?

It is said that 'Gnostics' believed that only the spiritually aware would be saved. However, it is surely a remarkable thought contained in The Gospel of Judas that Judas, who is for most of the gospel both outside 'the 12' (and therefore barred from joining the 'great and holy generation'), and the most condemned man on earth, is yet finally raised to that great and holy generation, most of all perhaps *because he really wants to be*.

That is to say, he was willing to have his mind changed. He was willing to stand up before Jesus, even though he was not yet able to look him directly in the eye, that is: to understand his mind, or bear the essential spiritual presence. Does not The Gospel of Judas suggest that it is we who stand in our own way? Does not the gospel show a way to all who have a will to go?

Anyhow, the doctrine of the Catholic Church has never said that everyone will be saved, whatever they do. For the wicked there is no straight ticket to heaven at the moment of death. Furthermore, there has always been a 'communion of saints'. If that communion is not an élite, why are the saints raised on pedestals and prayed to?

Is it not possible to consider, says one internet contributor, 'that God's plan included a component for the long-term education and evolution of human consciousness (considering its current pathetic state)'. Could this gospel not be a seed for a new step forward after years of spiritual error, something for which the human race, or at least part of it, may be ready for? Perhaps it is God who has sent this strange work back into our world in order to show up what we have been, what we have become, and what we may yet be?

Is the star of Judas rising? And if so, might ours too?

Remarkably, this idea that the figure of Judas has the capacity to lead people to a higher awareness of spiritual self-realization was voiced years before the publication of The Gospel of Judas.

Samael Aun Weor (1917-1977), born Víctor Manuel Gómez Rodríguez in Bogotá, Colombia, was a prolific writer and teacher of occultism. In 1973, he wrote of how, 'The Cosmic Drama of Christ would be impossible to represent without the role of Judas; this apostle is then the most exalted Adept, the most elevated amongst all of the apostles of the Christ Jesus.'

In a work called *Gnosis – The Practical Gnosticism of Samael Aun Weor*, the author was again moved to consider the spiritual significance of the 'greedy liar': 'Judas symbolizes a very specific aspect of the consciousness. To comprehend Judas in his full symbolic depth requires Meditation. The Intellect is simply too shallow and redundant to grasp the full impact of any spiritual truth, and Judas, who on the surface appears diabolic, escapes easy definition.'

This striking vision of Judas as an exalted adept of spiritual mysteries seems prophetic of the figure that emerges from The Gospel of Judas. However, it is more likely that the author of these intriguing words had been meditating on the esoteric teacher Gurdjieff's *Beelzebub's Tales to his Grandson* (Weor wrote a work called *The Revolution of Beelzebub* in 1950). Gurdjieff, spiritual guide both to the dancer Nijinksy and to the author of *Mary Poppins*, Pamela Travers, reckoned Judas was a most loyal disciple who sacrificed himself to save Christ's mission.

One fascinating – and not at all occult – contribution to the defence of The Gospel of Judas came from the translator of the gospel, Rodolphe Kasser, who as far as I know has no particular mystical or New Age axe to grind. In an interview with *Swissinfo*, Kasser was asked how he responded to Pope Benedict XVI's insistence that Judas was a traitor. Kasser replied: 'It was a rather stupid response to say that this new text confirms the idea that Judas betrayed Jesus through love of power and money. That's not the case at all. Judas is presented [in his gospel] as someone who wants to know more. That's what Gnosticism is about: it is knowledge that brings salvation, and false beliefs that prevent man from developing. The Bible itself is not opposed to this.'

Swissinfo then asked if the Church's reaction was motivated by fear. Kasser's answer was direct: 'It is motivated by intellectual laziness. People don't want to change what they have always believed. I noticed this reaction among people in the town of Yverdon where I live. Someone I know well told me they were against this new discovery because they didn't like the idea of Jesus and Judas plotting together.'

Elsewhere, some reactions held quite unusual interpretations of passages of The Gospel of Judas. Rather than interpret the phrase, 'You will sacrifice the man that clothes me,' as Bart Ehrman does, in suggesting a Gnostic dualism between spirit and flesh, one blogger with an interest in yoga reckons the gospel blends with the evolutionary thought of the yogi guru Sri Aurobindo and Patrizia Norelli-Bachlet: 'Jesus was talking about the *Man* – as in *us* – as in *this* temporary phase of Humanity.' According to this interesting interpretation, the 'man' that 'clothes' Jesus is the human world that hides or obscures the true being or nature of Jesus. The interpretation asserts that 'Jesus [via the author of the text] basically tells us that he is playing a divine joke on humanity. He tells Judas fairly clearly that by enacting his crucifixion, he would intentionally plant the seed of the dissolution of Man (Mental Man), in order to make way for *that* Generation or the Supra-mental Race as spoken of by Sri Aurobindo, which Jesus knew was coming in a future aeon or age.' The writer of these words describes him- or herself as an aficionado of 'Integral Yoga'.

It is worth noting that yogic practices were not unknown to the Graeco-Roman Egypt of the period in which The Gospel of Judas is thought to have been composed – if, indeed, it was composed in Egypt in the first place. To be frank, we do not know where it was composed and cannot be entirely certain that there was a Greek original, though it would seem most likely.

Against this particular yogic allegory, Professor Rodolphe Kasser, of the University of Geneva, prefers the same basic interpretation of the text as that held by Bart Ehrman. According to Kasser, 'Jesus says it is necessary for someone to free him finally from his human body, and he prefers that this liberation be done by a friend rather than by an enemy. So he asks Judas, who is his friend, to sell him out, to betray him. It's treason to the general public, but between Jesus and Judas it's not treachery'.

Supporting this view, Elaine Pagels believes that the so-called betrayal may have been 'a secret mystery' between Judas and Jesus. In an interview for ABC News (6 April 2006), Pagels added how she hoped that people would appreciate 'the excitement of this discovery and recognize that it's all right to ask the kinds of questions that sometimes they're afraid to ask, and say, "What else didn't we know about the early Christian movement? Could, for example, Judas be forgiven?" And when people start asking that question, they'll realize that it doesn't destroy faith, it actually can strengthen it. But it's a different kind of faith; it's informed by what we understand about our past.'

Gnostics Today

In all of this talk of age-old heresies and ancient documents, one is inclined to forget that a growing number of people today identify strongly with the Gnostic tradition. To them, the quest for *gnosis* is not something that disappeared under the stones of Egypt with The Gospel of Judas in the 4th century AD. Rather, it is something that has always been present somewhere in the world, popping up from time to time like the engulfed cathedral beneath the seas of Debussy's famous *Prelude*.

The gnostic of today likes the image of an underground river, or sacred stream, that occasionally emerges as a freshening spring in unlikely places and at unlikely times. Some of these people have chosen to associate themselves with Churches or societies that permit their ideas to grow in their own way and in their own time.

Los Angeles Times staff writer, Arin Gencer, posted an article on 22 April 2006 on (*Neo-*) Gnostic reactions to The Gospel of Judas, 'Gnostics Find Affirmation in Gospel of Judas'. Gencer said that while the National Geographic launch promised to 'challenge some of our deepest held beliefs', this was not the case for gnostics of today. For them the 'so-called revelation was just a confirmation of a long-held belief that there was more to Judas and the Crucifixion story than the Gospels of Matthew, Mark, Luke and John suggest.' Gencer quoted Bishop Stephan Hoeller, who leads a Gnostic congregation, the *Ecclesia Gnostica,* founded in 1956: 'Gnostics were inclined in this direction for a long, long time. The notion that Judas was this terrible villain ... that has never really been accepted in Gnosticism,' Hoeller said.

Author of *The Gnostic Jung,* Stephan Hoeller also turns up in an issue of *New Dawn* magazine (Special Issue No 2, 2006), an Australian-based publication that regularly and intelligently reports on Gnostic-type subjects for the non-specialist reader. In the article, Hoeller makes an interesting point. He reckons that in the first two centuries of the Church there was no orthodoxy; therefore there was no heresy. On this basis, The Gospel of Judas is simply an early Christian work – not as early as the traditional Gospels, but a genuine example of early Christian thought nonetheless.

In this regard, it is interesting that Ehrman uses the expression 'proto-orthodoxy' to describe the position of someone like Irenaeus, who wrote 'against the *gnosis* falsely so-called' around AD 180. Readers may judge how useful compound terms like 'proto-orthodoxy' really are. It might make more sense if the different emphases of early Christianity were simply named after those who we know taught them. For example, 'Pauline Christianity' (after

Paul), 'Johannine Christianity' (after John), 'Valentinian Christianity' (after Valentinus), and so on. The problem is trying to find the definitive 'Jesus Christianity' that all the strains of belief believe themselves to be.

As for The Gospel of Judas, we do not know the name of the person who was responsible for its special insights. We can be fairly certain it was not someone called Judas Iscariot. The work is not written in the first person and Judas is a character in a work that, as far as we can tell, is a creative reflection on the traditional accounts.

New Dawn magazine has clearly been highly stimulated by the appearance of The Gospel of Judas. In order to meet the demands of its readers, its special issue also contains articles on *The Da Vinci Code*, Mary Magdalene, the Holy Grail, the Nag Hammadi Library, the medieval Cathars, the New Age, as well as a carefully considered, non-committal article on The Gospel of Judas.

Two Gods?

The article in *New Dawn* about Judas ('Judas: The Greatest Disciple?'), is written by an American writer on esoteric subjects, Richard Smoley. He makes some interesting points about possible Jewish origins for the 'higher God' and 'lower God' idea that is such a striking feature of The Gospel of Judas. Smoley examines the work of Old Testament scholar Margaret Barker. She hypothesized that during the 'First Temple' period (c. 940-586 BC) of ancient Jewish history, Jews worshipped a kind of divine trio: *El*, the supreme God, *Yahweh*, the national God, and *Asherah*, a feminine consort.

According to the hypothesis, Asherah was discarded during priestly reforms enacted under King Josiah (c.640-609 BC) while El and Yahweh were ordered to be seen not as separate, but as one, only God. Barker believes this period marked the change from henotheism (a supreme god among a coterie) to monotheism (there is no god but God). According to Barker's hypothesis, this reformed structure of dual worship would dominate the Hebrew scriptures after the 7th century BC.

According to this idea, Yahweh could be seen as a usurper, who had 'got above himself' and equated himself with 'El' (the generic term for God and the supreme God of some Canaanites). Originally a 'national god' (every nation had one), Yahweh became the absolute deity in the interests of divine unity, as against the polytheism of the Jews' neighbours, the Canaanite (and others). That is to say, 'El' was too close for comfort and had to be, so to speak, 'Yahwised'. It is a theory.

As regards the origin of the higher and lower deities of 'Gnosticism', one theory suggests there was a kind of 'continuity movement' of older Jewish ideas, supported by those who clung to this dualist structure of a supreme deity and a secondary, national deity. They came to see the Jewish Law as inferior to the Gnostic way as a means of reaching the highest God. Thus, Paul's later criticism of the Jewish Law reflects contact with, or knowledge of, this continuity tradition. Since the so-called Gnostics followed Paul in their concept of the limitations of the Jewish Law, the Gnostic distinction of higher and lower deities also reflects an evolution of the priestly and prophetic conflicts of the old Jewish kingdom.

The hypothesis has plausibility, but it will be difficult to convince those who recall the patriarchal narratives concerning Abraham and his quintessential belief in one God (*but which one?*). However, the question of how truly monotheistic the ancestors of the Jews actually were is a matter of considerable debate among scholars – especially since the issue is so close to the heartfelt beliefs and wishes of so many religiously minded people.

Without a time machine – and for all the strides made in archaeology – we have no absolute knowledge of the complexities of belief as experienced in the Middle East, 1,500 years or so before Christ. We know what people came to believe, but we know very little about how they came to believe it. All the accounts favour the dominant interests of those who had their version of events and beliefs written down. This is as true of the so-called Old Testament, as it is of the so-called New.

This does not make life easy for non-specialist people – that is to say, the vast bulk of believers in Judaism and Christianity, or for interested atheists, agnostics or subscribers to other religions. As I hope you can see by now, there are no easy answers to any of the really big questions! That is why they are still Big Questions! And one of the biggest questions with regard to Gnostic beliefs is this whole issue of a higher and lower deity.

Irenaeus' attack on the followers of the speculative Christian teachers of his day – those for whom the word *gnosis* was especially important – centred on his conviction that they profoundly insulted not only the God of the Jewish faith, but also the creator God recognized by many pagan philosophers as well. Philosophers who revered 'the divine Plato' also accused *gnostikoi* (a nickname) of hating the fashioner of the universe. Then again, these same philosophers did not care for Christians of any type, as far as we can tell.

But Irenaeus, for one, seems to have wanted Christian beliefs to have intellectual respectability – at least as far as a 'realistic' picture of the *natural* universe was concerned. Irenaeus constantly accuses his targets of being irrational, self-contradictory and absurd. But in the world in which Irenaeus was operating, and in which The Gospel of Judas was composed, there could be no more irrational belief than that of 'the Word (*Logos*) made flesh'.

Followers of Plato's philosophy recognized the majesty of the universe, but never thought for a second that flesh could carry the full 'weight' or quality of the divine mind. Flesh, coming from a lower order of existence, could not inherit the spiritual. Rather like the readers of The Gospel of Judas, Plato's admirers believed the spirit would have to rise to higher levels to perceive the true home of spiritual reality.

So, this distinction between higher and lower deities (and the moral deficiency of flesh and the world) has always been the most controversial aspect of the specific beliefs associated with the word 'Gnostic'.

Just to complicate matters even further, the distinction of true (if remote) deity and lower (anti-spiritual) deity has also been subjected to a broad range of interpretation and questioning. For example, is the 'lower God' of the Gnostics wicked, or just deficient? Is he simply inadequate to deal with man's problematic nature? Is the 'lower God' really just a representative of *our* inadequate ideas about 'God' – our tendency to make Gods out of our own image?

Is not the case, rather, that it is not the 'lord of this world' who is the 'Fool' (*Saklas*), but *we* who are Fools for so imagining the highest God in such an inferior way?

Did these condemned versions of Christianity *really* hold that this world was thoroughly evil, and all material life dark and spiritually insupportable? Or, rather, were they using a shocking myth as a means of waking people up, and getting them to think about the deeper nature of reality? After all, in Gnostic writings, you were not encouraged to *believe in* the lower deity; you were encouraged to *transcend him*.

It seems that the condemned teachers were trying to develop the faculty of spiritual perception. In order to develop that faculty, they had to find ways of breaking the familiar coating of materialist perception. So they made a 'fool' out of the body and the world that sustains it. This notion is a staple of Brahmaic Hindu philosophy to this day.

If we think back to the narrative in The Gospel of Judas, Jesus tells Judas the disciples need to get the false god out of their system; but they cannot. They are psychically wedded to it. *He, Judas,* however, can. The reader was doubtless intended to get some encouragement from this. *If Judas can make it; so can I!*

In the lower-world perception, Jesus is the 'expected king-messiah', the deliverer of the people. This is a political idea. But in the higher world, in the spiritual perception, Jesus and his 'great and holy generation' show the true and original dimension of human potential. Judas is introduced to the great and holy generation: Man as he was *meant to be* – that is to say, a spiritual being, a reflection of the Father and His Wisdom.

It may be that a person who cherished The Gospel of Judas when it was fresh might say to the Lord Archbishop of Canterbury: 'You watch too many lurid TV news reports and read too many newspapers and committee documents. You're too involved with the image of the problems of this world. You think you're confronting reality, but you're not getting to the root of the matter. Giving to charity, doing good works is good, but you can do it forever and ever and the problems will remain, so long as you look at the world from the point of view of a person in the world. There is simply more to this revelation of Jesus than the moral religion and the life of faith that is dear to you. This is good news. Why do you reject it? What did Jesus say? *My kingdom is not of this world.* He wasn't an escapist; he had *seen through* the world. Do you think *you* can, so long as you continue to think you know what it's "all about"?'

When you think about it, it is truly astonishing that all of this debate and questioning has come about as a result of the publication of The Gospel of Judas and its swift injection into the world of popular culture. If it is rubbish, it is obviously powerful rubbish. There seems no doubt that the ripples caused by this immense reaction to the appearance of what is little more than a few scraps of ancient papyrus, will go on for a long time to come.

One thing may have been learned. There really is a very large audience for issues of religion and the spirit, if the material appears in the 'right shape'. That shape may be the wrong shape for some scholars, and the Churches may bitterly resent it, but it seems to be the shape that fits our world. Everyone can learn something from this process.

Is that a good thing or not?

Chapter Four

JUDAS – ANGEL OR DEMON?

'those who accept the humanity of Jesus as a dogma ...

do not grasp it as a historical fact.'

G B Caird, Oxford theologian

It was probably some time in the 9th century AD when a monk, writing in Irish Latin, penned the story of Irish saint, St Brandon, or Brendan. According to the story, St Brendan leaves his homeland in Ireland and goes on a perilous sea voyage. In the course of the voyage, Brendan's mind ponders on the mythical Island of the Blessed, separated into accessible and inaccessible portions. Will it be accessible to him?

Before he can find it, Brendan must pass by the mouth of hell. Both the island and the mouth of hell appear to be in the Atlantic Ocean. The mouth of hell was probably a volcano, located in Iceland. St Brendan does not risk landing on it. However, on a nearby rock, forever thrashed and washed by the crashing waves like Prometheus bound, Brendan encounters Judas Iscariot.

Brendan is understandably intrigued. What is Judas Iscariot doing stuck on a rock, so close to the mouth of hell? Is he not supposed to be well inside it? Judas explains to Brendan that his usual torment is indeed to burn like a lump of lead in a crucible, night and day, at the bottom of a crater. However, his miseries are not without interruption. Judas is permitted a holiday in the cooling sea, not only at weekends (from first to second vespers every Sunday), but also from Christmas to Epiphany, Easter to Whitsun, and on two festivals of the Virgin.

As holidays went, these must have been torture (even by 9th-century standards). Among a number of deductions the reader might make on reading this, dare I say, charming little story, one stands out boldly. There appears to be a curious ambivalence as regards Judas' qualification for eternal damnation. While it may have been torture to know that at the end of each sojourn on the rock he would have to return to the heat of hell, at least this mythical Judas knew he would be back again at regular intervals with the chance of meeting a passing saint.

Saints and the damned were supposed to be kept strictly apart: each could hardly be indifferent to the fate of the other. Furthermore, Judas' life was still governed by a divine order. Was he really damned for all time – or only between holidays?

While the reader or hearer of the story might speculate on whether Judas was entitled to any refreshing respites from damnation, one could hardly say that Judas was entirely forsaken. Perhaps, one day, in the mercy of God, *his* boat would come in too, for to leave him without any hope at all would be damnation indeed.

It is, one might suppose, much easier to be theologically creative when dealing with a mythical Judas than with an historically real one.

There was certainly more sympathy for Judas in the life of the Irish saint written over a thousand years ago than there was in the current Pope's response to The Gospel of Judas in 2006. And here we come to the point of this chapter. How can we disentangle the myth of Judas from the fact of Judas? Is the Judas Iscariot of The Gospel of Judas a mythical creation – a bit of theological creativity?

Or is the Judas of the traditional Gospels the product of a myth-making or propaganda exercise?

Will the real Judas – if there is a real Judas – *please stand up?*

Easy to say. When we attempt to find out who 'the real Judas' was, we are in very similar territory to that encountered when trying to find out who 'the real Jesus' was.

The Historical Jesus and the Historical Judas

For more than 150 years, biblical scholars have attempted to locate the 'historical Jesus'. Many have despaired of ever finding such a figure. Take away the mythology and theology surrounding the figure of Jesus, scholars assert, and there is very little to focus on. Sceptical scholars have argued that it is simply impossible to disentangle what has been believed about Jesus from any authentic figure 'underneath'.

Everyone who has encountered stories of Jesus has 'clothed' him one way or another. According to the Gospel accounts, Roman soldiers clothed his beaten body with a cloak either of red or purple, ridiculing him as a defeated and humiliated 'King of the Jews'. Paul clothed him in theology.

What's underneath? Even The Gospel of Judas seems uninterested in the 'man' that clothes the *real* Jesus: the spiritual saviour, the Great Seth. According to Judas' gospel, Jesus could hardly wait to get 'the man' off his back.

Did Jesus begin as 'Word' and then become flesh, or did he begin as flesh and then come to be seen as 'Word'? If Jesus was, as believers believe, fully God and fully human, then that humanity must have been fully involved in human history.

The Gospels are not biographies. There is very little contemporary non-Christian evidence by which it is possible to fix Jesus in time as an historical personality. We know that Pontius Pilate was a Procurator in Judaea with powers of life and death, but we have none of his administrative paperwork; the same goes for the other authorities in the region. Jesus' fame, the Gospels tell us, was widespread in his lifetime from Syria in the north to Judaea in the south, but we have no contemporary records from his lifetime to support this view. And yet, we have a number of accounts of other men in his lifetime who also caused problems for the authorities in Judaea and in Galilee: a number of them, incidentally, called Judas. But these men never raised anyone from the dead, as Jesus did in the case of Lazarus, according to John's Gospel. You might think such an occurrence would not go unnoticed in a world without chloroform.

Was Jesus 'written out' of history before he was written 'in' to it? Everything we have, everything we can read about Jesus, was written after his physical absence from the historical scene, and was written by people already convinced of the meaning and significance of his life. According to the traditional Gospels, Jesus talked to the disciples about what his life meant and what his life was intended to signify – even before he had completed it. Jesus, we are told (after the events) was living out a pre-arranged pattern, a plan. Everything that happened – including Judas' betrayal – had been pre-written. It had all been prophesied. This is very strange.

There were no objective committees of enquiry set up, as far as we know, to find out 'what really happened'. All the most immediate 'evidence' comes from those claiming to be Jesus' followers and the material is repeatedly of a miraculous nature. Attempting to reconcile historical knowledge with the demands of the 'Jesus of faith' has taxed excellent minds to the limit. The Churches have been prepared to accept historical contributions so long as they do not infringe on the territory of religion.

In fact, historical research frequently gives positive outcomes for believers. New historical information has tended to be employed to bolster people's faith in the religion. It is religious believers who pay for much of the archaeology going on in modern Israel.

Artefacts do not harm the religion – it is unwelcome *interpretation* that is threatening. It seems likely that if The Gospel of Judas had simply said that Judas and Jesus had a mutual understanding to fulfil the prophecies, then the Church would probably have welcomed the work as an 'interesting apocryphal gospel' that needs some studying. It is the Judas gospel's interpretation of Jesus' Crucifixion and the negative assessment of the disciples' witness that is so threatening. Is there anything in this 'new' scenario that suggests our historical knowledge is inadequate?

We have far more knowledge of the political, social and economic realities of life in 1st-century Judaea than most of our ancestors did. As a result, when we see movies or documentaries about the early Church or of Jesus' life, the plethora of detail gives us the illusion of having seen something like 'the whole picture'. It is undoubtedly *like* a whole picture, but if taken to be such it is an illusion. If you see Franco Zeffirelli's *Jesus of Nazareth*, for example, you might think we knew all there was to know about life at that time. The picture is so rich; the feeling of authenticity is so strong. All you need is a very good actor with enigmatic qualities, beauty and presence and soon the Word is made flesh once more.

The Gospel story seems to fit very nicely into all that background research. The same remarks apply to Mel Gibson's film about the Passion of Christ; authenticity is enhanced further by having actors speak in Aramaic. Once you have got the history looking (and sounding) right, it is a short step to begin injecting the meaning and interpretation. How much 'faith' does it take to be moved by a beautifully shot image of Jesus being put in a tomb, followed by the discovery, by talented actresses, of the empty tomb? Add a good musical score, and *hey presto*! – you have 'seen it' with your own eyes. The historical detail seems more and more to confirm the experience of faith.

The Christian Church has, as far as we can tell, always advocated the view that Christianity is 'an historical religion'. This means that its central message stems directly from its claims that certain things actually happened in the 'real world', as we know it. As St Paul said of the bodily resurrection of Jesus: if it did not happen, then Christ died for nothing and 'our faith' is void.

However, for some reason, these things that allegedly happened in the real world are often to be accepted 'on faith'. If these things happened in history, then the history must be recorded. If the Gospels are the records of that history, why should those events be accepted on faith? Why can't we just have a reasonable trust in the historical record? The answer to this possibly impious question is that the events of great significance are, in terms of our general knowledge of history and human life, incredible. They cannot be believed – without the will of faith. Do these events then really belong in human history?

History, however inaccurately told, however tendentious the event described, suggested or reconstructed, does not demand faith in order to be accepted. There is 'good history' and 'bad history', depending on the skills of the historian and the accuracy of his or her sources. Plausibility is a general arbiter of credibility.

But the Gospels are not history; they are Gospels: writings with a purpose. As St John's Gospel declares near its end: 'These things are written that ye might believe Jesus is the Christ, the son of God, and that believing ye might have life through His Name.' If I made a similar statement at the end of a biography of Romano Prodi, you would know I was not an historian.

The Church requires that our knowledge of history must include the extraordinary and the miraculous. Once this is accepted, rational demonstrations of real historical probabilities hardly matter. The Jesus of faith must triumph over the Jesus of history; salvation is at stake. Factual reportage will not get you into heaven. The Gospel writers were not trying to win journalistic awards or academic honours. This is what Professor Caird meant in the quotation at the beginning of this chapter: 'those who accept the humanity of Jesus as a dogma ... do not grasp it as a historical fact.' Accepting Jesus' humanity as a dogma, or fixed doctrine, does not incline believers to see its implications in the realm of historical fact.

How can one understand a being who is fully God and fully human, when we know from our own experience that *to be fully human* means precisely that we are unable to be fully God? The spirit may be willing but the flesh is weak. It cannot be fully human to add on, acquire or be seamlessly fused with, a vastly higher level of totally miraculous being. To be fully God would be to change what it would mean to be fully human. Nevertheless, this was the view ratified and sealed by the Eastern and Western Churches at Chalcedon in AD 451. Jesus' full humanity and full divinity became a dogma of the Church in both the east and the west.

The dogma only works within the concept of 'salvation history': a metaphysical concept. That is good news for believers but it does not help us find the 'Jesus of history'. Jesus would have to be *more than human* to qualify for the dogma's definition. In other words, the dogma would move you very close indeed to the very heresy it was intended, in part, to annul. The so-called 'Gnostics' contended that Jesus *was* more than 'human' and that, therefore, his apparent, or physical, humanity was a cloak. In Gnostic thinking, 'humanity' is a spiritual archetype, not a psycho-biological phenomenon. From this perspective, it is *we* who are not 'fully human'.

I repeat my earlier statement: *To be fully God would be to change what it would mean to be fully human.* For Gnostics, Jesus demonstrated the necessary expansion of our conception and consciousness of humanity, cloaked by the illusion of sense perceptions; cloaked, that is, by the flesh. As the old Christmas carol has it: 'veiled in flesh the Godhead see'. You could entertain a cardinal with the view that the dogma of Christ's full humanity and full divinity presupposes a logical heresy. But he would not believe you.

If fact must come second to faith in Church dogma, then Jesus' humanity must come second to faith in his divinity. Facts contrary to dogma may be dismissed as secondary or even irrelevant considerations.

But we cannot prove *historically* that salvation has taken place. It is a matter of faith and belief, guaranteed in theory by the authority of the Church. If the Church's authority is questioned, then according to its own theory, salvation is imperilled. Doubt can be a risky business. Historically, it has led to the rack and the stake.

Having said all of this, it is still the view of the Church that Christianity is an historical religion, built on events that happened in fact. Nevertheless, reliance on historical events has left the faith vulnerable to criticism from those who insist on an historical, evidential basis for taking the religion seriously. This did not matter so much in the Middle Ages when historical method was not very well developed and people had confidence that the Church had all the relevant facts. Belief and knowledge seemed to walk together. Perceived miracles were the obvious sign of God's presence.

Getting the history right did matter in the early years of the Church, however. That is because its enemies, such as the pagan critic Celsus, attacked the Gospels for historical discrepancies and illogicalities. Celsus made his case in about AD 175 in his book *True Logos*. There he argued that since Jesus knew what would happen to him, he had therefore *wilfully* enticed the authorities to deal with him; he had engineered his own downfall. The fact was, asserted Celsus, that the man worshipped by his followers as a god had been put to death by the Roman authorities for crimes against the state. Unfortunately we only know those parts of Celsus' argument preserved by the Christian writer Origen, who argued against him, and selected evidence to support his cause.

Since the widespread dissemination of printed books and education, many have questioned the historical basis for the Christian faith. However, the arguments for or against the faith (based on the evidence) merely go back and forth, since the area of debate is almost always the Bible itself. Critics of Christianity use the same material for attacking the faith as the defenders use for defending it.

Since the critics tend to question the historical validity of the Gospels in the first place, attempts to pick out discrepancies will frequently seem a matter of arbitrary choice. Anyone can find a text that supports their argument. If you doubt the Gospels, why use them as evidence for doubt?

The records themselves are written from the point of view of religious certainties. In order to discredit the Gospels permanently, you would need to find alternative records, but, so far, there are none stemming from precisely the same period.

So you can see that the discovery of so-called 'alternative' gospels opens them up to being used to criticize traditional views of the faith – especially if the new material casts either light or shadow on the established record. In the opinion of most scholars, using the new material for such purposes is unjustified. Scholars do not want to get into angry debates with believers. By and large, they just want to get on with enlarging the interest value of their chosen subject.

However, when a work such as The Gospel of Judas enters the mainstream world of popular thinking in such a sensationalist way, it soon loses its scholarly virginity and becomes a stick used by both defenders and critics of traditional religion. As we can see from the previous chapter, that is exactly what has happened.

Therefore, it becomes imperative that we investigate whether The Gospel of Judas has implications for our knowledge of the written evidence concerning the beginnings of the Christian Church.

Does The Gospel of Judas tell us things the traditional Gospels do not, or cannot?

Does The Gospel of Judas have a more accurate source than the traditional story?

Was Judas Iscariot a 'greedy liar', a traitor?

Was Judas really a good man, doing God's will?

Have we got our picture of Judas Iscariot wrong?

Did Judas Iscariot really exist, or was he invented for the sake of a story?

Does our understanding of the Christian religion rely on knowing the truth about Judas Iscariot?

In short, was Judas Iscariot an 'angel' or a 'demon'?

Hunting Judas

If trying to locate the 'Jesus of history' is a remarkably difficult task, attempting to locate the historical Judas Iscariot is almost impossible. In order to get anywhere at all with this problem, we simply have to ascribe some measure of historical actuality to the accounts of Judas in the traditional Gospels and The Acts of the Apostles. This is for one simple reason. There is absolutely nothing else in the 1st century that tells us anything about a disciple of Jesus called Judas Iscariot. If Judas was invented, nothing in the Gospels will tell us anything about him, because he did not exist.

We cannot prove that he existed, but we can work on the basis, as in the case of Jesus, that he probably did. If we find, on the other hand, that Judas probably did not exist, then we can at least attempt to understand why the figure was invented and – more importantly for our purposes – why the author of The Gospel of Judas found him so significant.

The Gospel of Judas and the Four Gospels

Imagine if The Gospel of Judas had been found, but we had never heard of the four traditional Gospels, Matthew, Mark, Luke, and John. We should not be very struck, I think, by the portrayal of Judas in the 'new' gospel. Nor would we be moved by the way he is separated from the other disciples. Who were these 'other disciples', anyway? They would seem a pretty bad lot, based on the account in The Gospel of Judas.

As for the religious understanding behind the account, how would we understand that?

If the Gospels had never been written, but Christianity had developed without them, it is possible that Christianity would have been rather like Hinduism, consisting of many different cults sharing particular moral and spiritual features – including mythical or semi-mythical characters. Everyone would have heard of Jesus, of course, but he would probably, after 2,000 years, have many, many different faces. There would be many sayings and stories, and some stories would probably take place in different parts of the world. You would have local stories, unheard of elsewhere, in which Jesus and figures from his stories would probably be thought to have once appeared nearby. Perhaps they might be expected to be seen again. There would probably be no distinction made between the characters of his stories (such as the Prodigal Son or Good Samaritan) and actual people who might have lived long ago. Pontius Pilate might be a saint and Saint Peter might be more of a mountain than a person.

People might not be sure of when some events happened, or whether they had happened in this world or another. There would be people who saw Judas rather like Set (or Seth) in the Egyptian religion – as the betrayer of his 'brother' Osiris – and there might even be the odd cultic centre for those who thought Judas was an angel. It might be believed that this angel only *appeared* as a traitor, but was really Jesus' closest friend. The 'Judasites' would be interested in the newly discovered work (though they might wonder what a 'gospel' was), but few others would be interested.

The Gospel of Judas would simply be accepted as another tiny part of the great mosaic. Perhaps it might even be seen as useful historical information, telling a world that had forgotten the original historical setting how the story started – not that they would have much to go on from the account in the gospel itself. Gnostic writings were never rich in topographical detail!

As another hypothesis, try to imagine The Gospel of Judas coming into a world where Christianity had never even got off the ground: a world where the infant faith had been defeated even before the end of the Roman Empire – defeated and forgotten. Scholars today (if there were any) would look at The Gospel of Judas and accept the story as being something like a myth told by Brahmins or by Buddhists. There might be some speculation about whether Jesus was a bit like the Buddha, or more like the Hindu

Krishna, or even some kind of 'far-out' Jewish prophet. Perhaps it would be recognized as a 'Gnostic' work, a small cult of that name having hypothetically survived in tiny pockets in the obscure places of the Middle East.

One thing is fairly certain, the publication of The Gospel of Judas would probably only have been noted by a few of the more serious newspapers and scholarly journals.

What may be deduced from these two imaginary, and strangely dispiriting, scenarios? Just this: the whole power and significance of The Gospel of Judas relies upon the existence of the four traditional Gospels.

It is the relation of the Judas text to those four Gospels of Matthew, Mark, Luke and John that provides the whole meat and creative spark of the drama we are here investigating. A similar point is made by Bishop Irenaeus of Lyon. In Book 3, chapter 11, section 7 of his work, *Against Heresies*, Irenaeus writes, 'So firm is the ground upon which these Gospels rest, that the very heretics themselves bear witness to them, and, starting from these, each one of them endeavours to establish his own peculiar doctrine.'

Even more to the point is the realization that The Gospel of Judas really does not make much sense unless it is seen in relation to the traditional Gospels. This is because the figure of Judas is presented in The Gospel of Judas in deliberate contrast to the figure of Judas known in the traditional Gospels. The reader is *meant to be surprised* by the appearance of this 'secret account'. It may have been intended to shock; it succeeds.

The gospel is intended to overturn assumptions about 'what was really going on' at the time of the Crucifixion. The gospel's special interpretation of those events is drawn up almost entirely from meditating on the events described in the Gospels. This was indicated in Chapter Two and will be demonstrated vividly in this chapter.

This issue of its relationship to the Gospels must affect our view of the historical authenticity of the account of Jesus and Judas given in The Gospel of Judas. Is this an historical account of what happened between Judas and Jesus? If it is not, does it matter?

One thing is certain. *The four Gospels came first.* There was not a big bag of 1st-century gospels from which the four were taken simply because Church authorities in later years liked them best or thought they best suited their purposes. This is an important point to grasp because some people will be of a mind to imagine that The Gospel of Judas, as well as other 'Gnostic gospels', were simply 'alternative' gospels that the Church rejected. They were rejected, but a long time after the other four Gospels had been used widely and become generally accepted.

How do we know this?

Dating the Gospels

The dating of the four traditional Gospels is an amazingly difficult business. This is in part because we only have copies produced much later. The oldest complete New Testaments, the *Codex Vaticanus* and the *Codex Sinaiticus*, were written down around AD 300, in either Syria or Egypt. Before that time, we have fragments from the New Testament, and many Latin and Greek quotations from the Gospels in works of commentary, apologetic and polemic.

We can never be entirely certain that the Gospels in the earliest known complete versions were substantially identical to the Gospels that bore their names 200 years earlier, but we have no compelling evidence to think otherwise. The Gospels were used in weekly worship all over the Empire and innovations would not have passed unnoticed. There are of course minor variations, omissions, scribal errors, odd additions and unattributable sayings in the surviving ancient manuscripts. The John Rylands Library in Manchester has a papyrus fragment from what appears to be The Gospel of John from around AD 100, though more likely after that date than before it.

From internal comparison of the Gospels, we can be sure that Mark is the first Gospel, since both Luke and Matthew use it. Mark is usually dated around the year AD 65, a year after the Emperor Nero's persecution of Christians, during which Mark's supposed principal source, St Peter, was martyred.

According to an early Church Father, Papias (c. AD 60-130), Mark wrote down faithfully everything he could gather from the apostle Peter. Papias had been a close friend of Polycarp, Bishop of Smyrna (born c. AD 65), who was martyred in AD 155.

Polycarp was a very old man when young Irenaeus (later bishop of Lyon) sat at his feet and heard - as did Papias - of how Polycarp had heard the memories of John, disciple of Jesus, speaking at Ephesus. This reminiscence is recorded by Irenaeus in his *Epistle to Florinus*. There is still some dispute as to whether this was the John who was part of Jesus' inner circle in the Gospels or whether he was one of Jesus' other disciples. The author of The Acts of the Apostles mentions some 120 disciples convening at the time Judas' replacement was discussed - a fact often overlooked in people's imaginations. John, then as now, was a common name.

According to Irenaeus, Polycarp had heard not only from John, disciple of Jesus, but also from others who had seen Jesus. Polycarp wrote a letter to Christians living in Philippi in Macedonia. In this letter, Polycarp quotes from Matthew, Luke and the First Epistle of John, among other works that are now included in the New Testament. These works had apparently become familiar scripture by about AD 105.

It appears that Irenaeus accepted The Gospel of John to be the work of the one whom his old martyred teacher Polycarp had heard. Otherwise, we might ask if Irenaeus should have wondered why Polycarp had not suggested that the Gospel bearing his teacher's name was an imposture. In Book 3, chapter 11 of *Against Heresies*, Irenaeus, without any shadow of doubt, attributes The Gospel of John to John, 'the disciple of the Lord'.

There is, however, a slight problem here. We have part of the writings of Papias, friend of Polycarp, writing about AD 120. Writing about how he has recorded the sayings of those who saw Jesus,

Papias refers in the same paragraph to John (in relation to the 12) and to 'the Elder John', also called one of 'the disciples of the Lord'. They are both disciples of the Lord, but one is called 'Elder John' and the other, who by inference is no longer alive, was almost certainly one of the 12 apostles.

No one has satisfactorily solved the issue of how there came to be this tradition of two disciples called John. We can only be reasonably secure in thinking that Irenaeus was sure that one of them wrote, or was in some way responsible for, the Gospel that bears his name. John's Gospel has been dated as late as between AD 120 and 150, partly in view of its developed Christology (speeches on the nature of Christ and his relation to the Father) and partly due to fundamental differences to the other three Gospels.

Longer versions of letters from Bishop Ignatius of Antioch contain quotations from this Gospel (as does the spurious epistle of Ignatius to the Tarsians). Ignatius was martyred in about AD 114, but the longer letters may have been expanded by a hand other than that of Ignatius. They come from a later date.

The usual compromise is to say John's Gospel was probably written by about AD 90 but took time to be accepted or broadcast widely in the Church, perhaps on account of its strangeness and therefore doubted provenance. Luke and Matthew are usually dated after *Mark*, between about AD 70 and 85.

Another reason for a later dating of John is because the language seems to reflect a period after the heyday of a Jewish Christian Church in Jerusalem. References to 'the Jews' almost as a separate or foreign people in John suggest a time when links between the Church and a rebellious Galilee and Judaea had become dangerously embarrassing. This factor may also be important in the treatment in John's Gospel of the figure of Judas Iscariot.

It would seem reasonable to suppose that the four Gospels were well in circulation by the time Irenaeus sat at the feet of Polycarp around AD 150, while Matthew, Mark and Luke had been around for well over 50 years before then.

But what of The Gospel of Judas? When was that work written?

In Book 1, chapter 31, of *Against Heresies*, Irenaeus gives us our first ever reference to a gospel of Judas:

> Others again declare that Cain derived his being from the Power above, and acknowledge that Esau, Korah, the Sodomites, and all such persons, are related to themselves. On this account, they add, they have been assailed by the Creator, yet no one of them has suffered injury. For Sophia was in the habit of carrying off that which belonged to her from them to herself. They declare that Judas the traitor was thoroughly acquainted with these things, and that he alone, knowing the truth as no others did, accomplished the mystery of the betrayal; by him all things, both earthly and heavenly, were thus thrown into confusion. They produce a fictitious history of this kind, which they style the Gospel of Judas.

Now, the first question is, was this 'Gospel of Judas' the same work as that which we have come to know in a Middle Egyptian dialect of Sahidic Coptic? It has to be said that The Gospel of Judas we have seen published in 2006 does not have anything to say about the Sodomites, Esau, Korah or the role of Sophia saving Cain and all the others from injury. Nevertheless, Irenaeus does not say that these matters are mentioned in the book; only that it is a history 'of this kind'.

However, Judas is presented as one who knew the 'truth' as the others did not, and how he 'accomplished the mystery of the betrayal' could be the subtitle of the work we now possess. Irenaeus has not said that he has read the book he refers to. Furthermore, it is always a possibility that someone read Irenaeus' work against this heresy and decided to write his own version of Judas' gospel.

It is also possible that whatever Irenaeus referred to in about AD 180 underwent substantial revision between that time and the writing of it in Egypt in about AD 300. Who is to say that there were not *apocryphal* apocryphal gospels?

However, it is the only reference we have from this early period, and while we cannot say with absolute certainty that we are referring to the same work, there are important elements of consistency. The business about Judas being curiously responsible for throwing earthly and heavenly things into confusion by his act does ring bells with the final stages of the gospel.

If this work is the same, or substantially the same, all we can say of its date is that it was in existence by AD 180, but we have no copies – or even quotations – earlier than about AD 300. The work is consistent with known thought forms of the 2nd century, but there is no known reference to Barbelo in the surviving literature of the 1st century.

It is safe to conclude that a gospel of Judas was not available to the writers of the traditional Gospels. Had it been so, it would have given rise to a consternation since it makes absolutely clear that the disciples of Jesus were unaware of the secret plan by which Jesus would defeat the lord of this world – and, indeed, were incapable of grasping such a plan.

We can be reasonably sure that the writer of The Gospel of Judas was familiar with at least some of the accounts of the four traditional Gospels – and wrote consciously against, or rather, *above* them. But could it be that there were elements within those four Gospels that could justify the extraordinary, terrific, and rather frightening twist that the author of The Gospel of Judas gives to the tradition? Is it possible to build the strange theology of The Gospel of Judas from the four Gospels?

In order to find out, we must take a closer look at the Judas of the Gospels – the Judas we think we all know.

Judas in the Gospels

A number of scholars have taken the view that there must be more to the picture of Judas Iscariot than that derived from the traditional Gospels as an aggregate witness. The scholarly case for Judas' innocence or relative innocence has been well summarized in James M Robinson's 2006 book, *The Secrets of Judas*.

Robinson recognizes that the picture of Judas held by the Church may be too harsh an interpretation of Judas' possible motives. The writers of the Gospels, especially after Mark, may have missed some important nuances of the tradition regarding Judas.

A lot of stress is laid on the Greek verb *paradidōmai*. This verb is usually translated as 'I hand over,' or 'I pledge,' or 'I hand down,' or 'I betray.' It has been argued that 'handing Jesus over' does not necessarily carry the implication of treachery. This line of analysis is given greater weight by other observations concerning Judas' true role in the *dénouement* of Jesus' ministry, as told in the traditional Gospels.

One of the translators of The Gospel of Judas and a leading scholar in Nag Hammadi Library studies, Marvin Meyer, has made the point that the treatment of Judas gets more critical and condemnatory over the period of the formation of the Gospels. This view is also highlighted in Hyam Maccoby's 1992 book, *Judas Iscariot and the Myth of Jewish Evil*.[1]

That is to say, if Mark is the first Gospel, and John the last, the difference between the two in their treatment of Judas and his alleged crime is striking. Between the two, Luke and Matthew also seem more emphatic than their common source, Mark, in respect of Judas' guilt. Luke is even more hostile to Judas than is Matthew, if that were possible.

Meyer then posits a time-line from *c.* AD 65 through to c. AD 100. It would appear that Judas gets 'stitched up' more and more as the years go by. It is a bit like the coverage of a murder in the newspapers. The original charge may be based on a suspicion, but once it has been told and retold, the more lurid elements are emphasized. As a result, witnesses' memories are influenced by additional embellishments arising from inflated suspicions, and by the time of the final judgement, the jury may find it very hard to separate fact from fiction.

Our legal system is supposed to protect jurors from being influenced by gossip and the press. Those who wrote and talked about Judas Iscariot in the 1st century were not protected from talk. Indeed, as Papias, and Irenaeus' records show, the Gospel writers and their audiences got their principal ideas from listening to people talking.

One might ask the question, who among Christian communities would dare to say that Judas had been misjudged in, say, AD 120? Such a view would be regarded as gross impiety. Once the Gospels were written, speculation was supposed to cease. Only people with no great vested interest in 'sticking in' with the mainstream Christian communities would have felt free to speculate, or even, as in the case of The Gospel of Judas, completely 'trash' the accepted story. But in order to trash the Judas story, it would be necessary to trash the entire Church structure that supported it; this The Gospel of Judas effectively does. In this gospel, Church leaders are presented as perverts and blind men, products of a lack of contact with the 'immoveable race', the 'great and holy generation' of Seth.

Still, it is a long way from saying a convicted man's crime has been magnified to saying that as a result of the exaggerations he is necessarily innocent! The issue is whether the trial has been fair. Meyer and other scholars think Judas may have had an unfair process in the trial of history and the appearance of The Gospel of Judas gives us an opportunity to re-open the case.

So let us re-open the case.

First, we need to be presented with the evidence. The only evidence we have is the Gospel accounts. How far they reflect eyewitness testimony is much disputed. Having said that, The Gospel of Judas does not take issue with the eyewitness; The Gospel of Judas is interested in the *mind*-witness. That is to say, it is not what the disciples *saw* that matters, but precisely what they *failed to see*. The clues to find what the disciples failed to see were *already* secreted in the Gospel accounts, if one had the eyes to see. This appears to have been a contention of the author or authors of The Gospel of Judas.

The Gospel of Mark

As far as we can tell, the first written mention of the name of Judas Iscariot comes in Mark, chapter 3, verse 19, at the end of a list of the 12 disciples chosen to be with Jesus, to preach, to heal and to cast out devils:

> And Judas Iscariot, which also betrayed him. (Greek: *kai Ioudan Iskariōth, hos kai paredōken auton.*)

The earliest (4th century) Greek versions agree with this phrasing, though the spelling of the 'surname' is recorded as *Iskariōtēn* (Iskarian) in the 5th century *Codex Alexandrinus,* and as *Skariōth* in the *Bezae* manuscript of the 5th to 6th century.

Here is the name of the accused: Judas Iscariot. Judas is distinguished from the other disciples by being given a surname. This may have been done to distinguish this Judas from Jesus' brother, also called Judas in Mark 6, v3.

As we have seen in Chapter Two (in 'Jewish-Christian Relations'), 'Judas' means 'praised' (Hebrew: *Yehudah*) and has the same root as the name of the old southern kingdom, Judah, which the Romans called Judaea. 'Judaeans' was translated into English as 'Jews'.

Judah, Juda, Jude and Judas are all the same name. Judas was a very common name and it is significant that the author of Mark wishes to distinguish this particular Judas. He distinguished him with a surname and then a reputation. Judas is the one who betrayed him. There is almost the implication of *'You remember! Judas Iscariot is the one who betrayed Jesus.'* This story has been told before and it is important for the rest of the story (which people would hear) that they remember this character and mark him out.

The story of Judas doing a specific deed is right there in the tradition at the start. Whether he 'handed Jesus over' or 'betrayed him', this Judas had done something memorable. The author has only to say these few words and the hearers of the Gospel are expected to know what he is talking about – or, if they have not heard it before – they must remember this person.

Judas has a reputation. Readers may judge what might promote this sort of language. Judas, one way or another, is a marked man. Had he become a bogeyman to Christians before Mark's Gospel was compiled? Was Judas' guilt part of the original Gospel message preached by the 12 and the other disciples?

But what does Iscariot mean? Is the name significant or is it just his surname, added to distinguish him from another?

'Iskarioth' (in Mark) is simply a proper name. The *Codex Alexandrinus* reading of 'Iskarian', or possibly 'of Iskariot', suggests a place-name. The place often suggested is 'Karioth' in Judaea, on the basis that the Hebrew *Ish-Qriyoth* would mean 'man of Karioth'. Karioth is nowhere mentioned in the New Testament. A place called Kerioth is mentioned in *Joshua* 15, v25 in a list of towns. The etymology might also stem from the plural of 'small city', possibly indicating some kind of suburban environment.

Another leading possibility is that the name derives from the Latin *sicarius* or dagger man. The *sicarii* were the assassins who worked along with the militant Zealots against the Romans. They would go into crowds, mingle with perceived collaborators, then stab them to death before making a quick escape.

Since another disciple of Jesus, Simon 'the Canaanite' (Greek: *ton Kananaion*) was almost certainly a member of the Zealot movement, this designation would fit with Mark's apparent hesitancy in revealing who some of Jesus' disciples were. The word transliterated from the Greek as 'Kananaean' comes from the Aramaic *Qanna'im*, meaning Zealot. It is possible that two of Jesus' disciples were what the Romans would consider, in today's parlance, terrorists, or at least, insurgents. Either way, Zealots were crucified when captured in pursuance of their armed struggle with Rome.

The scholar S G F Brandon wrote an essay on the Zealots in his interesting book of collected papers, *Religion in Ancient History.*[2] Professor Brandon thought it likely that Mark did not translate the Aramaic word meaning 'Zealot' into Greek because the Gospel was composed shortly after, or even during, the Jewish revolt that began in AD 66.

Jewish Zealots were as popular in Rome during those years as Osama bin Laden is in Washington today. Mark therefore hid the name by transliterating it, not translating it. The idea that Jesus could easily be described as part of the Jewish resistance movement was too dangerous to contemplate. It would scare new Christians and put off potential Gentile members. In the event, Nero would persecute Christians anyway. As far as hostile Romans were concerned, the 'whole bunch' (of Christians) was part of the movement against good Roman values.

If Mark was prepared to obscure Simon the Zealot's name, then 'Iscariot' could be a way of obscuring Judas' dismal trade also. What seems convincing in the one case, however, does not altogether convince in the second. It might be that the activity of Judas had already been obscured in the past. 'Iscariot' might have been a nickname for Judas used by other disciples, the meaning of which is now lost to us.

Furthermore, as we shall see, The Gospel of John makes no bones about blackening Judas' reputation – even before the 'act of betrayal'. What better way could be found of blackening it further than to say, 'Well, after all, Judas was *always* the dagger man' – the one prepared to knife his countryman in the back!

On the other hand, John takes the view that while Judas had a potential for dishonesty, it was Satan that entered a crack in his soul and inspired his dark act. In Zeffirelli's well-researched TV version of the life of Jesus, this idea of Judas being motivated by nationalist and violent interests, and his willingness to push the game against the authorities further than the other disciples, seems to draw something from the idea of a Zealot Judas.

The Zealot Judas is a dagger-bearing Judas; a man who had the ability to do the deed, coldly, professionally – for a fee, if necessary: a hit-man. This picture has become over time a quite common view of Judas. He has been made to fit in with our more detailed knowledge of the protracted crisis in Jewish-Roman affairs in the 1st and early 2nd century. In this regard, Judas the *sicarius* seems to have a lot going for him: dodgy contacts, ruthlessness, a possible cause.

When Israeli archaeologist Yigael Yadin excavated the fortress and palace of Masada, the whole world learned that in AD 74 pious Zealots, in their determination to keep their religion pure of Roman contamination, were prepared to commit suicide *en masse*, rather than surrender to Roman soldiers. 'Never again!' Perhaps Judas hanged himself in order to avoid surrender to Roman soldiers. The more detailed political picture that emerged from this archaeology gave another twist to the idea of Judas the suicide. He was a man caught between conflicting emotions of love, hate and fear: love of his country, love of Jesus, hatred of Rome, fear of failure – and fear of himself. Judas has run away from the Church's traditional picture of him caught in a straightforward moral and spiritual conflict – the 'greedy liar'.

Nevertheless, for all its steely – and bloody – modernist characteristics, this gritty picture still has its more romantic sides. Judas is a man disappointed by Jesus' unwillingness to grasp a political opportunity, and yet tortured by the way Jesus seems to know more about him than he knows himself. Jesus is 'on his case' and it drives him to terrible acts. He is a haunted man. He seems to know too much, yet knows nothing at all. What is his Master really doing?

Judas 'the Confused' in today's moral landscape puts him on a kind of par with Thomas 'the Doubter'. There may be more in this than meets the eye.

It must be said, however, that while the evidence for a Zealot Judas is not conclusive, we cannot dismiss it either. It certainly did not seem to mean anything to the writer of The Gospel of Judas – but, of course, by the time he/she or they wrote it, Judaea had been erased, as such, from the Roman map: the sheep were scattered. The Zealot cause was absolutely finished.

Or was it? Have we gone too far? We have seen in our journey through the text of The Gospel of Judas that there may well be distinct messianic references within it. Remember the reference to Judas' star, and to the raising of his horn? The Judas of The Gospel of Judas does have apocalyptic characteristics – and apocalyptic was the favoured interpretation of history of the Zealot movement.

Apocalyptic, and even Gnosticized messianism, may have kept the Zealot light going after the total terrestrial failure of the Zealot challenge to the powers of this world (the Roman Empire). It is possible then that the Judas gospel was translating a disappointment in the worldly hopes of establishing a messianic kingdom into the pure realm of spiritual salvation and a collective messiahship of the elect.

While a Roman temple to a Roman god now stood on the site of the Temple of the Jews, had the true Israel been assumed to a higher world?

So far, this must remain a speculation. One thing is certain, the historical Judas can hardly have been motivated by things of which he could have known nothing, that is, the catastrophe that would befall the Jewish people after his mysterious death.

Establishing a motive for Judas is one of the most difficult aspects of this whole investigation and has led some good writers to speculate imaginatively as a way of filling in the mystery. The thing about mysteries, however, is that we cannot get to the bottom of them, no matter how hard we try. That is why they are mysteries. Nevertheless, we need not give up; a little light is better than no light at all.

There is one other possible way of accounting for Judas' name which has few supporters. It is a simple explanation, but no worse for that.

The Lost Tribe

To anyone looking at a map of ancient Israel, 'Iscariot' would immediately sound like the tenth division of Solomon's kingdom, namely Issachar. Issachar was the fifth son of Jacob, or Israel. Jacob had 12 sons and they became the fathers of the 12 tribes of Israel.

In the Old Testament book, I Kings, chapter four, verse 7, we read that 'Solomon had 12 officers over all Israel, which provided victuals for the king and his household: each man his month in a year made provision.' Each officer was linked to a tribal area of the kingdom. Jehoshaphat was linked to Issachar. Issachar was the area on the southwestern side of what in Jesus' time was called the Sea of Galilee.

It seems possible that when Jesus chose his own 12 he had in mind both the tribes of ancient Israel and Solomon's designation of officers; whether he was thinking about the signs of the zodiac is unknown. It may be inferred that each man had a specific role. John's Gospel informs us – with what historical justification we cannot tell – that Judas was in charge of the collective purse.

The members of the tribe of Issachar were among those Israelites described as the 'Lost Tribes of Israel'. This is because the northern kingdom of Israel was conquered by the Assyrians in 722 BC (the Hebrew peoples had been divided into the kingdoms of Israel in the north and Judah in the south). After the Assyrian conquest, many of the northern tribesmen intermarried with foreigners and some of them came to be called Samaritans, after the region of Samaria where they lived. They were looked down on by aristocrats and their distant kin in the south. The old northern tribes of Israel had effectively been lost.

As the famous parable of the Good Samaritan makes clear, the Samaritans were regarded as low-breeds by many of the Jews of Jesus' time. They had married outside the Israelite gene pool. But Jesus is recorded as having said he came to look for the lost sheep of the house of Israel. He came, he said, to preach to the lost, not to the righteous. A good Samaritan was God's idea of a neighbour to be loved. In the political and social picture of 1st-century Judaea, this attitude of Jesus would have been understood as a ministry to those people in the north who were despised by the uptight authorities of the south.

Galilee was full of the descendants of the old lost tribes of Israel, not all of whom were Samaritans by any means. There were Galileans who had not married outside the old nation, but the old tribal borders had been effectively obliterated; Greek was a common language in Galilee and the urban culture had been Hellenized.

Judas may well have been a person whose family remembered their ancient tribe and were proud of it. They were 'of Issachar'. A natural shortening of the name - or nickname -would give us a Greek word *Iskariōtēn* or *Iskariōth*: Iskariot or Iscariot.

A person who knew he came from one of the great 'lost tribes' of yesterday - of the Solomonic Golden Age - may well have been a person who looked forward to the return of the messianic kingdom: the unity of the ancient nation. He would be a person very interested in his status in that kingdom, the status of his tribe, his people. He would want to know when the Star of Jacob (James) and his 12 sons would rise again.

He would have heard about the revolt of Judas the Galilean that took place in AD 6 against Herod Antipas, the foreigner, the Idumaean Arab and friend of Rome. The 1st-century Jewish historian Josephus says that Judas the Galilean 'was a teacher of a peculiar sect of his own, and was not at all like the rest of their leaders'. Josephus wrote for a Roman audience, so this represents a rare and curious moment of (possible) approval of a man who led a revolt.

Annoyingly, Josephus does not tell us anything more about Judas' peculiar sect, only that Judas believed one should submit to the lordship of men only after God was properly reverenced; he fought against a Roman tax. He would not render to Caesar things that were God's (taxes came from the fruit of God's land). It is possible that the 'sect' referred to by Josephus pursued the cause taken up by what we know as the Zealots (or at least one branch of the movement).

Another namesake of Iscariot, this time from Sepphoris, just west of the old tribal area of Issachar, is described by Josephus as the son of 'the arch-robber' Hezekias. This Judas raided an Herodian armoury and set about arming his men for an abortive military strike. It might seem surprising to us that anyone could grow up in Galilee in the 1st century AD and not see the world as a place more characterized by continual armed struggle than lilies of the field that neither toil nor spin, but yet remain more glorious than Solomon.

'Robber' is a term that the Roman collaborator Josephus used of Zealot fighters. It is quite possible that when The Gospel of John (and the Pope) refer to Judas as a thief, they are merely echoing this assessment of the moral status of the Zealots' efforts to liberate themselves from foreign domination.

Just for the record, at the time of these two fighting Judases (when an historical Jesus would have been a little boy), there was another Galilean who took the sword. He put a crown on his head, but was afterwards killed by Herod's soldiers. His name was Simon. Simon was the name of Judas Iscariot's father. Of course, there were many Simons around at the time.

Could Jesus have called his Judas after the tribe of Issachar as an endearing nickname, as well as a reference to the man's ancient lineage?

According to I I Chronicles 12, v32, 200 men of Issachar came to King David at Hebron (David, like Jesus, was of the tribe of Judah). It is said that they were 'men that had understanding of the times, to know what Israel ought to do' – this distinction marks them out from the other tribal leaders. Did Jesus (of the House of David) think of Judas like that – as a man of understanding who knew what Israel ought to do? Was he a man who could get things done: Jesus' number one for the hard job?

There may be more to this 'Issachar' idea than we first thought. According to the Jewish *Targum* (a commentary on the Jewish scriptures), the reference to the men of Issachar having 'understanding of the times' meant that they knew how to ascertain the periods of the sun and moon. They also understood the intercalation of months, the dates of solemn feasts, and could interpret the signs of the times.

These men knew *when* to act.

In the apocryphal *Testaments of the 12 Patriarchs*, first written some time around the late 2nd century and early 1st century BC, there are some interesting associations with the names of both Issachar and Judah (Judas). In this work, the *Testament of Issachar* tells the biblical tale of Issachar's mother Leah's purchase of Jacob's night-time services by the giving of mandrakes to Rachel. There is a night-time exchange for profit. Is there resonance here with the betrayal scene where a kiss is purchased for money at night?

In the remainder of the narrative Issachar himself is portrayed as leading a godly and simple agricultural life. This account comes from the Greek version of the Old Testament, the Septuagint. In the Hebrew version, Issachar is condemned to forced labour on the fields (Genesis 49, vv 13-15). Could there be some link here with the idea of Judas Iscariot buying a field and suffering in it (as told in *Acts*)?

The Testament of Judah concerns itself with courage, financial greed, and apostasy by fornication (with non-Israelites). All of these attributes have been applied to Judas Iscariot.

In case anyone should think that these apocryphal writings may have been a long way from the minds of the writers of the Gospels, it is worth noting that scholars have drawn attention to several parallels with the Gospels. These parallels show that either parts of the *Testaments of the 12 Patriarchs* were adapted by Christian writing, or Christian writing was influenced by these texts.

There is a great deal of interest in the coming of the messiah and in references that seem to chime in with events in the life of Jesus. In *The Testament of Levi*, for example, we read of how:

> The heavens shall be opened, and from the temple of glory shall come upon him sanctification, with the Father's voice as from Abraham to Isaac. And the glory of the Most High shall be uttered over him, and the spirit of understanding and sanctification shall rest upon him in the water. (Levi 5, vv21-2)

This passage compares interestingly with Matthew 3, vv16-17:

As soon as Jesus was baptized, he went up out of the water. At that moment heaven was opened, and he saw the Spirit of God descending like a dove and lighting on him. And a voice from heaven said, 'This is my Son, whom I love; with him I am well pleased.'

There are some interesting astrological aspects attached to Issachar, especially if we are disposed to see Iscariot as a kind of pun on Issachar. After all, Judas in his particular gospel is told to look to his star. In Jewish astrological lore, Issachar is the sixth tribal member answering to Cancer. Cancer has four stars sometimes called *Aselli*, which is Latin for donkeys. At the summer solstice, the sun enters Cancer. This is when the light of the day begins to diminish. Judas' key operation takes place in a world of diminishing light, until the final act that takes place while the world is asleep.

Some scholars of astrology have perceived astrological allegory in the New Testament. Traditionally, God's word is written in the stars. This is how the Magi came to Bethlehem. The idea would not seem strange to the author of The Gospel of Judas. Scripture had to be fulfilled. That is a keynote of all the Gospels' treatment of Judas. As is written in *Acts*:

Brethren, the scripture had to be fulfilled, which the Holy Spirit spoke beforehand by the mouth of David, concerning Judas who was guide to those who arrested Jesus. (*Acts* I, vI6)

It might seem we have taken a great deal from one verse of Mark's Gospel - the first word that announces the arrival of Judas Iscariot on the stage of literature. But it is only right that we look at his name. It has long been believed that a person's true identity is hidden in their name. Jesus, for example, is given a name, Yeshua, signifying that he would be a deliverer of his people. Perhaps Iscariot, among other things, signified that this man would be a leader of the people to be delivered.

But something seems to have gone wrong.

Betrayal

The next time we encounter Judas Iscariot in Mark is immediately after a scene set in the house of Simon the leper, at Bethany. Jesus has been anointed by a woman and some have complained that the ointment of spikenard could have been sold instead and the proceeds gone to the poor. In John, the one who complains is *Judas*; not in Mark. Is this an example of Judas getting a bad press in the later work – that is, as time goes on, Judas gets progressively demonized?

Mark 14, vio re-introduces Judas Iscariot as 'one of the 12':

> And Judas Iscariot, one of the 12, went unto the chief priests, to betray him unto them.

The word 'betray' could also be rendered 'hand over', but whichever translation is chosen, it seems the high priests can hardly contain their delight. Common sense might tell one that this is because Jesus is being betrayed by one of his own. If you can get inside the inner circle of your opponent, you are half way to catching him. In fact, they might not even have to catch him. Judas is going to save them the trouble. Perhaps they offer him money to keep him in this remarkably co-operative mood:

> And when they [the chief priests] heard it, they were glad, and promised to give him money. And he sought how he might conveniently betray him. (Mark *14*, vii)

The writer of the Gospel seems in no doubt that Judas is betraying his master. But no reason whatsoever is given. The word translated 'conveniently' can also mean 'opportune' or 'due season'. For some reason, the timing has to be right – but it is Judas who is making the decision about when would be the right time. (This implication is absent from John's Gospel, where Jesus is well ahead of Judas' game.) On the other hand, Jesus' preparations also have the feeling of a pre-arranged plan:

> And he sendeth forth two of his disciples, and saith unto them,
> Go ye into the city, and there shall meet you a man bearing a
> pitcher of water: follow him. (Mark 14, v13)

This plan involves what to the 12 disciples appear to be total
strangers, and yet, somehow, Jesus appears to have arranged for
their presence at pre-timed and pre-planned locations. This reminds
one of the guys in spy films who must meet the man with the pink
carnation in his buttonhole. Another collaborator, unknown to the
disciples, appears shortly afterwards. Jesus seems to have got the city
'covered' with his team. Again, the disciples know nothing about
this operation. They have a role and they must fit into it:

> And wheresoever he [the man with the pitcher of water] shall
> go in, say ye to the master of the house, The Teacher saith,
> Where is the guestchamber, where I shall eat the passover with
> my disciples? And he will show you a large upper room
> furnished and prepared: there make ready for us. (Mark 14,
> vv14-15).

Does Judas know what is going on? Has he been pre-warned? Is he
part of the set-up? The author of The Gospel of Judas may have
seen this gathering set of events happening almost over the heads of
the disciples and come to his own conclusion. The disciples did not
understand what was going on. Judas, who had already gained the
confidence of the high priests, did. Of course, the writer of Mark's
Gospel does not understand either, because he has got his Gospel
from the disciples. The next scene adds to the picture of the
disciples floundering about in incomprehension:

> And as they sat and did eat, Jesus said, Verily I say unto you,
> one of you which eateth with me shall betray me. And they
> began to be scornful, and to say unto him one by one, 'Is it I?'
> And another said, 'Is it I?' And he answered and said unto
> them, 'It is one of the twelve, that dippeth with me in the dish.'
> (Mark 14, vv18-20).

The Greek literally says, 'he shall hand me over [or betray me], he who is eating with me.' When Jesus says 'one of the 12', the Greek emphasizes: '*the* one of the 12'. The phrasing is curious. Is 'the one' the 'leader' of the 12? Is he someone who thinks he is above the others? Is he above the others?

Readers of the Gospels will be familiar with scenes wherein the disciples argue with each other for who is going to be enthroned closest to Jesus, or have leading roles in the messianic kingdom they are expecting.

Could it be that those incredulous questions that are translated as 'Is it I?' might be translated as 'Not I, surely?', implying that even now the disciples are wondering who is top dog? Are they fighting for the honour of handing Jesus over? A lot hangs on whether the word is 'betray' or 'hand over'.

Do the disciples think Jesus is joking? Has the enormity of what he has said not sunk in? Or could it be that they have all had misgivings, that they have all been tempted to betray him – and their denials are guilty ones? We know that Peter later will make a big point of saying that he has got what it takes to stand by Jesus in his hour of need. And we know that Peter disowns him. He buckles, leading one to ask the question: could he have ever done what Judas was asked to do, according to The Gospel of Judas' interpretation? (It is clear that the writer of The Gospel of Judas knows this scene, or something like it, because he is so merciless in parodying the confusion of the disciples.)

'He who is eating' with Jesus, may mean the one who is closest to him. This could be taken in a physical sense, or as the one who Jesus regards as the top of the 12. It could also mean that Jesus and the one of the 12 are 'chewing' on the same problem, or taking sustenance from a different cup. In the garden, Jesus begs his heavenly Father to take the cup away from him.

The author of The Gospel of Judas seems to have decided that Jesus had made his choice of who was his number one. The next verse is taken by all those familiar with the story as a straight statement of Judas' guilt. It appears that Jesus condemns Judas:

> The Son of man indeed goeth, as it is written of him: but woe to that man by whom the Son of man is betrayed [or handed over]! Good were it for that man if he had never been born. (Mark 14,v21)

Well, the author of The Gospel of Judas gave this prediction his own twist. Judas will be able to reach the kingdom, but he is going to have to grieve a great deal. Far from Judas being condemned to an eternal torment for his actions, the fact that he is going to have to carry the burden of guilt - while knowing he is innocent - will make him wish he had never been born!

Whether it is 'handed over' or 'betrayed', it is always going to *look* as if he has betrayed Jesus. The prophecy has to be fulfilled. The expected one has to be taken in the house of his friends. The magic of the ritual, so to speak, requires it. It is no good trying to explain it to the other disciples; they just wouldn't understand. It is beyond them. But those to come, those who can see beyond the obvious picture, they will understand. Until that day, woe unto the one who does the deed.

It should be noted that nowhere in this scene does Jesus - or the author - refer to Judas by name. The implication might be that the role of 'betrayer' is an office. The author of The Gospel of Judas seems to grasp this. The man who does the deed will suffer, but the *Name* of Judas will be vindicated. The names of the righteous, as Jewish custom knows, are written in the Book of Life.

The scene moves over to the Garden of Gethsemane. There may be a link between this scene and the scene *in* The Gospel of Judas where the disciples talk of their bad dreams while Judas dreams of being stoned by the disciples. The disciples are asleep. Again, their weakness is demonstrated. Judas, we know, is wide awake. He's on his way.

> And he [Jesus] cometh the third time, and saith unto them,
> Sleep on now, and take your rest: it is enough, the hour is
> come; behold, the Son of man is betrayed into the hands of
> sinners. (Mark 14, v41)

I think at this point we can end this ambiguity about 'betray' and
'hand over'. While the possible literal ambiguity *might* have appealed
to the author of The Gospel of Judas, it is quite plain by now, with
all the incremental force of the story, that as far as the author of
The Gospel of Mark is concerned, Jesus is going to be betrayed. He
is going to be betrayed by Judas Iscariot.

The only question then is whether Judas knew it was *supposed* to
look like that, or whether he knew he was being treacherous to his
Teacher and to his companions:

> Rise up, let us go; lo, he that betrayeth me is at hand. And
> immediately, while he yet spake, cometh Judas, one of the 12,
> and with him a great multitude with swords and staves, from
> the chief priests and the scribes and the elders. And he that
> betrayed him had given them a token, saying, Whomsoever I
> shall kiss, that same is he; take him, and lead him away safely.
> And as soon as he was come, he goeth straightaway to him, and
> saith, Rabbi; and kissed him. (Mark 14, vv42-5)

You may notice Judas is giving the orders. Or is he? He tells his little
army to take Jesus away 'safely'. That sounds interesting. *Safely*... Is
Judas concerned they do not hurt his Rabbi? The Greek word can
also mean 'lead him away *securely*.' Again, an annoying ambiguity
where we would have liked perfect clarity. We don't get it.

Perhaps the armed men have other orders, for we then read that
they lay their hands on Jesus, whether roughly or not we hear not.
Anyhow, at least one of the disciples takes it as provocation and a
skirmish erupts. A servant of the high priest has his ear cut off.
There is nothing here about it being healed by Jesus.

There has been a bloody fight that only seems to end when
Jesus tells them they are low-life for getting him at night because

they were afraid of taking him when he was in public. The disciples flee. Are they outnumbered? Are they expecting to be taken as well? Where does Judas go?

We do not know. That is his last appearance in The Gospel of Mark.

The Gospel of Matthew

The Gospel according to Matthew is well known to have been directed chiefly at a Jewish audience beyond Judaea: more scattered sheep of the House of Israel. This assumption lies in the fact that few opportunities are lost for the author to show that such and such an event is 'in fulfilment of the scriptures'. Jesus says that the Jewish scriptures 'testify of me'.

Inevitably, this hunting through the Old Testament for tie-ins between events or sayings in Jesus' life and ancient sayings has affected the presentation of the author's account of Judas Iscariot.

Indeed, most scholars are of the opinion that details of Jesus' story have not only been shown to be 'in fulfilment' of scripture, but have been lifted bodily out of scripture and made into features of the New Testament story. The author did not think this was a case of invention. The habit of seeing Jesus' life prefigured in scripture was such a feature of Jewish Christianity that it seemed the pious thing to do. Jesus had, according to Matthew's Gospel, told people to search the scripture for indications of who he was.

The story of Judas gets the Old Testament treatment. As in Mark, the first notice we have of Judas Iscariot actually doing something is when he goes to the chief priests. In this account, possibly based on Mark, the presentation of Judas' visit is 'cranked up' in intensity. The Greek appears to have been changed to put Judas at a distance from the reader in personal significance.

Mark's 'the one of the 12' has become 'the one called Judas *Iskariotes*' (not Judas *Iskarioth*, as in Mark). Perhaps the author was troubled by Mark's Greek which seemed to give Judas some special place in the 12. Matthew is having none of that:

> Then one of the 12, called Judas Iscariot, went unto the chief
> priests, and said unto them, What will you give me, and I will
> deliver him unto you? And they covenanted with him for 30
> pieces of silver. And from that time he sought opportunity to
> betray him. (Matthew 26, vv14-16)

As in, Mark, this scene takes place straight after the curious
anointing of Jesus at Bethany. The anointing might look like the
spontaneous action of a woman entranced by Jesus' presence, but
the link is with messiahship (the anointing of a king) – and so is the
scene with Judas and the high priests.

Like so many things, the connection can be read in several ways.
Has the author of Matthew simply followed the traditional order
established in Mark? Is the delivery of Jesus over to the authorities
part of a kingship ritual? Or is Judas disturbed by the anointing,
fearing things have gone too far, and deciding he is going to force
the action, either because he wants Jesus arrested, or because he
wants Jesus to confront his enemies and traduce them with his
power?

Unfortunately, we never get the motive. Well, in Matthew, we get
a motive: money. We hear about these 30 pieces of silver. Where did
they come from? They came straight out of the prophecies of
Zechariah:

> And I said unto them, If ye think good, give me my price; and if
> not, forbear. So they weighed for my price 30 pieces of silver.
> (Zechariah 11, v12)

Chapters 9 to 14 of the prophecies of Zechariah are thought to
have been written between the 4th and 3rd centuries BC and deal
with messianic themes of redemption after the division of the
kingdom (the scattering of the sheep). The paltry 30 pieces of silver
is all God is offered for his services to his people. Again, there are
two ways of looking at this.

We know Jesus was aware of these prophecies because when he entered Jerusalem on an ass, he set it up carefully in conformity with the prophecy of the messiah's humble arrival, in Zechariah chapter nine, verse nine. This is a kind of ritual re-enactment (unless of course the whole thing was invented by Gospel writers because they followed the prophecies and innocently 'made them history').

If Jesus knew the prophecy concerning the entry into Jerusalem, then he knew the one concerning the 30 pieces of silver. It may be, of course, that Matthew has simply added this detail because it seemed to him that there was a dark symmetry between the price offered to God, and the price paid for the betrayal of God's precious Son.

This is the usual understanding and I am not saying that it is not a correct inference. However, there is another possibility. The passage in Zechariah is all about God's patience being exhausted with his people. God is going to *break* the precious covenant with his people. The prophet uses the image of staves being broken:

> Then I cut asunder mine other staff, even Bands [its name],
> that I might break the brotherhood between Judah and Israel.
> (Zechariah 11, v14)

Taking this into consideration, we get an extra resonance in Matthew's use of the word 'covenanting', going beyond the arrangement between Judas and the high priests. We may see a possible motive for such action.

As has been suggested earlier, Judas, the man of Issachar, may have been part of Jesus' plan to seek the lost sheep of the House of Israel. The lost sheep were those who had been cut off from the kingdom at the time of the Assyrian conquest of Israel. The plan seems to have involved uniting the kingdom once more in a divine blessing, so that all nations would eventually descend upon Jerusalem in awe of the One True God. But the centre, the Temple, must first be purified – perhaps even destroyed. In this context, the use of these prophecies makes perfect sense. For we read in Zechariah, just after the symbolic breaking of 'the brotherhood between Judah and Israel' (the old southern and northern kingdoms), God's raising of a false shepherd:

> For, lo, I will raise up a shepherd in the land, which shall not visit those that be cut off, neither shall seek the young one, nor heal that that is broken, nor feedeth that that standeth still: but he shall eat the flesh of the fat, and tear their claws in pieces. Woe to the idle shepherd that leaveth the flock! The sword shall be upon his arm, and upon his right eye: his arm shall be clean dried up, and his right eye shall be utterly darkened. (Zechariah 11, vv16-17)

We know from all accounts that Jesus did everything this false shepherd did not do: he visited those 'cut off' (Samaritans, lost tribal remnants, the rejected), he healed the sick, had compassion for the hungry and spoke of the good shepherd who cares for his 'flock'. Who, then, could this bad shepherd be? Everything points to the religious authorities of Jesus' day being identified as a collective 'bad shepherd'. *Woe unto them!* says Jesus so many times in Matthew's Gospel. They had failed. The arrival of the Romans was a plain judgement on them. The rot was within:

> Behold, I will make Jerusalem a cup of trembling unto all the people round about, when they shall be in the siege both against Judah and against Jerusalem. (Zechariah 12, v2)

In order to fulfil the prophecy, Judas *has* to be paid a price for the delivery of the King. Only then, after the high priesthood has been destroyed, will the covenant be restored between God and the righteous and the lost.

If this is a sound reading of the situation, the only question perhaps is whether Judas knew what he was doing. It would make sense, in the context described, that Judas was told the price he would have to ask – if, that is, he had not worked this out already for himself. Why did the disciples, and therefore the Gospel compilers, never realize this? They were not told – any more than they were told the identity of the man with the pitcher of water, the woman who anointed Jesus at Bethany, the master of the house who organized the 'last supper', and the man who provided the ass on which Jesus was to ride to Jerusalem. They were not told, perhaps, because their job was to *preach* the new kingdom, not understand how it had happened. Jesus knew their limitations; they would have to come to see for themselves in their own way.

It may be that we are never given a clear motive for Judas' actions, other than mere greed (so unconvincing), because the other disciples never understood his motives themselves. All they knew was what their eyes told them that dark night.

Returning to the text in Matthew, there is some confirmation of the view of Marvin Meyer and others that the Gospels show an incremental build-up of Judas' evil profile. The account of the Last Supper is similar to that of Mark, but there are differences. Chief of them is that, in Matthew, after Jesus has told the disciples that the one dipping into the (common) dish with him will betray him, it is not the disciples who ask 'Not I?' but only Judas. He, apparently, is the only one with the guilty conscience.

Judas says: 'Not *Me*, Rabbi?' The Greek is exceptionally emphatic. This could be a response to Jesus' words that it would be better for the betrayer never to have been born. In fact, the money has already been exchanged. In the Gospel account, Judas is guilty as hell.

Also, Jesus answers Judas' question, 'Not *Me*, Rabbi?', with the answer, 'You have spoken.' This would not work if the other disciples had all asked the same question, as it is written in Mark. The short phrase, extraordinarily heavy, has extra resonance.

'You have spoken' could mean 'Well, you're the one who's talking,' as well as 'Your asking the question answers it,' or even 'You have *already* spoken.' Wherever one places the emphasis, Matthew takes Judas as guilty from his own mouth. As Meyer rightly concludes, Matthew adds more force to the impression of Judas' personal responsibility. Forensic re-creation of the facts was not a priority of the Gospel of Matthew. Jesus must be delivered, and

Judas is the guilty man who made sure it happened.

And this extending of Mark happens again with the taking of Jesus in the garden. As with Mark, Judas turns up with the armed band from the chief priests, having told them of the recognition sign. 'Lord, Rabbi' says Judas, and kisses Jesus. In Matthew, Jesus responds, 'Comrade, from where have you come?' Rather enigmatic. It might well have struck the author of The Gospel of Judas, for in this gospel Jesus takes time to explain what world Judas has come from and to which world, if he can bear the grief, he will be going.

Incidentally, the idea that something is enigmatic is alien to many readers of the Gospels. Because we have been taught Jesus spoke in parables so that ordinary people could understand him, we tend to forget that Jesus also spoke in parables so that some people would not understand. The Archbishop of Canterbury railed against the idea of Jesus being seen as a 'guru, a mystery man'. I do not know about *guru* (the Hindi form of 'rabbi') but if Jesus was not a mystery man, I do not know what a 'mystery man' is!

Jesus had to explain the parables to the disciples. Unfortunately, we have no one (at least not a contemporary authority) to explain to us exactly what was happening with Judas Iscariot. We have to work it out for ourselves. *Comrade, from where have you come?*

In Matthew 26,v56 we are told that all this was done that the scriptures be fulfilled. We are told that all the disciples forsook Jesus, and fled. They gave him up. Was it because they were outnumbered? According to Matthew, Jesus tells everyone he could pray for 12 legions of angels to assist him, if that was the right thing to do. The disciples could only have been non-plussed. Jesus did not seem to need them. He says it is all to fulfil the prophecy in Zechariah:

> Awake, O sword, against my shepherd, and against the man that is my fellow, saith the LORD of hosts: smite the shepherd, and the sheep shall be scattered: and I will turn my hand upon the little ones. (Zechariah 13, v7)

The last phrase is not mentioned in Matthew, nor is the first.

Matthew seems to think the 'shepherd' that is smitten must be Jesus, the sheep being the disciples who run away. However, we have seen from Zechariah, chapter 11, that it is the bad shepherd, 'the idle shepherd that has left the flock', that God has sent as a judgement on his people. The prophecy may be saying that the bad shepherd will be smitten – a hopeful sign.

Who is 'the man that is my fellow', in this verse? Could it explain the famous moment when the servant of the high priest has his ear cut off? The sword is awoken against the high priest, and his fellow, is a reasonable interpretation.

By the way, in Matthew the ear is not healed. There is blood here and it is not tidied up. This is a messianic conflict, but exactly what is going on, seems impossible to reconstruct.

Matthew adds more guilt to Judas than Mark. But Judas also shows what looks like profound remorse. In Mark, Judas does the deed and that's an end of it. Matthew gives us a picture of the aftermath. The 30 pieces of silver reappear:

> Then Judas, which had betrayed him, when he saw that he [Jesus] was condemned, repented himself, and brought again the 30 pieces of silver to the chief priests and elders, Saying, I have sinned in that I have betrayed the innocent blood. And they said, what is that to us? see thou to that [meaning: 'that's your business; keep us out of it']. And he cast down the pieces of silver in the temple, and departed and went and hanged himself. And the chief priests took the silver pieces, and said, It is not lawful for to put them into the treasury, because it is the price of blood. And they took counsel, and bought with them the potter's field, to bury strangers in. Wherefore that field was called, the field of blood, unto this day. Thus was fulfilled that which was spoke by Jeremiah the prophet, saying, And they took 30 pieces of silver, the price of him that was valued, whom they of the children of Israel did value; and gave them for the

potter's field, as the Lord appointed me. (Matthew 27, vv3ff.)

Here the author of Matthew seems to have got his prophecies mixed up. It is from the prophecy of Jeremiah (chapter 32, verses 6 to 9) that one Hanameel will come to Jeremiah to suggest he buys a field. Jeremiah does so – for 17 shekels of silver. But the main prophecy is from Zechariah again:

> And the LORD said unto me, Cast it unto the potter: a goodly price that I was prised at of them. And I took the 30 pieces of silver, and cast them to the potter in the house of the LORD. (Zechariah 11, v13)

Not only is the prophetic background confused here, suggesting the author has done his own conflation of texts to suit other available material, but the story does not tally with Judas' fate as given elsewhere in the New Testament. Judas does not hang himself in The Acts of the Apostles, as we shall see. Did any of the Gospel compilers *really* know what had happened to Judas? Or were they guessing?

One can only guess whether the author of The Gospel of Judas would have been struck by the allegorical potential of the 'field of blood' and the place 'to bury strangers in'. Those of a 'Gnostic' cast of mind were encouraged to see themselves as strangers in the world. The world *itself* would be the place to 'bury' strangers in. Judas has become a 'stranger', an outsider and alien. He is 'Allogenes', 'of another race', in terms of his destiny in The Gospel of Judas. As for the 'field of blood', The Gospel of Judas has Jesus explain to Judas that the ruler of the lower world is Nebro, 'whose appearance was defiled with blood'.

On a more prosaic level, if there was any historical basis to this account in Matthew chapter 27, this image of Judas 'throwing down the gauntlet' by casting the 30 pieces of silver in the Temple has definite signs of a ritual enactment of Zechariah's messianic drama. According to the prophecy, the disgusting price paid for the services of God is thrown at 'the potter' in the Temple. This is a prophetic act. In Zechariah it precedes the breaking of the brotherhood between Judah and Israel. It amounts to a declaration of divine war.

Was Judas perhaps continuing the ritual of divine king-making? We can only speculate, given the confused nature of the tradition that has come down to us.

It is also worth mentioning that the dream scenes in The Gospel of Judas, which take place in the Temple and show a corrupt priesthood with blood on their hands, may perhaps represent a *Sethian* rendering of the scene described above with Judas in the Temple: a powerful scene for sure.

The remorse, in this context, should have been coming not from Judas, the executor of the divine prophetic will, but from the high priests. They get their blood money back. Knowing that is what it is, they condemn themselves, and try to 'bury the evidence' by providing a new cemetery in Jerusalem – perhaps in preparation for what is to come.

The layers to this story are many and tangled.

What does the Gospel according to Luke add to our understanding of whether Judas was good, bad or plain misunderstood? Does Luke intensify the picture of Judas' crime?

Luke and Judas

The moment of the fatal kiss in the Garden of Gethsemane is handled differently again in Luke. Luke's Jesus does not call Judas, 'Comrade' – even sarcastically. After the kiss, Jesus says (for any reader who had not worked this out perhaps): 'Judas, betrayest thou the Son of man with a kiss?'

This is putting the matter plainly. One feels that by the time the author of Luke was writing, the familiar image of Judas has been set in stone with no ambiguities. Judas does in Luke what people expect Judas to do. Should anyone question motive, such questions are dismissed by the simple following device. In Luke, the real culprit – to whom Judas surrenders – is revealed:

Then entered Satan into Judas surnamed Iscariot, being of the number of the 12. And he went his way [followed Satan's path not Jesus'], and communed with the chief priests and captains, how he might betray him unto them. (Luke 22, v3)

In *Luke*, the plan is cooked up between Judas and the chief priests in conference – there is no hint of any symbolic activity or messianic ritual here; this is a straightforward conspiracy. And *Satan* is behind it. If you have doubts about Judas' guilt, take it up with *him*.

And they were glad, and covenanted to give him money. And he promised, and sought opportunity to betray him unto them in the absence of the multitude. (Luke 22, v6)

There is no mention of 30 pieces of silver, either. Would this prophecy muddy the story? Possibly. Why? Because if we take the author of Luke as being the person who wrote The Acts of the Apostles, then there can be no scene of Judas taking the silver into the Temple and throwing it down. Judas cannot possibly throw back the blood money in an effort to redeem the one for which it was paid. There can be no question of the money having symbolic, prophetic power; of it being cast down in the Temple as an act condemning the high priests and their regime: a declaration of God's impending judgement and the annihilation of the old order.

There cannot even be the idea Matthew puts forward of a repenting Judas, horrified that Jesus has actually been taken, astonished at what he has done, filled with the feeling that it were better had he never been born, so, logically, hanging himself as quickly as possible.

No. The Gospel of Luke has been called the romantic Gospel, and none of the above fits his view of the story. Tradition says that Luke acquires much of its outlook from Paul and would want no shilly-shallying about the meaning of the Crucifixion. Judas appears again in the first chapter of *The Acts of the Apostles* in a little speech given by Peter 'in the midst of the brethren', recorded as numbering about 120. He is announcing that they must choose a successor to Judas. Even though we are told that the assembly had all accompanied Jesus in the time he was with them, Peter proceeds to tell them what had befallen Judas. He says it was all to fulfil a prophecy; not Zechariah this time, but Psalms:

> Yea, mine own familiar friend, in whom I trusted, which did eat of my bread, hath lifted up his heel against me. (Psalms 41, v9)

Judas is a traitor; he betrayed his best friend:

> Now this man purchased a field with the reward of iniquity; and falling headlong, he burst asunder in the midst, and all his bowels gushed out. And it was known unto all the dwellers at Jerusalem; insomuch as that field is called in their proper tongue, Aceldama, that is to say, The field of blood. (Acts 1, vv18-19)

Peter then quotes another 'prophecy', also from Psalms (69, v25): 'Let their habitation be desolate; and let none dwell in their tents.' For good measure Psalm 109, v8 is thrown in: 'Let his days be few; and let another take his office.' No repentance, no forgivenness. Psalm 109 has quite a few other tortures that the psalmist hopes will be visited on his enemies. One of these psalms begs God to turn his enemy's bowels into water and his bones into oil. Furthermore, 'Set thou a wicked man over him: and let Satan stand at his right hand' (v6). Perhaps this is where Luke got the idea of Satan entering Judas from. It is as though someone said to the Gospel compiler: 'You want to know about Judas? Read Psalm 109 – it's all there.'

There can be very little of an historical nature in this account. This account is supposed to have taken place shortly after the ascension of Jesus, and yet we hear of this field, *Aceldama*, as if it were an old story – 'And it was known unto all the dwellers of Jerusalem.'

This is not surprising. This Gospel was written after Jerusalem had been destroyed by the Romans in AD 70. The author is dealing with hearsay about events in the past. It does not seem likely then that Luke had read Matthew – if Matthew had been written yet. The story of the potter's field with all the prophetic nuances is not present. In fact, Judas was apparently enjoying his ill-gotten gains when he was finally felled in a punitive prophetic judgement.

It makes absolutely no historical sense at all.

If Judas survived the trial of Jesus long enough to purchase an agricultural opportunity, he would, according to Luke's own account, have hardly been unaware of the resurrection, later appearances of Jesus, and so on. Are we to believe he suddenly preferred farming to being a messianic officer? – only if we accept things on faith, perhaps.

It is plain to the logic of this investigation that the fate of Judas was of no real interest to those who came after Jesus. They had heard of a betrayal. The story became more refined, more definite. Judas' role becomes formulaic; his judgement certain. How did he die? It was written in the prophecies. He died. Who cares?

Well, someone writing in the 2nd century seems to have cared. I hope we can see how a writer with a peculiar cast of mind could interpret the established records. Perhaps it was not so difficult to begin this process of re-interpretation and reformulation. There are so many holes in the Gospel accounts, all you would need would be a well-honed critical consciousness – and a good, working, alternative theory. These tools the writer of The Gospel of Judas had.

The writer of The Gospel of Judas also seems to have had access to one other invaluable asset. Paradoxically, where Judas is concerned, Professor Meyer has considered that asset as the most damning Gospel of all. For Meyer and other scholars, the Gospel of John represents the 'end of the story' in the evolution of the guilty Judas, damned for all time.

The Not-So-Secret Gospel of John

The 20th-century German scholar, Rudolf Bultmann, considered John's Gospel a halfway house to Gnosticism, so ethereal and spiritual had the figure of Jesus become.

John's Jesus talks in great speeches about who he is, where he comes from, where he is going; that no one gets to the Father except by him; that he is the true vine, the true bread, the light, the love of God, the way, the truth and the life. And to cap it all, Jesus is the *Logos* ('Word') made flesh.

In case you did not know, the 'Word' does not mean the *words* of the Bible, it was a Greek word meaning the divine intelligence that created the universe. It is reflected in the mind of the true seeker and it is revealed in the intelligent study of God's creation. The *Logos* is the creative mind of God. Without the *Logos*, the universe and the natural world would be unintelligible.

In The First Epistle of John, the Word is shown as part of a trinity: 'For there are three that bear record in heaven, the Father, the Word, and the Holy Spirit: and these three are one' (I John, 5, v.7). However significant the mysticism of John might have seemed to those who appreciated The Gospel of Judas, there was one sticking point, at least. The idea of the Word becoming flesh was not an idea they could stomach – at least in its blunt terms. The Word was spiritual; flesh was flesh – just a passing thing that is, and is not.

It may be that the first chapter of John – opening, 'In the beginning was the Logos' – was written with the so-called 'Gnostics' in mind (of course, the latter had their own 'secret book' of John – The Apocryphon of John). It is also possible that the treatment of Judas in John's Gospel was also intended to dissuade anyone from thinking Iscariot might have known better than the other apostles did. Nevertheless, the writer of The Gospel of Judas – as well as writers of works probably read in connection with it – were prepared to see things in John's Gospel that even the author had not intended!

The Son of Perdition

> While I was with them in the world, I kept them in thy name:
> those that thou gavest me I have kept, and none of them is lost,
> but the son of perdition; that the scripture might be fulfilled.
> (John 17, v12)

Judas, of course, is the 'son of perdition' referred to in this prayer of
the Johannine Jesus for the apostles. The reason Judas has been
lost is to fulfil the scriptures; there was no real choice in the matter:
lost he had to be. Would he have to be picked up later, after the
grief? The author of The Gospel of Judas seems to have noticed a
certain lack of charity in this prayer. He is having none of it. When
Jesus shows Judas the generation of the universe from within the
divine energies of God in The Gospel of Judas, he has this to say
about 'perdition':

> The multitude of those immortals is called the cosmos – that
> is, perdition – by the Father and the 72 luminaries who are with
> the Self-Generated and his 72 aeons.

Yes, Judas is a 'son of perdition' all right! He is a child of the
cosmos. His home is with the immortals. 'So', the author seems to
say, 'the Word was made flesh and dwelt among us, as you put it.
But who could see it? Only Judas! Judas has the courage to get up and
say to Jesus that he comes from the immortal realm of Barbelo' –
and Barbelo in the language of Sethian *gnosis* corresponds to the
Logos, the *Sophia* or Wisdom of God. The point about Jesus is not the
man, but the hidden God in man.

For the author of The Gospel of Judas, the evidence was lying all
over the scene of the 'crime'. Of course there was truth in the
Gospels, he might say. But the truth had become irredeemably
twisted: twisted by the lord of this world.

If the disciples could not understand what Judas was trying to
do, then how could they understand enough to write an accurate

gospel? If they missed the point about Judas, they would miss the point about everything. They would see Jesus in their own image, according to their own perceptions and expectations. They would be confused. They would write as they saw; they had not seen enough. Nevertheless, in writing about the one that came from Barbelo, truth was bound to 'come out' in the Gospels, at least for those who could see it. The Gospels were littered with clues.

It is a curious paradox that the very Gospel that would appear to have the worst possible picture of Judas and his damnable guilt – John – is the one that seems to have inspired the writer of Judas' gospel the most. In the following passage, we have an image for the classic Gnostic dichotomy:

> When Jesus therefore perceived that they would come and take him by force, to make him a king, he departed again into a mountain himself alone. (John 6, v15)

There are those who see Jesus as a king: an earthly power. In The Gospel of Judas, these people would be the disciples. But Jesus wants to get away from them; he wants to get higher. He goes to the mountain. Judas will have to be led apart from those below if he wants to perceive the truth.

> But there are some of you that believe not. For Jesus knew from the beginning who they were that believed not, and who should betray him. ... From that time many of his disciples went back, and walked no more with him. (John 6, vv64-6)

If Jesus knew who would betray him, why did he not stop it? His disciples would have been only too glad to stone a traitor.

Why did he not stop it? Because Jesus *had* to be betrayed. Either Judas had come independently to the same idea or he was willing to fall in with the necessity. The author of The Gospel of Judas simply deduced that for Judas to fall in with the plan, he had to have seen what the others could not. Here was the proof. Many of Jesus' disciples, according to John, went back. They walked no more with him.

There is nothing like that in the other Gospels: people walking out on Jesus, giving up. Well, there was the rich young man who could not live without his income, but he was not a disciple; he did not even get *that* far. But here we have a large number giving up the fight before it had even begun. Was it because there was to be no fight?

Jesus was too 'far-out' for some of the disciples. Furthermore, the author has given the game away: there were those who *believed not*, and there was Judas. Simple. The sentence clearly divides Judas from the non-believers. The non-believers were disciples who would walk no more with Jesus. They are the same ones who fled the garden, who forsook him. Judas had what it took.

> Jesus answered them, Have I not chosen you 12, and one of you
> is a devil? (John 6, v70)

Right! Judas is a devil, all right! He is the 'thirteenth daimon'. The Gospel of Judas turns what looks like a rebuke into a badge of honour. A *daimon* is the genius of a man; Judas is a genius! The reading 'in the *gnosis*' then is: I chose 12, and it is the one who breaks away from you who is the *daimon* I can work with! Jesus can handle a devil when he wants to; he comes from above, devils are below. Devils do as he tells them. *Daimons* know what they are doing. (Daimons and demons were confused even then.)

> He spoke of Judas Iscariot, the son of Simon: for he it was that
> should betray him, being one of the 12. (John 6, v71)

Being one of the 12 ... Judas is *the* one of the 12. Outside the 12, he becomes the thirteenth and therefore attains his true, hidden, divine nature.

> Ye are from beneath; I am from above: ye are of this world; I am
> not of this world. (John 8, v23)

The Gospel of Judas is happy to take this statement absolutely at face value. It was Judas who saw this very thing. Judas' gospel seems to ask, *What is all this about the Word made of flesh?* Look, he says it himself: *Jesus is not of this world.* Anyone who disagrees with this statement is 'from beneath'.

The Gospel of John is the only Gospel that puts Judas out as the spoiler of Jesus' anointing at Bethany. The author may have observed in the other three Gospels – if he had read them – that Judas' visit to the religious authorities in Jerusalem immediately follows the anointing. This may explain why the evangelist goes 'one further' than the other Gospels and has Judas already beginning his evil career as traitor and turncoat by verbally attacking the woman who anoints Jesus with the ointment of spikenard. (It is, of course possible that John is relying on more accurate eye-witness testimony, as he provides the names and some extra setting.) The discomfiting scene takes place in the presence of Lazarus who has recently been raised from the dead, and we are told it was Mary, a disciple, who wipes the ointment into the skin of Jesus' feet, so soon to feel the agony of crucifixion. Then we are told that Judas Iscariot can contain his sense of disgust no longer:

> Then saith one of his disciples, Judas Iscariot, Simon's son, which should betray him, Why was this ointment not sold for 300 pence, and given to the poor? (John 12, vv4-5)

In case we might think Judas is experiencing a sudden burst of charity, the writer of the Gospel is quick to explain:

> This he said, not that he cared for the poor; but because he was a thief, and had the purse and bare what was put therein. Then Jesus said, Let her alone: (John 12, vv6-7)

Here you have almost the whole indictment: Judas Iscariot, betrayer of Jesus, thief, liar, spoiler of a sacred ritual, ignorant and embarrassing guest, hypocrite and oppressor of women. And so the conclusion follows: 'Now is the judgement of the world: now shall the prince of this world be cast out.' (John 12, v31)

Again, there is nothing here that the author of The Gospel of

Judas would not joyfully concur with. The defeat of the prince of this world is at hand. But in order for this to happen, John requires that it is Judas who is the servant of the lord of this world. The lord of this world thinks he can defeat the power of Jesus through killing him; Judas is the means. Not so, says Judas' gospel, Jesus would not let the prince of this world trick him with Judas; he can see right through this. The prince of this world is the one who is to be outwitted.

What any of this has to do with the historical Judas, we can barely tell. Wherever we look, Judas is being exploited for theological purposes: 'And supper being ended, the devil having now put into the heart of Judas Iscariot, Simon's son, to betray him' (John 13, v2). According to this, Judas is the devil's disciple. One can only wonder if the eyes of the author of The Gospel of Judas passed over this misunderstanding (for in The Gospel of Judas, Judas' 'devil' was his hidden god). Perhaps he suddenly grasped the symbol staring out at him from the next few lines: 'He [Jesus] riseth from supper, and laid aside his garments...' After the supper, *Jesus laid aside his garments*. That is to say, Jesus laid aside his body, offering the lord of this world his fake victory. Perhaps this is the verse that inspired in Judas' gospel those striking words: 'But you [Judas] will exceed all of them. For you will sacrifice the man that clothes me.'

The Beloved Disciple

It cannot be stressed strongly enough that the traditional Gospels are composite works. Textual analysis has proved that the Gospels are 'patchworks' of disparate material. They have been 'sewn together', edited, 'cut and pasted'. Pieces have been removed from other sources. What those sources originally were, we do not know.

Sometimes the reader may feel there is material missing. A train of thought is begun and then seems to cease abruptly just where we might expect an explanation. Maybe the explanation did not suit the mind of the compiler. Maybe, he felt the material had already been used, or was too familiar to bear repetition.

As a result of identifying material shared by Matthew, Mark and Luke, scholars believe there was an original sayings source common to them. They did not know what it was, so they called it 'Q' from the German *quelle* (meaning 'source'). But 'source' could mean several works, a collection of sources.

What this means for us is that none of the Gospels was written 'at a stretch'. Do not imagine the original compiler sitting down and dictating the work to a scribe, line after line. There might have been such a work in the first place, but if there was, it has been added to enormously, such that it would now be impossible to deconstruct the Gospel down to a supposed first, consistent draft.

While we know that there are themes special to each individual Gospel – John seems to be the most systematic in this regard – the Gospels do not represent the working out of *single* ideological purposes. They are not apocalypses, revelations or visions, though they do contain elements of such material. Imagination has been used to reconcile or blend different sources. There are themes; there are emphases. Definite choice has been made on the sources – on what words to emphasize, or even change. There is a mind, or minds, at work on this material.

So to call them a patchwork in the sense of an almost random selection or aesthetic design would be a mistake. However, material is sometimes included because, for whatever reason, the compiler of the gospel simply felt he *ought* to put it in. Maybe because he knew his readers liked this story, or even because he could not see why he should *not* put it in. Or perhaps it interested him – even, because it meant something significant to him that we cannot ourselves immediately comprehend.

Scholars have often drawn attention to odd little details and peculiar sayings that seem difficult to 'fit in' with the rest of the narrative, however disjointed those narratives often are.

One thing is certain. We do not read the Gospels in the way that their first readers 'read' or heard them. They lived in a different psychological landscape. Things that appear incidental or even meaningless to our time may have had a vast impact on the minds of people all those many years ago. We can never be certain we have got the message in the precise way the message was intended to be received.

One of the more curious features of John's Gospel, remarked on many times by scholars, and a source of perpetual intrigue to laypersons alike, is the occasional references to a 'disciple whom Jesus loved'. One of the disciples has been singled out in John; he is generally called the 'beloved disciple' and has frequently been associated with the apostle 'John', the alleged principal source of the Gospel.

Now, while this conclusion has much good research behind it, it does not end the mystery. As we have seen, mysteries are mysteries, but we can try to shine a torch down the bottomless well.

We may have an advantage over the compiler of John's Gospel. It is perfectly possible that he did not know the identity of the disciple whom Jesus loved either. Of course, he may have *thought* he did. After all, Jesus was supposed to have loved all his disciples – except, perhaps, Judas Iscariot.

Who would have claimed in humility to be the disciple whom Jesus loved? Can you imagine it? 'Oh! That was *me*! I'm the one he loved!'

I should not be surprised if some of you were now beginning to think about *The Da Vinci Code* or works with a similar theme. Could the disciple whom Jesus loved possibly have been... *Mary Magdalene*? Well, we do not know. We do know that contemporary writers who shared insights with the author of The Gospel of Judas did make a fascinating case for Jesus having loved Mary Magdalene more than the other disciples, saying (in The Gospel of Philip) that he kissed her often on the mouth.

Incidentally, the word 'mouth' is missing from the original papyrus – but even if it were there, close study of the Nag Hammadi Library reveals that when Jesus kisses a person on the mouth, it means that the words spoken by that mouth were true and holy. It may also mark the transmission of the holy spirit, as we shall see. It is not an erotic sign! (The Jesus of *Gnosis* sometimes appears as a child, but the writings of that tradition know nothing of physical progeny.)

Anyhow, the author of The Gospel of Judas shows no interest in Mary Magdalene, being quite clear in his or her understanding of the primacy of Judas. If indeed Jesus did love a disciple more than the others, then it was Judas. He was the one who would exceed the rest.

> Truly, truly, I say unto you, that one of you shall betray me. Then the disciples looked one on another, doubting of whom he spake. Now there was leaning on Jesus' breast one of his disciples, whom Jesus loved. Simon Peter therefore beckoned to him, that he should ask who it should be of whom he spake. He then lying on Jesus' breast saith unto him, Lord, who is it? Jesus answered, He it is, to whom I shall give a morsel, when I have dipped it. And when he had dipped the morsel, he gave it to Judas Iscariot, the son of Simon. And after the morsel Satan entered into him. Then said Jesus unto him, That thou doest, do quickly. Now no man at the table knew for what intent he spake this unto him. For some of them thought, because Judas had the purse, that Jesus had said unto him, Buy those things that we have need of against the feast: or, that he should give something to the poor. He then having received the sop went immediately out: and it was night. (John 13, vv21-30)

This confusing passage led one scholar[3] to the conclusion that the beloved disciple was Judas Iscariot – a lone voice speaking before his time, perhaps. Noack stuck his neck out and argued that Judas was the only disciple who really understood the mind of Jesus. He argued that the so-called betrayal of Jesus was not a treacherous act, but a deliberate playing into Jesus' hands, in order to allow Jesus the fulfilment of his purposes. It is striking that Noack had never seen The Gospel of Judas.

However, the Johannine passage quoted above has been cited in refutation of what other scholars have sensed as the offensiveness of Noack's theory. In that passage there seems to be a distinction between the guilty man and the disciple leaning on Jesus' breast. However, even a cursory reading shows that the passage cannot be taken as being either logical or historical. The beloved disciple asks who will betray him. Jesus says it is the one to whom he gives the morsel. He then gives it to Judas Iscariot. If the other disciples heard this, they would have felt compelled to deal with Judas there and then. They would not have been left wondering why Jesus tells Judas to do what he has to do, quickly.

Furthermore, if Judas had heard Jesus' instructions to do what he was going to do quickly – and he was being genuinely treacherous – he would have to have had second thoughts because the whole plan depended on secrecy to work, and so now it would have fallen through. He would have had no reason to believe Jesus wanted him to succeed.

Even if Jesus had only given the morsel-dipping clue to 'the beloved disciple' (and this disciple was not Judas), then the beloved disciple would surely have told the others, unless he wanted Jesus betrayed also. If he had known already what Jesus wanted to achieve by permitting the betrayal, he would not have needed to ask the question.

None of this adds up at all. Even the oft-voiced pious solution – that though Judas is effectively accomplishing God's will, he is still guilty because he surrendered to Satan – just does not take account of the contradictions. Even the author seems at pains to try and explain some illogicalities – like the business about the disciples wondering if Judas might have gone out for some late-night holiday shopping. No, it does not add up.

What we have is a composite description serving different purposes. The explanation about the disciples wondering why Jesus should tell Judas to do his work quickly looks, frankly, like a cover to explain why the disciples do not just beat Judas up. Of course, there might have been a lot of noise at the occasion and they might even have been drunk, as well as confused, and therefore misheard what was going on. But however you look at it, it is a confused and confusing narrative, manifestly contradictory to the other Gospel accounts. In none of the other three Gospels does Jesus give the morsel to the alleged guilty man, thus making the identity of the traitor plain.

One has got to imagine Jesus and his disciples reclining on their left elbows, taking their nourishment with their right hands. If the beloved disciple was leaning on Jesus' breast, then he was on Jesus' right hand, the chosen place. Peter asks this disciple to ask the question of Jesus. Apparently, Peter dares not ask it. That also shows primacy, as though to say: 'You know him best; you ask him!'

Now if the disciples are not meant to know it is Judas who is going to do the deed, then Jesus would speak his answer into the beloved disciple's right ear. Jesus' right arm would have to be around the beloved disciple's front if the disciple were leaning on his breast, as we are told he was. This would not give Jesus a lot of room for manoeuvre in dipping his morsel of bread and putting it into a disciple's mouth (or hand). The betrayer would have to be pretty close – in fact next to the beloved disciple (at most) if Jesus was not going to have to pull away from the beloved disciple, get up and take the morsel around to the betrayer. This would have alerted everyone. Would Judas have got out of the building in one piece?

In this scenario, a detective might be inclined to think that the circumstances required that Jesus put his arm round the front of the beloved disciple and feed him the bread. The words, 'Take this, this is my body' come to mind. The idea of Jesus being 'betrayed' by the one he loved makes great dramatic sense. The ultimate moral dereliction: *betrayed by his best friend*!

How much historical actuality there may be in all of this is a mystery. However, the author of The Gospel of Judas may very well have put this picture together and come to the same conclusion as Herr Noack, the 19th-century German biblical scholar.

Again, one may argue: 'But this is ridiculous. The compiler of John's Gospel would never have countenanced such an implication!' Well, we have seen that he has 'worked' his source to fit – for example, the explanation of why the disciples do not understand the fateful words that Judas should do what he has to do quickly.

Is it possible that the author of John's Gospel did not understand the allusions in his 'beloved disciple' source material? We get a little clue of something strange in this regard a little later in John 14, v22. Something very odd happens here. We actually hear 'Judas', the disciple, ask Jesus a question. This is practically unheard of! Throughout the Gospels we hear from Peter, John, James, Andrew and a snippet from the others here and there – but *Judas*! He is not even mentioned in the rest of the Gospel. Here is the passage:

> Judas saith unto him, not Iscariot, Lord, how is it that thou wilt manifest thyself unto us, and not unto the world?
>
> Jesus answered and said unto him, If a man love me, he will keep my words: and my father will love him, and we will come unto him, and make our abode with him. (John 14, v22)

The question attributed to Judas ('*not Iscariot*') could have served for The Gospel of Judas as an opening line: *Lord, how is it that thou wilt manifest thyself to us, and not unto the world?* It also sounds like a quotation straight out of that bright gem of the Nag Hammadi Library, The Gospel of Thomas. At this very moment, I reach for my copy of the Nag Hammadi Library. I open it at a random page. It is a page from The Gospel of Thomas. My eye alights onto one line:

> Jesus said, 'He who will drink from My mouth will become like Me. I myself shall become he, and the things that are hidden will be revealed to him.'

All very interesting. *He who will drink from my mouth...* Then we turn to the first line of The Gospel of Thomas: 'These are the secret sayings which the living Jesus spoke and which Didymos Judas

Thomas wrote down.' Who is this Judas Thomas? We hear in the traditional Gospels of a Thomas, and a Didymus, but not a Didymos *Judas* Thomas.

For him, we have to turn to the apocryphal Acts of Thomas, a product apparently of the Syriac Christian Church in the 2nd or 3rd century. That community, to the north of Galilee, held Judas Didymos Thomas in high esteem.

In The Gospel of Thomas, in the Nag Hammadi Library, Jesus asks the disciples whom he is like. Simon Peter and Matthew both answer rather weakly. Then Thomas says: 'Master, my mouth is wholly incapable of saying whom You are like.' This response is practically identical to that given by Judas Iscariot in The Gospel of Judas: 'I am not worthy to utter the name of the one who has sent you.'

At this moment, in The Gospel of Judas, Judas is taken aside for unique spiritual instruction from Jesus. Exactly the same thing happens in The Gospel of Thomas. Jesus says that he is not Thomas' master, meaning that *he*, Didymos Judas Thomas, has understood; he has become like Jesus: 'Because you have drunk, you have become intoxicated from the bubbling spring which I have measured out.'

Judas Didymos Thomas has drunk from Jesus' mouth. Is this a proper interpretation of the kiss – the sharing of the morsel? – the drinking from the common bowl, the cup of sorrows? According to The Gospel of Thomas, when Thomas has returned from instruction the disciples want to know what he has been told, that they have not. They are jealous. The picture is effectively identical to that in The Gospel of Judas. In there, Thomas says to the disciples, who have been left out: 'If I tell you one of the things which he told me, you will pick up stones and throw them at me; a fire will come out of the stones and burn you up.' I need hardly remind readers of Judas' dream in his gospel where he is stoned by the disciples after having received unique instruction.

Did the author of The Gospel of Judas understand Didymos

Judas Thomas to be the same person as Judas Iscariot?

Was the author of John's Gospel using sources in which the figure of Judas was significant for reasons other than betraying Jesus? Could that explain why John has a sudden question coming from Judas, who, he has to emphasize in his text, is *not* Iscariot. He could not be Iscariot – because in John's narrative line, Judas Iscariot has already left the scene. Who is this Judas who asks why Jesus is only manifest to the few?

It might come as a surprise to those who think the writers of the Gospels were very close to the events and personalities they describe to realize that even the names of the 12 disciples are not uniform in the Gospels. Their information is apparently second-hand, at least, on this issue and plainly inaccurate, since they cannot all be right.

Whereas Luke refers to a Judas, the brother of James, as one of the 12 (in addition to Judas Iscariot), this figure is unknown to Mark. Mark has a disciple called Thaddaeus where Luke has Judas, brother of James. Matthew has a Lebbaeus, 'whose surname was Thaddaeus', but no Judas other than Judas Iscariot. Luke has James being the son of Alphaeus, whereas in Mark, Levi is son of Alphaeus. All the Gospels have a Thomas.

Then there is Jesus' family. In Mark (6, v3), Jesus' brothers are James, Joses, Simon, and Juda (Judas). Matthew has the same brothers, except 'Juda' is spelt with the more familiar 's', *Judas*. It is possible that either the author of Mark did not like the mention of a Judas who was Jesus' brother, or some such thought occurred to a subsequent scribe.

Jesus had a brother called Judas. Could the Judas referred to in John (indicated as 'not Iscariot') be Jesus' brother, or one of the 12 – or both? Is the Didymos Judas Thomas of the Syriac Church to be identified with Judas the brother of Jesus, or Judas, one of the 12, or Judas Iscariot, or could he be Thomas? Could it be that this figure, Didymos Judas Thomas, is 'the disciple whom Jesus loved'?

There is undoubted confusion here. How much did the Gospel

writers really know about the subtleties governing Jesus' entourage which, by all accounts, included not only 'the 12' but between 70 and some 120 'disciples', a large number of women (including one, Joanna, associated with the Herodian court), and various members of Jesus' family?

There also seems to have been a group of people involved with Jesus' Jerusalem operation who were unknown to the disciples. These people did special jobs and seem to have been part of a network. Taken as a whole, this was a big organization – it threatened the religious and, therefore, civil authorities of the day. Did everyone involved know what everyone else was doing? It would appear not.

The Sunday School – or Hollywood – image of Jesus wandering around a landscape that often looks like Arizona, like a hippy with a dozen robed fellows walking behind him, waiting on his every scripted word, is totally inadequate. If you want to know the facts, do not watch movies! Even the brilliant images of poet Pasolini's great *Gospel according to Saint Matthew* do not give us much more than a romantic – if gritty – image of the Great Outsider.

Some of these guys who walked with Jesus carried swords (the Jesus in Luke reckons two swords would be enough to take to the Garden of Gethsemane). In the 1st century AD, a sword was equivalent to a Kalashnikov today. These were deadly weapons. Whatever Jesus' personal convictions, he became a target for people who wanted him to become a king, and was surrounded by people expecting real political action.

Where does 'Didymos Judas Thomas' fit into all this? It is very difficult to say, but if you thought the plot was thickening, just bear this in mind. 'Thomas' comes from the Aramaic for 'twin'. *Didymos*? That also means 'twin', in Greek. *Twin Judas the Twin*? What's going on? Is this Jesus' twin brother? Is this the disciple whom Jesus loved? No wonder the Gospel writers were confused!

Gnostic writers were not. The Syriac *Book of Thomas the Contender*, thought to come from Edessa in the first half of the 3rd century, contains a conversation of 'secret words' between Jesus and 'Brother Thomas' – Judas Thomas – written down by one Mathaias (Matthew). In this fascinating book (part of the Nag Hammadi Library) the reader seems to be intended to reach spiritual identification with Jesus – not to have him as a 'master' but to reach where he has reached, to take the holy words direct from Jesus' mouth into oneself:

> Now since it has been said that you are my twin and true companion, examine yourself that you may understand who you are, in what way you exist, and how you will come to be. Since you are called my brother, it is not fitting that you be ignorant of yourself. And I know that you have understood, because you had already understood that I am the knowledge of the truth. So while you accompany me, although you are uncomprehending, you have (in fact) already come to know, and you will be called 'the one who knows himself'. For he who has not known himself has known nothing, but he who has known himself has at the same time already achieved knowledge about the Depth of the All. So then, you, my brother Thomas, have beheld what is obscure to men, that is, against which they ignorantly stumble.

This is a wonderfully erudite account of the significance the author attaches to profound self-knowledge as the prerequisite for the path that leads to eternal life. That last line, by the way, about perceiving what has been obscure to men, is an intriguing reference to a little known saying of Jesus from the Gospels:

> And he beheld them, and said, What is this then that is written, The stone which the builders rejected, the same is become the head of the corner? Whosoever shall fall upon that stone shall be crushed; but on whomsoever it shall fall, he shall be winnowed. (Luke 20, vv17-18)

This is one of Jesus' better jokes. It is not the stone that falls from heaven that will crush the ignorant, but the one you do not see in your way. As Jesus says to Judas Thomas, you have seen that 'against which they [unenlightened men] ignorantly stumble'. The stone from above 'winnows' the one on whom it falls: it separates the wheat (goodness) from the chaff (darkness) – an alchemical image perhaps. The one who knows himself has been 'hit by the stone'. His head has been sorted out.

There is little doubt that by about the middle of the 2nd century there existed a perception of Judas or Thomas, or Judas Thomas, as being 'the twin' – possibly Jesus' real, or symbolic, brother.

It must be said that symbolic spiritual (Sethian) brotherhood was of more use to the spiritual redemption philosophy underlying the Judas Thomas literature – but that does not mean it was not originally based on a genuine familial kinship. However, to make the step of associating this beloved figure with the betrayer of Jesus appears to be the special insight of those who valued The Gospel of Judas. Were they on the right lines? Is there anything more in The Gospel of John that might have encouraged this spectacular association?

Another Disciple

Judas then, having received a band of men and officers from the chief priests and Pharisees, cometh thither with lanterns and torches and weapons. Jesus, therefore, knowing all things that should come upon him, went forth, and said unto them, Whom seek ye? They answered him, Jesus of Nazareth. Jesus saith unto them, I am he. And Judas also, which betrayed him, stood with them. As soon then as he had said unto them, I am he, they went backward, and fell to the ground. Then asked he them again, Whom seek ye? And they said, Jesus of Nazareth. Jesus answered, I have told you that I am he: if therefore ye seek me, let these go their way: That the saying might be fulfilled, which he spake, Of them which thou gavest me have I lost none. (John 18, vv3-9)

Contrary to what he has said before in this passage, he *has* lost one. Judas is standing with the enemy. But that is all he is doing. Perhaps he has not lost him after all.

In the other Gospel accounts, Judas' task is to identify the leader. This he does by kissing Jesus. *There is no kiss in* John. Jesus is so far ahead of the game that he goes forward to meet the armed band and offers himself. The act of betrayal in John lies in the fact that Judas has told the chief priests and Pharisees where Jesus customarily goes – to a garden 'over the brook Cedron'. Jesus is not handed over at all.

Another motive for Jesus offering himself is presented here – to fulfil the scriptures while at the same time preserving the lives of his disciples. 'It's *me* you want', he seems to say, which carries a double meaning: that it is him they *need*, but they cannot see it.

It still seems strange that the extremely dramatic kiss of Judas is missing, the betrayal of the friend. *The betrayal of a friend... Ah!* Is it that John does not want to show Judas as having a close relationship with Jesus? Is John aware of another tradition about Judas being a specially close friend of Jesus? Is he perhaps aware of a tradition that Judas has drunk the words of life from Jesus' mouth? With an apparent cavalier disregard for what must have been an established tradition regarding Judas' kiss of betrayal, John tells it the way *he* wants. We shall probably never know exactly why.

There is another fascinating detail, one that might well have influenced the structure of The Gospel of Judas. When Jesus says to the armed group, 'I am he,' we are told that 'they went backward and fell to the ground.' They cannot bear his presence; Judas is with them.

'Surely', The Gospel of Judas seems to cry out, 'you've missed something!' Perhaps the author of the Sethian gospel has recognized the absence of Judas going straight up to Jesus' face and kissing him. Perhaps he has sensed the unease from the author of The Gospel of John about the prospect of Judas being in control of the situation, his strength. Is this why John has cut the kissing scene?

In The Gospel of Judas, this scene between Jesus and the men who come to take him away seems to be transposed into a confrontation between Jesus and his unknowing disciples. In a possibly parallel scene in *Judas*, Jesus taunts the disciples:

> Any one of you who is [strong enough] among human beings, bring out the perfect human and stand before my face.
>
> They all said, 'We have the strength.' But their spirits did not dare to stand before [him], except for Judas Iscariot. He was able to stand before him, but he could not look him in the eyes, and he turned his face away.

The author of The Gospel of Judas has looked at the Judas who comes before Jesus from outside the circle of the disciples, and he has seen a figure of rare strength. On the other hand, he has also perceived a weakness that must be remedied. One thinks of the question of Jesus to Judas in Matthew: 'Where do you come from?' What is your spiritual level? You come before me, but you and I do not yet see eye to eye. *Yet...*

The author of The Gospel of Judas seems to treat the traditional Gospels as visions, almost dream-scapes, full of pregnant, unexplored meanings. The 'secret gospel' consists of that which may be extracted from them. It is not given for all to see.

There are other curious details in John, following the arrest scene. In these we return to the question of the beloved disciple and Judas Iscariot. After Jesus is arrested, the account in The Gospel of John has Jesus taken first to the palace of high priest Annas, then to his son- in-law, Caiaphas:

> And Simon Peter followed Jesus, and so did another disciple: that disciple was known unto the high priest, and went in with Jesus into the palace of the high priest. But Peter stood at the door without. Then went out that other disciple, which was known unto the high priest, and spake unto her that kept the door, and brought in Peter. Then saith the damsel that kept the

door unto Peter, Art not thou also one of the man's disciples?
He saith, I am not. (John 18, vv15-17)

Who is this 'another disciple' who was known to the high priest,
and who goes into the palace of the high priest? It would appear
that the woman at the door also knows him. Given what little we
know, it might seem likely that the other disciple – who (like the
beloved disciple) cannot be named for some reason – may be Judas
Iscariot.

Why these characters cannot be named is anyone's guess, unless
they are intended as clues for eventual solution. Needless to say, a
number of scholars have identified this intriguing other disciple
with the disciple whom Jesus loved. Whoever he is, he is quite high
up in the administration. He (or she?) can come and go to the high
priest's palace, while poor Simon Peter has to wait outside. The
other disciple can get Peter into the courtyard.

But if the figure is Judas Iscariot, and Peter has seen Judas with
the enemy, why would Peter be prepared to accept favours from
him? Unless, of course, Peter had not noticed that Judas Iscariot was
with the crowd of soldiers, for in John, Judas does not come
forwards. Judas is 'with them', not in front of them.

It has been speculated that the other disciple was part of the
high priest's family, and that would explain the various details given
in John. Such details as the name of the high priest's servant who
has his ear cut off, the story of Nicodemus, the meeting of the
Sanhedrin and other matters might also have come from such a
privileged source.

The other disciple uses his (or her) influence with the
doorkeeper to let Peter through. Why is Peter brought in by this
'other disciple'? Furthermore, what is Peter doing there anyway?
He is skulking about within spitting distance of the men who have
just arrested Jesus – and he is the man who drew his sword and cut
off the ear of Malchus, the high priest's servant. Would they have
left him alone? We are told they ask him if he is one of the disciples.

Peter denies it. This is the same question asked by the woman at the door. It is also the question put to Judas Iscariot at the very end of The Gospel of Judas: 'What are you doing here? You are Jesus' disciple.'

Curiously, the traditional role of Simon Peter is transposed in The Gospel of Judas to that of Judas Iscariot. Is Judas the 'other disciple'?

In The Gospel of Judas, the arrest of Jesus appears to be made not in the 'garden', but in the guest-chamber, where Jesus is spied on by 'scribes'. It is they who approach Judas and ask him what he is doing there. 'You are Jesus' disciple.' Not a question. A statement. Judas is Jesus' disciple. He is the one who has followed Jesus.

In John, Peter has followed Jesus to the palace of the high priest as well. But he is kept *outside*. He does not have the power to enter by himself. When the 'other disciple' entreats the woman to let him in, all Peter can do – when asked if he is one of Jesus' disciples – is to deny it. When the chips are down, the 'other disciples' are not up to it. When the author of The Gospel of Judas makes these extraordinary cross-references, he or she knows that the theological lineage that has gained authority in the Church is that of Peter, the denier of Christ.

The climax of The Gospel of Judas is extraordinarily enigmatic. Following the question 'What are you doing here?', asked not by Jesus in the Garden, as he did in Matthew with the similar question 'Wherefore art thou come?', but by the spying scribes, Judas answers them 'as they wished'.

The curious resonance of this scene with that of Peter's famous denials of Christ leads one to speculate on whether a tradition might have gained currency that it was Judas who had denied Christ. It is all very mysterious. Very deep.

The author of The Gospel of Judas could point to John's Gospel and bring out its obscured truth, that Peter was the outsider: 'Peter stood at the door without' (John 18, vi6). In The Gospel of Judas, Judas is *with* Jesus at the arrest. Even in John, the 'other disciple' 'went in with Jesus into the palace of the high priest' – but Peter, the one who is supposed to hold the keys to the kingdom, what was he doing? He was warming himself by the fire provided by those who had bound Jesus.

Didymus Was Not There

You might think that after the terrible events of the Crucifixion and the amazing appearance of the saviour to Mary Magdalene in John, chapter 20, we would hear no more about betrayal. This is not the case, however.

After Mary Magdalene's breathtaking news, Jesus suddenly appears in the midst of the disciples. He breathes on them, and they receive the Holy Spirit (a variant account to that of The Acts of the Apostles with its Pentecostal tongues of flame and cast of thousands).

A little word on this breathing scene. The word 'breath' in Hebrew is *ruach*, which is also translated as spirit, the breath of life. The breath of Jesus is holy breath. Among the Yezidi people of northern Iraq and the Kurdish Autonomous Region today, the word for spirit or life-breath is *ruh*. It is believed that when true lovers kiss, the *ruh* of one passes into the other. When Jesus 'breathed on' the disciples, it means he breathed *into* them, mouth to mouth. This is the life-giving drink received from the mouth of Jesus in The Gospel of Thomas.

Nonetheless, according to John, 'Thomas, one of the 12, called Didymus, was not with them when Jesus came.' According to John, Thomas missed out on the Holy Spirit. This seems odd.

Where had he been? We do not know, but you probably know the rest of the story. Thomas says he will not believe unless he can actually put his hands into the wounds of Jesus. This means that even though the disciples have seen Jesus, Thomas thinks it cannot have been a physical presence of flesh and blood. This is the origin of 'Doubting Thomas'.

But was there a doubting Thomas? Could he not have been a *Knowing* Thomas, to begin with? Most of those who valued the tradition of *gnosis* believed that the resurrected Jesus was a wholly spiritual being, freed at last of the limitations of flesh and death. For them, the resurrection was proof that Jesus *was* a spiritual being. That men might follow him to this glorious estate was their hope and gospel. Judas in his gospel does not want an eternity on earth, he wants to join the great and holy generation in their more beautiful 'house'.

It has been speculated that this presentation of Thomas and the weird scene of him plunging his hands into the wounds of Jesus, was an early Church polemic against those who did not recognize holiness in the idea of a physical resurrection. Jesus says to them, according to John: 'blessed are they that have not seen, and yet have believed.' The 'children of the resurrection', as some Gnostics called themselves, did not accept this put-down. For them, blessedness comes from seeing for oneself. You do not need to believe; you can *know*.

A Coda

Then Peter, turning about, seeth the disciple whom Jesus loved following; which also leaned on his breast at supper, and said, Lord, which is he that betrayeth thee? Peter seeing him saith to Jesus, Lord, and what shall this man do? Jesus saith unto him, If I will that he wait till I come, what is that to thee? (John 21, vv20-2)

According to The Gospel of Judas, Judas would have to wait until the end of time for his eventual ascension. Perhaps he is still, in some sense, with us.

Jesus said, The Kingdom is like a shepherd who had a hundred sheep. One of them, the largest, went astray. He left the 99 and looked for that one until he found it. When he had gone to such trouble, he said to the sheep, 'I care for you more than the 99.'

Jesus said, 'He who will drink from My mouth will become like Me. I myself shall become he, and the things that are hidden will be revealed to him.'

'These are the secret sayings which the living Jesus spoke and which Didymos Judas Thomas wrote down. And he said, "Whoever finds the interpretation of these sayings will not experience death."' (The Gospel of Thomas)

Chapter Five

THE VERDICT OF TIME

The book of the generation
of Jesus Christ, the son of David
the son of Abraham,

Abraham begat Isaac, and Isaac
begat Jacob; and Jacob begat
Judas and his brethren.

(Genealogy of Jesus, Matthew I, vv1-2)

And Jesus himself began to be about
30 years of age, being (as was supposed)
the son of Joseph, which was the son
of Heli, ...

... which was the son of Seth,
which was the son of Adam,
which was the son of God.

(Genealogy of Jesus, Luke III, v, 23, v 28)

PART ONE

A Judgement

We have seen the evidence. I hope there is sufficient for readers to form their own judgement as to whether Judas Iscariot was innocent or guilty of the betrayal of Jesus.

It has been suggested that I should offer my own view as to the guilt or innocence of Judas. I do not attempt this in order to guide you, the jury, in making your own decision, but merely to satisfy your curiosity as to what the author may himself think. I am in no position to make anything like a final judgement on Judas Iscariot and I hope that my opinion – and it is only an opinion – will not be regarded as being in any way authoritative.

This is an exceedingly slippery case. All the players have vested interests in the outcome. Battles have been fought over differing interpretations of the events surrounding the Crucifixion of Jesus. It should be noted that these battles have been fought chiefly within Church circles.

It is not enough to say that 'all these issues were settled years ago'; *why drag it all up again now?* The fact is that only in the last 50 years or so has professional study of theology to the highest level been available to those outside the Churches. University places to study theology and biblical history were regarded as the preserve of the Churches. Who else would want to study religion that did not wish to be a minister or priest of religion, or who was one already? The idea that high-level scholarship in religious matters might interest those who had no particular religious ministry – or even religious conviction – would have seemed very strange before the Second World War.

The Churches had a great advantage should any of their 'non-professional' members dare to challenge accepted beliefs. Theologians could look down on them from on high and condemn their uninformed, impious ignorance. The reward for challenging accepted ideas was frequently social ostracism and, before the 19th century, imprisonment or death. Beyond the bounds of the Western religious settlement, these constraints still apply in many places.

Occasionally, a clever and well-educated person might challenge the Church, but throughout the Middle Ages and Reformation period, to do so was also to challenge the state. Heretics were usually people trained within the Church: Giordano Bruno and Pico della Mirandola, for example, were both members of monastic orders.

So the privilege of investigating religion from as objective a position as possible is really a recent opportunity. In order to understand the case of Judas Iscariot, such a position is vital. Responsible theologians from the largest Churches try very hard to conform to scientific standards of enquiry, but there are some questions on which too great a weight rides to expect an objective judgement. It is safer to look backwards at what has been pronounced in the past and hope that the irritating question is quietly forgotten. Who would wish to demolish a great and useful edifice for the sake of a few faulty bricks?

Well, it might depend on where the bricks are placed: supporting wall? Foundations? A window frame? One might have to bring the builders in!

So, what do I think about this extraordinary case?

Where there is a crime, there is almost always a motive, unless the perpetrator was mad. There is no indication that Judas was mad, unless we take the report that Satan entered into him as a sign of possession or madness. If Judas was mad, then he was not responsible for his actions.

However, the account of diabolical influence does not belong to our earliest account. Diabolism seems to be part of the gradual move to blacken Judas as time went on. I do not think it is a factor for judgement. Accusing enemies of devilish activity seems to have been a regular slur for the period. Jesus' opponents also accused him of having relations with devils. If Judas was mad, then he is innocent. Besides, if he was mad, Jesus should have cured him, as he is reported to have had great skill in curing madness by expelling devils. If Jesus knew Judas was mad, and did nothing, what would this tell us about Jesus?

It is difficult to establish a convincing motive for Judas' treachery on the basis of the extremely biased evidence we have to examine. Biased? Yes, Judas' guilt is taken as a fairly established part of the oral tradition that pre-existed the writing of the Gospels. Before we look at the status of that tradition, let us continue with the question of motive.

The motives ascribed to Judas seem to be as follows. According to Mark, Judas was the one who betrayed Jesus; no motive is offered, other than the implication that he was the kind of man who did that sort of thing.

Why then would Jesus have chosen Judas? Jesus is supposed to have been able to look into people's hearts and know their mind. If he deliberately chose a traitor, how could he have controlled the key moment of treachery? The timing of the 'betrayal' was absolutely crucial; all the Gospels say so. It was to fulfil the scriptures.

Besides, if Jesus deliberately chose a traitor, then the culpability for the 'betrayal' must lie with the one who knowingly took on a traitor. This is close to what the police sometimes call 'entrapment' – deliberately setting up a situation in full knowledge that a crime will be committed. Again, what would this tell us about Jesus?

Matthew introduces the idea of money. Personal profit is a common motive for crime, even for betraying one's friends. It does happen. However, as we have shown, the accounts of the money concerned have other implications. The figure of 30 pieces of silver was not a conventional price or exchange, but a prophetic, symbolic figure; it was a price paid by ungrateful people for the services of God; in the prophecy, the figure is a pittance, not a fortune.

A simple bargain of information in exchange for cash would hardly involve such symbols. If Judas thought he was betraying 'God' he was almost certainly mad, and therefore deserving of compassion, or at least a cure.

It is a general opinion of scholars that the account of the silver exchange was simply lifted out of the prophetic writings and used as a 'fulfilment' story, to fill in a lack of knowledge after the event. If this is so, it can have no serious bearing on the alleged guilt of Judas.

On the other hand, as I have explained in the previous chapter, the prophetic drama of the exchange could just as easily have been part of an arrangement understood both by Jesus and Judas as something that had to be done as part of the bigger plan. Details of the account in John – if they have any historical value – may suggest that Judas Iscariot may have thought he could control events in the high priest's palace. It is possible he was tricked. This might explain a sudden departure (if he was the 'other disciple') and his letting Peter into the high priest's courtyard. It is also possible that the 'other disciple' was another member of Jesus' special Jerusalem support team, about whom the disciples seem to have known nothing. (Joanna, married to a man of the Herodian court, would be one speculative possibility.)

Perhaps there had been a deal with the high priest that would have brought Jesus before him to demonstrate his true intentions or to enact some miraculous action. However, a meeting with the chief priests could have been arranged without Jesus having to be taken by force. It is possible that the 'forced arrest' was also an illusion that had something to do with convincing the *disciples* of something. But what? Was there meant to be a fight? Did the disciples back down? If we continue down this path, speculation will outrun the evidence of the accounts altogether.

Furthermore, Jesus' opinion of the Jerusalem priesthood seems set; he did not care for them. A careful reading of the Zechariah prophecies suggests that Jesus may have seen the priesthood as representatives of the evil shepherd sent against Israel as a punishment. This was a view that we know was held by some educated Jews whose writings were secreted in the caves at Qumran, providing part of the famous Dead Sea Scrolls collection.

Jesus was at odds with the priesthood. They must have known it. Judas must have known it. Did Judas have a change of heart? Had he been a member of the priesthood himself, then gone over to Jesus – even as a spy – and then been 'brought back in', like an agent seeking a protection programme after a major intelligence operation. Judas operating as a spy is certainly a possibility.

However, this explanation does not properly account for the conviction represented by all the Gospels that the arrest and Crucifixion of Jesus was absolutely vital to Jesus' understanding of what was required in the saving messianic action of God.

If Judas was a spy, then we might have to jettison the notion that

Jesus intended to be killed. If the belief in salvation through Jesus' death is regarded as a later explanation of the events, we should have to doubt very large parts of sayings attributed to Jesus in all of the Gospels. The necessity of the Crucifixion is one theme that, arguably, binds them all together.

One highly debatable hypothesis should not be used to demolish the far greater quantity of evidence: evidence that upholds the view that Jesus knew what he was doing when he travelled to Jerusalem – the very place, he is supposed to have said, where prophets can expect death.

No other motives for betrayal, other than greed, or service of the Jerusalem priesthood, are present on the surface of the Gospels. There is really only one motive that runs counter to acts of genuine treachery that is also present in the Gospels – the classic one for those who think Judas might have been set up as the guilty one after the events. That motive is that Judas was simply motivated by a deep sense of service to his Teacher, his Lord. He did as he was told, even though it grieved him greatly.

The idea of remorse and repentance is to be found in Matthew. The Acts of the Apostles has nothing to say about this. In *Acts*, Judas buys his field and then suffers what looks like a punitive miraculous sudden death, 'that he might go to his own place' (Acts I, v25), as the enigmatic phrase has it. The implication seems to be that Judas Iscariot got his just desserts, but where 'his own place' was we cannot be sure. Hell? The author of *Acts* leaves it in the judgement of God, which is to say, he does not know.

It would be helpful in establishing motive, if we knew what happened to Judas after the alleged betrayal. But the two accounts of his death – hanging and dying later – cannot be reconciled. He went and hanged himself from remorse, says Matthew. He bought a field and then at some time fell headlong and his guts exploded, says *Acts*. We are at liberty to suspect that the Gospel writers did not really know what happened.

The earliest account, Mark, has nothing to say about what

happened to Judas Iscariot. If he had known, and it had served the purpose of the Gospel, then we may suppose he would have told us. John seems to lose sight of Judas altogether in a series of very peculiar events that seem to partake more of the psychology of vision than of history.

This matter brings us to the question of the status of the evidence before us. It has become clear in the course of this investigation that the Gospels are far from ideal accounts of the events of Jesus' life and those around him. The Gospels were employed to preach, effectively, a new religion. That is their purpose. Jesus is the star and the rest are supporting players.

Jesus did not authorize the Gospels. The Gospels were not written for experts in political and social analysis. Had they been so, we may suspect they would have been long forgotten. No, they tell a story of a triumphant overcoming of the world by the providence of God in the figure of Jesus. You are intended to come to one conclusion when reading or hearing the Gospels: *Jesus is Lord*. The facts speak for themselves. This is indeed the response of many millions to the words of Jesus and the story told about him. The Gospels have succeeded mightily in their purpose.

We are not here to question the religious significance of the Gospels but to try to ascertain whether the story told in The Gospel of Judas may have some basis in fact. The Gospel of Judas also has a purpose; this we have explored in Chapter Two.

If, as I think we have proved to a reasonable degree of certainty, that the author of The Gospel of Judas has used the four Gospels known to posterity as sources for his very different spiritual vision of Judas, then there must be *something* in the Gospels which admits of such an interpretation.

The author of The Gospel of Judas does not seem to have been impressed by the Gospels' historical credentials. He sees their accounts as swimming in contradictions: contradictions that can be resolved only when one sees that Judas was not the traitor he has been painted as being.

There seems little doubt to me that much of the Gospel accounts are not only highly selective accounts – sufficient for their purpose – but also at some remove from their subject matter. While many people used to believe that the Gospels were 'fairy tales' written 'hundreds of years' after the events, it is now generally understood that people who had known Jesus and his disciples could still have been alive at the time when the Gospels were written.

I do not doubt that people who are used to oral teaching and not subjected to the mass media have better developed memories than most of us today. Speaking for myself, I should find it very difficult to remember the actual words of a conversation I heard 35 years ago, or even much of the topographical detail; the odd, inspiring phrase comes to mind from time to time. Stories are easier to remember, of course. They inhabit their own imaginative space. But, as the saying goes, times change. The world in AD 65 (the earliest date for Mark) had changed a lot from the world of AD 30-33 (the Crucifixion); people had changed – a new generation had emerged, with new expectations and views of their parents; fresh political and social challenges and crises had emerged.

Now, if we consider that Jesus' operation in Galilee and Judaea was more extensive than popular mythology might suggest, then we may ask the question: whose view of events is represented in the Gospels?

The Gospels bearing the names of Mark and Luke are generally thought to derive from material stemming from words overheard or conveyed at sundry times by Peter and by Paul. Paul was a Johnny-come-lately to the cause of Jesus and we know he was regarded by many Jewish Christians as holding the wrong ideas. Peter we know was a man born to preach and inspire, but he was by no means sure of everything. He had arguments with Paul and, according to tradition, Paul persuaded him he was wrong to avoid eating at table with Gentiles who followed Jesus.

As for John, scholars are at variance as to its apostolic authority (in terms of its authorship). That it conveys a profound mystical and spiritual religion is not in doubt, but few scholars would believe it was written by the same disciple called John who is reported to have been invited to see Jesus transfigured on a mountain.

The earliest records (such as Papias) all involve problems – at least for us. John was accepted into the canon because there was no convincing tradition *against* its attribution to the apostle, because it was widely used by mainstream Christians and because its religious content was regarded as important to the Church.

Nevertheless, while there is much fascinating detail of Judaean and particularly Jerusalem life before AD 70, it is clear that the Gospel is a 'spiritual Gospel'. Its message is to the spirit, not to historians.

An Alternative Reading

I think that Jesus chose 12 men in conscious awareness that Solomon had chosen 12 officers to run his kingdom. I am disposed to think Jesus was intelligent and psychologically acute in his choice of men. I believe he chose each one for a specific purpose, according to his talents. What those specific talents were, we do not hear in the Gospels, but for a few scraps, such as giving Simon a new, mystical name, *Stone* – which may also have been a joke. These little details give us an inkling of Jesus' treatment of these men. Sometimes, I think too much is made of them and later interpretation has discoloured and distorted their meaning.

I think it likely that Jesus' activities were in fact far more complex than the Gospels suggest. We have all kinds of details that suggest this and here is not the place to record them all. To give just one example, one of the women who gave money to help Jesus was a member of the Herodian court. The Herodian court was a place of ceaseless political and familial intrigue, but also of religious superstition and much cruelty.

I doubt very much whether all of the disciples knew why each of the others had been chosen. I suspect Jesus operated on a 'need to know' basis. I think of words attributed to the Duke of Wellington at the Battle of Waterloo: 'If I thought my right hand knew what my left hand was doing, I'd cut it off.'

There was reticence among the disciples in asking Jesus questions. The disciples argued amongst themselves, shy of confronting their leader with their thoughts. They were intrigued by Jesus, compelled to follow. They were probably afraid much of the time – not that they lacked physical courage, but they must have been aware of how their world was separated from the society around them. Also, we must recall that there were dozens of people around Jesus most of the time. We do not have their names. Occasionally, a name pops into the Gospel narrative with no explanation. Joseph of Arimathea, for example, seems to come out of nowhere to provide the freshly made tomb for the crucified body of Jesus.

I suspect that Judas Iscariot was central to Jesus' organization. We are told he kept the purse. We have no reason to think that the organization was poor. I do not believe Judas was short of the necessities of life and I think that if he had wished to be rich he would have chosen a different path in life – if, that is, he was not well-off in the first place. The idea of him selling out his beloved Master for cash strikes me as a disgraceful slur, coming from someone who either did not know what was really going on, or who simply had heard it from someone who was misinformed and confused over identities.

The Pope is a poor biblical scholar to accept uncritically the idea that Judas was greedy – but then, the Pope's pronouncements are meant to be the voice of canonical tradition and the beliefs of the Church as a whole.

It is clear from the Gospels that the compilers were confused over who exactly was important to Jesus' organization – even the variance in the names of the 12 tells us something about how distant we are in the Gospels from Jesus' authentic plans. I think most people can remember the names of 12 people over a long period of time, if the list was precise at the beginning.

If Judas could be replaced by drawing lots (as is told at the beginning of Acts), then there could have been other replacements. However, I find this story of 120 people gathering around Peter to vote for the new apostle extremely suspect. The whole point about the 12 was that *they were chosen by Jesus himself.* I take it as an article of faith that Jesus knew what he was doing – and *only* Jesus knew what he was doing.

It was presumptuous to choose a new disciple. Besides, why did they not ask the allegedly bodily resurrected Jesus to choose a twelfth? This story does not make sense. It has been put together long after the events – if indeed there ever was such an event. If Jesus had not planned for a replacement, then the 'betrayal' must have been a surprise.

I am inclined to take the view that Judas was in some way connected with the ancient tribe of Issachar (Greek: *Issakar*) or that Judas fulfilled a role consistent with the biblical tradition that King David perceived special gifts of timing and decision-making in the elders of that tribe. The other members of the 12 may also have been chosen according to tribal origin. I think that Judas was well aware of the messianic potential of the images both of David (from whose House the messiah should come) and of Solomon (the wise lord of a golden age). It is likely that he identified Jesus with these images.

The prophecies of Zechariah provided the axis for the messianic movement's ideology. Impiety on the part of the leaders of Yahweh's children had (according to Jewish records) led to the 'breaking of the brotherhood' between Judah (in the south) and Israel (in the north). This division within had led inexorably to attacks from without. The northern kingdom of Israel was lost to Assyrian conquest in 722 BC. It is strongly to be suspected that Jesus' message to the lost sheep of the House of Israel was part of a plan to re-awaken the spirit of the ancient united kingdom according to the more glorious visions of the prophets.

Whether Jesus' envisioned kingdom was an earthly kingdom or a purely spiritual one, I cannot be sure. According to the general psychology of prophecy at the time, a heavenly restitution would in turn be reflected on earth below. The heavenly pattern would descend, as it were, to earth. That is to say, the restitution of the holy kingdom could not be effected by earthly methods alone. The spiritual work had to be accomplished first. Once that great work was achieved, the divine pattern could be restored. John the Baptist had already set a pattern of baptising into a *coming* kingdom. Jesus appears to have fully acknowledged this work of repenting and 'signing up' (through baptism) to what was not yet visible in the world. Blessed were those who had not seen but believed.

It is clear to me that the two kinds of kingdom – heavenly and earthly – were fused in his mind: the latter utterly dependent on the former. The spirit gave life, not the earthly letter. This conception was, we may say, something of an alchemical one: unity through the divine restitution and transformation of the lower elements of life.

On the principle of *as above, so below*, it is possible that Jesus recognized an earthly kingdom subsisting wholly on the spiritual bread of a higher kingdom above. What was preventing this fabulous fusion?

Jesus had read of the evil shepherd in Zechariah who does nothing for his people. I am convinced this was taken as an image of the Jerusalem priesthood who had made so many accommodations with the powers of the world, they had cut off the people from the true spirit of God's will. Behind this obstacle, Jesus saw the activity of the 'prince of this world': the one who dispenses silver and gold, but whose spiritual treasury is empty.

I think it is likely that Jesus and Judas Iscariot shared this vision, but mediated its implications to the other disciples according to their capacity to understand it. The parable of the talents may have been told to address this point about the unevenness of the disciples' capacities. 'You may have a little, but you can do more with it than you might think.'

This was an operation that could easily be misunderstood. There were enough tragic stories of brave warriors in Galilee, zealous for

God, going full tilt against the enemy and being swiftly and unceremoniously unseated. This operation was going to succeed where the others had failed; secrecy was essential. Close planning and co-ordination were vital for success. Not even the closest disciples knew what was going to happen – maybe even Judas only knew as much as he needed to know.

There is another possibility. Jesus let it be known that someone was going to have to hand him over. Nobody wanted to do it. Thus the '*Is it I's?*' at the last supper would mean: 'Please don't ask me! I won't do it! I'd rather die than do that!'

Judas, the man he can rely on, is chosen. And the rest, you can say, is history. Except, it is not. The history has become deeply confused.

I do not intend to go into the interpretation of subsequent events to the arrest of Jesus. Whether things went 'according to plan' would be the subject of another investigation. I only make one small suggestion. If Judas was made a scapegoat – as he may have been – then certain questions do arise. Nobody looks for a scapegoat unless things have gone wrong. Could the plan have gone wrong?

Or did it go miraculously right? Either way, the risks were enormous.

Was Judas Betrayed?

I began this section by comparing quotations from Luke's and from Matthew's contrasting genealogies of Jesus. It will be noticed that Matthew's genealogy goes back to Abraham, whereas Luke's goes back – *via Seth* please note! – to Adam , 'the son of God'.

Commentators on the Gospels usually attribute this principal difference in the genealogies (there are others) to the fact that Luke was written for a Gentile audience and Matthew for a Jewish audience. Thus, Adam, being the first example of humanity encompasses all humanity, whereas Abraham was principally a patriarch of the Jews.

If Luke did extend his genealogy back to Adam for this reason, it is rather sad. Abraham in Genesis is not just a father of the Jewish people; Abraham has been called 'father of peoples'. It is a principle of Genesis that Abraham had universal significance. According to the Jewish historian Josephus, Abraham went to the Egyptian priests and court with his belief in a single divine principle that ruled above all other deities. He had a message for all mankind.

It would appear that by the end of the 1st century, 'Abraham' had too much Jewish content for Gentiles to accept him as the progenitor of Jesus. Jesus had become a universal, stateless figure. He had taken a revelation from its 'bondage' among the Jews and exploded it into the whole of humanity. The Jewish cocoon had become a kind of historic burden.

The Church felt it had to keep the Jewish scriptures, but that was because they prophesied Jesus. The vision of a new Jewish golden age – a purified Jerusalem to which all the nations would come, according to the prophecies of Zechariah and Jeremiah – was broken. Curiously, the prophecies that Jesus wished to enact seem to have been applied to Jesus personally without reference to their original meaning.

If Jesus based his plans upon what the Christian world calls the Old Testament, then one might think that the role of a 'betrayer' might also be found in the Old Testament: a kind of model for Judas to fulfil. While there are sundry references in the Psalms to the psalmist being let down by one in his own house, the real breaker or betrayer of the covenant in the Old Testament is either the apostate people of Israel, or particularly, as in Zechariah, the false teachers, the 'bad shepherd'.

It makes more sense that Jesus would regard the viper in the nation's bosom as being the Jerusalem priesthood, particularly the Sadducean party, rather than one of his own. If Judas had contacts with that power-base, that could explain how he came to be tarred with the black brush. The ones who betrayed Jesus were the religious leaders of his own country. They did it because Jesus was their enemy; he planned their end. They and their Temple would fall. This was one of the first prophecies to gain currency after the Crucifixion. According to the story in Acts, voicing it gave the Church her first martyr, Stephen.

It has been said that the priesthood of Israel would never betray one of their own to the grisly, blasphemous death-rites of the Roman occupiers. This may well have been the norm. This may well have been the thought of Judas: part of the calculation. Giving Jesus to the Romans was the 'unthinkable option'. To do such a terrible thing, to collaborate with the occupier on such a hideous level, could, quite literally, 'bring the house down'. (Living memories persisted of the bloody riots in Jerusalem when King Herod had 'merely' permitted the appearance of Roman standards on the outside of the Temple walls.) Jesus was popular.

Politically speaking, Judas may have thought Jesus was 'safe' – even in the 'house of his friends' – if they were his friends. The supporters of Jesus would never let the authorities destroy him; there would be a riot. Maybe that was the idea: get the people of Jerusalem to demand his release. It could have led to a political crisis in the religious leadership of the country – even, who knows, a *coup d'état* of the Temple hierarchy. This was a consummation devoutly wished by many – and had been for a long time: a clean, if perhaps bloody, sweep of the ruling priestly party and then... messianic glory.

The chief priests knew the dangers. The question was: 'what do you do with Jesus now you have him?' They were in a bind. In what sense did they have him? Could it be, rather, that now, he *had them*?

Could they support him? Out of the question. Could they kill him? Difficult.

Maybe Jesus was supposed to have been cut down in the Garden; maybe that was the story Judas had told them: he would be cut down while resisting arrest. They could tell the people that Jesus had died in a night-time attack, betrayed by one of his own. The priests were innocent. Instead, Judas told the armed band they must take him to the high priest's house, safely. Judas landed the priests with a major problem. What were they going to do with Jesus?

It may be that in the appalling heat of crisis, the ruling party did something extraordinary – something unthinkable. They would give him over to the Romans, their oppressors. Perhaps they thought this was a political masterstroke. Perhaps it was a last resort. They only had one card up their sleeve to avoid the wrath of the people. Jesus had blasphemed almighty God. He had claimed to be divine.

This was the worst they could throw at him.

In the confusion and horror that followed, Judas was separated from the other disciples. He may have felt he had been tricked. Had things got out of hand? One can easily imagine a number of scenarios stemming from a tight situation such as this.

Was Judas betrayed? It is such an unexpected question. By whom? By his political contacts? By his friends? Who is to say Judas liked the other disciples? Jesus told them to love one another. How many times, one wonders? Were they always falling out? Did they trust one another? They looked to Jesus. When he was gone, they were afraid. They would believe anything.

Was Judas betrayed?

It is ironic that the split between the north and the south of holy Israel would never be healed in a great messianic deliverance. One result of this, sadly, may have been the eventual split between Christian Jews and non-Jewish Christians – and then between Jews and Christians altogether.

If Judas' hope had been for a united kingdom with a messiah who was both priest and king, then his hopes were certainly betrayed. He might not have wished to live to see it all come apart. It did come apart. The cauldron that was Roman Judaea would explode 30 years later, culminating in the destruction of Jerusalem – but where was the messiah to lead the purified kingdom?

Paul had taken Christ to a new audience. He had taken a package of mysticism, God, Jesus and universal salvation, and delivered it to the Gentiles, in defiance of other followers of Jesus. He wrote of how the Gentiles had been grafted onto the tree of Jesse (King David's father) – the holy generation (on earth) of Jesus. Soon the Gentile Church would no longer be a branch of that tree, but practically the whole trunk, with Gentile priests running the new body of Christ.

The whole history of the Jews would become 'BC'; their holy scriptures, the 'Old' Testament, their prophecies would become footnotes to the New Testament. 'Love one another' – a perfectly sensible piece of advice to offer bickering disciples – became the badge (if not the practice) of a new world religion. Jews who refused to accept the new order were alienated; even aspects of their own culture were removed from them. By the 4th century, Jewish Christians were regarded in the West as heretics.

Surely, there is something in the view of Professor Hyam Maccoby and other Jewish scholars who have seen in the figure of Judas Iscariot a 'necessary Jewish betrayer', created from meagre sources to epitomize the Jews' 'failure' to recognize the messiah of the Gentiles. It is so often the oppressor who blames the oppressed.

It is perhaps time for an historic reconciliation. Is it possible that The Gospel of Judas may yet help to effect such a reconciliation?

The Church may have to meet itself, face itself in those hours of mysterious betrayal between the sleep of the disciples – when only Judas was awake – and the first nails being hammered into the flesh and bone of the one called King of the Jews.

PART TWO

The Persistence of Judas

What happened to Judas Iscariot?

There is a massive amount of confusion and ignorance concerning the 20 to 30 years that followed the Crucifixion. We hear from the Church Father Clement of Alexandria, quoted at length in Church historian Eusebius' *Ecclesiastical History*, that the first 'bishop' (head of table, as 'bishop' originally meant) of Jerusalem, was James the Righteous. James (properly called 'Jacob') was Jesus' brother. One can only speculate on whether there is any connection between Jacob's leadership and the tradition that the 12 tribes of Israel derived from the 12 sons of Jacob (Israel). The presence of the Lord's brother also suggests a dynastic component to Jesus' organization that has been completely obscured as a result of the later fissures and competitive fractures within that organization.

Clement of Alexandria says that James the brother of Jesus (along with John and Peter) was given Jesus' tradition of *gnosis* (knowledge) after the Resurrection. Eusebius (c260-c340) received his information from Clement of Alexandria's now lost *Hypotyposes* (late 2nd century) and from the *Five Treatises of the Acts of the Church* by Hegesippus (mid- to late 2nd century). Clement's account of the stoning and clubbing to death of James, the brother of the Lord, is also referred to in the memoirs of Hegesippus. Most interestingly, the vicious public martyrdom of James (Jacob) that took place in Jerusalem is also related in The Second Apocalypse of James, possibly written early in the 3rd century, the first part of which was found with The Gospel of Judas in Middle Egypt.

In the Jewish Christian apocalypses of James, James, the brother of the Lord, is presented as a Gnostic redeemer and guide figure. It is noteworthy that in the gospel of Didymos Judas Thomas (or Gospel of Thomas), James the Righteous is given special prominence. In that collection of 'secret sayings', the disciples say to Jesus that they know he will soon depart. 'Who is to be our leader?'

they ask. Jesus says to them, 'Wherever you are, you are to go to James the righteous, for whose sake heaven and earth came into being.'

It is significant that the Western tradition of Peter being the principal foundation stone of the Church is not reflected in these early traditions. The Acts of the Apostles does not tell us who the leader of the primitive 'church' was – if that word has any meaning in this period – but so much attention is given to Peter's activities one might think he had taken over; this would be an error. After Peter, Paul completely dominates The Acts of the Apostles – to the degree that the book should really be called *The Miraculous Adventures of Paul and Some of his Associates and Former Enemies*.

The fact is that we know practically nothing of a non-miraculous nature about the critical period between the Crucifixion and the period of Paul's letters to the Gentile Christians (AD 50s). It is strange that this great lacuna is so seldom remarked upon. If ever there could be said to be a 'formation period' of the Christian Church, this must be it. A lot can happen in 20 years. What happened to all those other disciples? There are later stories of Thomas and Thaddaeus going to Syria, Armenia, Persia and India; Philip develops a connection with Ethiopia, but the rest is vague or increasingly legendary. The organization established by Jesus seems to be centred pretty well in Jerusalem until at least the Jewish Revolt that began in AD 66. What its precise primitive purpose was is extremely difficult to discern; logically, it should not be.

What seems fairly certain is that James the Righteous continued an established pattern of traditional hostility towards the priests, scribes and Pharisees of Jerusalem. It is they, according to Hegesippus, who engineered James' murder, as they had done his brother's. Eusebius dates the murder of James to as late as AD 62. He goes further than that. Eusebius quotes Hegesippus to the effect that many Jews in Jerusalem believed that the attack on the city by Titus, son of Emperor Vespasian, was a direct consequence of God's judgement with respect to the killing of Jacob, the 'righteous' (member of the Zadokite priesthood) brother of Jesus. Jesus' prophecy of the end of the Temple priesthood had come true.

In all of this time, we hear nothing of Judas Iscariot. But, then again, we hear very little of any of the dozens of disciples, and only snippets concerning a small number of the '12'.

It is generally accepted by New Testament scholars that there was an attempt in The Acts of the Apostles to underplay the split in the primitive Christian assemblies over the issue of Gentiles coming in to the fold of this Jewish movement. The author of Acts is completely biased towards the Gentile communities. He takes the side of Paul and portrays those who tried to frustrate Paul's attempts at universalism as unacceptable troublemakers – enemies of God's will, in fact. When I was at school, these zealous Jewish Christians were called 'Judaizers'. What was their sin? They were trying to make the proclamation of the new spiritual message 'Jewish'. *How dare they?* But the message *was* Jewish!

The victors write history; Paul's cause would eventually triumph – at a high price. If Judas did survive the events surrounding the Crucifixion, it is clear that, if he was a person involved in an authentic Jewish spiritual, political and messianic cause, then he would have had no place in the Gentile-dominated churches of post-AD 70. He would simply disappear from history along with those who thought like him. Whether Judas disappeared from the historical scene between AD 30/33 and AD 66 is an open question.

The story in Acts of his having fallen headlong, his bowels bursting forth, sounds very much like a garbled picture based on mixed prophetic messages: one being the Psalm that wished the psalmist's enemies' insides would turn to water quoted earlier. Conversely, but not without significance, there are also prophecies that talk of fountains of living water coming from the insides of the righteous. Take John 7, v38, for example: 'He that believeth on me, as the scripture hath said, out of his belly shall flow rivers of living water.'

The business about the field bought with ill-gotten gains is almost certainly a conflation of the account of the 'potter's field' in Matthew, with the Zecharian and Jeremian prophecies concerning the 30 pieces of silver, the potter and the field.

Perhaps there was at the time a cemetery in Jerusalem called *Aceldama* – a place to bury 'strangers' in – and maybe Judas was buried there. It would be appropriate for Judas, for he has certainly become something of a stranger to us. According to The Gospel of Judas, his glory was that, like Jesus, he was a stranger to the world.

Did he hang himself? If he did, it may have been less from remorse for a sin than a feeling that he had bungled his mission. This is possible. There is also the possibility that he may have done it out of profound sympathy with Jesus – 'if Jesus is to be hanged, then I shall hang with him.' 'If he is to rise again, then perhaps I shall rise with him.' Judas' death would then be a kind of martyrdom – one perhaps that no one would understand but himself.

If the other disciples had no idea of Judas' real role in the drama, they could never have understood him. If he was dead, then he could never explain it to them – or, perhaps, anyone. But we cannot be sure that the man who played such a pivotal role on the night of the arrest of Jesus did not survive.

Was there a tradition concerning Judas held among the members of Jesus' family? Information on Jesus' family is surprisingly sparse; his revered kin seem to have become inconvenient to the Gentile Church during the 2nd century, at least that is, according to Eusebius of Caesarea's *Evangelical Preparation*, when their claims to the patriarchate of Antioch were given short shrift by the orthodox.

In Book 3, chapter 22 of his *Ecclesiastical History*, Eusebius mentions grandsons of Jesus' brother Judas surviving to the reign of Trajan, during which time Jesus' relative, Symeon, son of Clopas, was second bishop of the Jerusalem Church – again and significantly, a relative of Jesus.

Symeon was, according to Hegesippus, martyred like his predecessor in AD 106 or 107. Why have we heard so very little of Jesus' family? It has been said that the Jerusalem Church ceased to be significant after the destruction of AD 70, but here we find these Jews being masters of the Lord's table in the reign of the Emperor Trajan.

Unfortunately, we cannot say whether Judas Iscariot was ever confused with Jesus' brother, Judas. Nor do we have access to the annals of Jesus' family. We do not know what happened to his family in the long term. There are some unpleasant sayings attributed to Jesus in the traditional Gospels that seem to put Jesus at a great distance from his family. These may in part be a result of the gradual *dis*-personalizing of Jesus that took place after the end of the 1st century, and possibly before. This is a very complex issue.

The presence of family members compromised growing doctrinal positions regarding Jesus' nature. We have no record of any member of Jesus' family saying that Jesus' mother was impregnated solely by the Holy Spirit and remained a physical virgin ever afterwards. That the Holy Spirit was somehow involved in the matter of Jesus' calling, or even birth, they may not have denied. But they would surely have been surprised to learn that their beloved relative, Mary, had somehow acquired the attributes of the goddess Isis and other mythological female figures.

The process of turning Jesus' nature into a church dogma could only be accomplished when there was no more threat of familial reality. The end of any influence from Jerusalem's Jewish Christians, led by members of Jesus' family, must be dated around the final defeat of Jewish resistance (the Bar Kokhba rebellion) in AD 135, after which Jews were deemed to be no longer welcome in Jerusalem.

Had the Jews simply disappeared after that, most Gentile Christians would not have been surprised, or, perhaps, bothered. But, like Judas, the Jewish people have endeavoured to persist despite ferocious attempts to blacken and annihilate them.

Some 45 years after that rebellion, we hear from Lyons' Bishop Irenaeus of a group of Christians who have in their possession a gospel of Judas. How long they had possessed it, we do not know. Was this a community of Jews? We cannot say. Irenaeus leaves the issue of Jewish Christianity aside. This gave later commentators the idea that Gnosticism represented 'the acute Hellenization of Christianity' (Harnack). This is not a view that would find many adherents today.

It is estimated that there were in the 1st century some two million Jews living throughout the Empire; Jews were excluded from Rome by order of Claudius, emperor from AD 41 to 54. Herod Antipas, who was only part Jewish, was exiled to Lugdunum (Lyon, France) in AD 39 by Gaius Caligula, so there may have been a Jewish community there. We cannot be sure if the Christians who possessed a gospel of Judas were inhabitants of Lyon.

However, one may legitimately ask why it is that the Judas Iscariot of The Gospel of Judas that we now have in *our* possession wishes to join that great and holy generation of Seth. It is clear from the gospel that this great and holy generation of Seth, this immovable race, is a spiritual generation. It is a generation of angelic character, born of the will and being of God. However, we should not discount traditions of Jesus' ancestral lineage that put his family in direct descent from Seth, 'son of Adam, son of God'.

Could it be that the so-called Sethian Gnostics were linked to a sacred tradition of Jesus' family, who had the power and authority to make new sons of Seth?

No scholar has yet given a rational account of the origins of the 'Sethian' *gnosis*. We know that it was a central tradition to a large number of the books of the Nag Hammadi Library. We know that it was linked in some way (but when?) to a sacred serpent cult of healing and wisdom (later nicknamed 'Ophites' or Naassenes) some of whose off-shoots seem to have developed some libidinous ideas to a degree that scandalized members of the orthodox Church.

However, within the pages of The Gospel of Judas, there is no florid excess of luxuriant or exotic myth – nor anything resembling sexual libertinism or demonic magic so often associated with

'Gnostic' beliefs by the enemies of the movement, then and now.

The interest of a Christian community in Judas has not been accounted for. He disappears (apparently) in AD 30/33; he reappears in defiant contrariness to the stories of the disciples of 'John' (Irenaeus' teachers) and Peter in about AD 180.

Judas is placed within the orbit of interest of the Sethian generation, among whom the 11 other disciples have little or no spiritual authority – with the notable exception of the 'twin' Judas Thomas. Thomas was a hero of the Jewish Christian Church of northern Syria; in the Western Church, as we know, he was the 'doubting Thomas'. But in the East, he would become the patron saint of masons, architects, builders: a man not of doubt, but of knowledge.

However, by the 4th century AD, the testimony of those who found something of spiritual value in the life of Judas would disappear. This can only be the result of the triumph of orthodoxy in the Roman Empire.

In AD 380, the Emperor Theodosius I (379-395) decreed the following addition (*Cunctos populos*) to his legal code:

> It is our desire that all the various nations which are subject to our Clemency and Moderation, should continue in the profession of that religion which was delivered to the Romans by the divine Apostle Peter, as it hath been preserved by faithful tradition; and which is now professed by the Pontiff Damasus and by Peter, Bishop of Alexandria, a man of apostolic holiness. According to the apostolic teaching and the doctrine of the Gospel, let us believe the one deity of the Father, the Son and the Holy Spirit, in equal majesty and in a holy Trinity. We authorise the followers of this law to assume the title of Catholic Christians; but as for the others, since, in our judgement, they are foolish madmen, we decree that they shall be branded with the ignominious name of heretics, and shall not presume to give to their conventicles the name of churches. They will suffer in the first place the chastisement of the divine condemnation, and

in the second the punishment which our authority, in accordance with the will of Heaven, shall decide to inflict.

A year later *Nullus haereticus* (AD 381) granted local officials the power to suppress by such means as were deemed necessary those outside the faith as established by the Council of Nicaea (AD 325). It had been at Nicaea that the Emperor Constantine had ordered the bishops of the Church to settle their differences and define the limits of orthodox Christian belief.

In *Nullus haereticus*, Theodosius lays down the penalty for non-conformity:

> ... Let them [heretics] be entirely excluded even from the thresholds of churches, since we permit no heretics to hold their unlawful assemblies in the towns. If they attempt any disturbance, we decree that their fury shall be suppressed and that they shall be expelled outside the walls of the cities, so that the catholic churches throughout the world may be restored to the orthodox bishops who hold the faith of Nicaea.

What this meant in practice was that if a Catholic objected to a group of people who were considered heretics, he or she could assemble a group of people and attack them. If the heretics resisted, that is, 'attempted any disturbance', they could be beaten as hard as might be necessary to prevent further active resistance; to expel people outside the walls of cities was to condemn them to poverty, homelessness and attack by brigands. They no longer had the protection of a state now indifferent to their survival.

By definition, a heretic was not a Christian, therefore you did not have to love them – because God did not love them either. How did you know this? *Because the scriptures were clear.* Which scriptures? *The approved scriptures.* Who approved them? *God's own representatives.* How do you know who they are? *They are the ones the Emperor has approved of.* If you do not agree, you are an enemy of the state. The Church has condemned you already.

Judas in Hell

In spite of the fact that there is no official Catholic doctrine insisting that Judas Iscariot is either a heretic or condemned to perpetual hellfire, hell is where he seems to have been dispatched. Of course, if he is in hell, then in some sense he is still alive, otherwise, how could he be suffering the punishments of hell? If we are to believe in the legendary voyage of St Brendan, Judas not only saw out the Dark Ages in a place enlightened by fire, but was also permitted occasional moments of respite on a lonely rock in the north Atlantic.

Unlike St Brendan, St Thomas Aquinas, the great Catholic theologian (c1225-74), never set sail for the Island of the Blessed and so took it that Judas was confined to hell without holidays. Aquinas was not a vindictive man and received no pleasure from the thought of Judas in a state of endless torture. However, he was, in his *Summa Theologiae*, keen to show that the justice of God was philosophically consistent with his essential, revealed nature.

Aquinas looked at the problem of free will and predestination. God, by definition, knows everything. He can see all possible consequences and knows all probable consequences with a certainty that even encompasses the vagaries of human freedom. Free will is a gift, but it carries with it the responsibility to do as God wills us to do. There would be no free will if God could choose to make us do what we would otherwise not be free to do.

The case of Judas illustrated his point. While it is just to say that God knew what Judas was going to do, and, furthermore, God's will included the knowledge that Judas would do what he did, then Judas is still responsible for his actions. He chose to do them by free will. But was not Judas' action predestined? Could Judas claim that he had no choice in the matter? No, he could not, because it was not his will to do God's will, but to do his own will. In his own mind, he acted contrary to what he thought Jesus would have wanted. In his own mind, he was ignorant of the predestined drama that God was unfolding. He was blind to it; Satan had entered into him.

A commentator might argue that Aquinas was condemning Judas for saving humanity. How could he save humanity (by enabling Jesus to die for our sins) and condemn himself simultaneously? Why should Judas have to suffer for his role in the plan?

Aquinas thought he was preserving something important for human beings. God's omnipotence does not mean we have to behave like clockwork soldiers or robots. We can fulfil our deepest possession of free will by opening our lives up to the will of God. This is what Jesus did when he accepted the cup of surrender to his destiny in the agony of Gethsemane.

Judas, on the other hand, had closed himself up in self-interest. How did Aquinas know that Judas had acted without knowledge of the vital consequences of his actions for salvation? Aquinas believed so because he held the Bible to be the revealed word of God in which there can be no essential contradiction.

Had Aquinas seen The Gospel of Judas, he would probably have consulted Irenaeus' *Adversus Haereses* and called for the burning of the gospel, declaring it to be a Satanic snare released (with the pre-destined knowledge of God) as a temptation – and test of the free will of the believer.

Dante Alighieri (b1265) had no, or little, choice but to accept the logic of Aquinas on this issue. The great poet was a great lover – of love. Dante's love for Beatrice is well known; his admiration for Occitan poetry likewise. But when it came to Judas Iscariot, Dante's *Inferno* (chapter 34, vv28-67) withholds any natural compassion and presented the most terrifying picture of Judas' destiny in the most vivid language:

> The Emperor of the dolorous realm [Lucifer] stood forth from mid-breast out of the ice; and I in size am more like a giant than the giants are to his arms... Oh, how great a marvel it seemed to me when I saw three faces on his head! The one in front was fiery red... and the right seemed between white and

yellow; the left had an aspect like the people who come from where the Nile descends. Under each there issued forth two mighty wings... sea-sails I never saw so broad. No plumes had they; but were in form and texture like a bat's: and he was flapping them, so that three winds went forth from him, whereby Cocytus was kept frozen. With six eyes he wept, and down three chins gushed tears and bloody foam. In every mouth he champed a sinner with his teeth ... 'That soul up there which suffers greatest punishment,' said the Master [Vergil], 'is Judas Iscariot, he who has his head within, and outside plies his legs. Of the other two, who have their heads beneath, that one who hangs from the black visage is Brutus ... and the other is Cassius ...

It is not every day that one great artist gets the opportunity to comment in detail on the work of another. The English visionary artist William Blake (1757-1827) spent time before his death learning Italian so that he could read *The Divine Comedy* of Dante in the original language. In old age he began work on conveying each canto of Dante's work in paint and pencil. Sadly, the project was never completed, but sketches exist for all the projected artworks and those few that he finished are very fine indeed.

Blake had a tendency to put his own mind into whatever work he was illustrating, giving subtle twists to his representations of well-known themes. Confronting Dante's poem was a great challenge to him. Blake found Dante's representation of hell morally abhorrent and deeply repugnant.

Blake, who shared many of the insights that we see in The Gospel of Judas – without ever having seen it – believed that the hell envisioned by Dante 'was originally Formed by the Devil Himself & So I understand it to have been'. Hell was not made by God for the torture of the damned.

This was not the way that the true God who is revealed in Man behaved with respect to sinners. In his visionary poem *Jerusalem*,

Blake cries out against those who cannot tell the difference between Satan's selfish works and those of God:

> Where are those who worship Satan under the name of God! Where are they? Listen! Every religion that Preaches Vengeance for Sin is the Religion of the Enemy & Avenger; and not of the Forgiver of Sin, and their God is Satan. Named by the Divine Name. (*Jerusalem*, v52)

He would have found The Gospel of Judas' condemnation of the god of the spiritually blind disciples an example of the 'everlasting gospel'. In *A Vision of the Last Judgement*, written in about 1810, Blake wrote:

> In Hell all is Self Righteousness; there is no such thing there as Forgiveness of Sin; he who does Forgive Sin is Crucified as an Abetter of Criminals, & he who performs Works of mercy in Any shape whatever is punished, if possible, destroy'd, not through envy or Hatred or Malice, but through Self Righteousness that thinks it does God service, which God is Satan. (*A Vision of the Last Judgment*, p93)

For Blake, 'Satan' is the 'Selfhood'. True forgiveness shows that one has overcome the ego-enshrining self. If Blake had heard that the Satan of Self had not *entered* Judas but rather had *come out of him*, he would have clapped his hands with joy. For Blake, as well as for the people who loved The Gospel of Judas, the world was a distortion: the cracked mirror of truth. If the tradition of the selfish claimed Judas was the criminal, take it that he was among the righteous. If Judas was Satan's prisoner, take it he would be redeemed in glory. This was the logic of those condemned by Irenaeus and all his spiritual followers.

In Blake's vision, Satan had his place. He was the 'Limit of Opacity'. Satan represented the boundary of materialism, below which it could not sink into complete chaos. He is the binding power of the material universe – great in his way, gilded with stolen light, but not the true God. This vision of Satan is very close indeed to the image in The Gospel of Judas of 'Saklas', or Ialdabaoth, the deity blind to anything above himself.

If, as the Catholic Church believed, Satan had Judas in his grip, then it was a kind of jealousy. The grip would be extinguished when the reign of the false god and his opaque world ended.

The Gospel of Barnabas

The Gospel of Barnabas is a highly problematic writing. Much used by Islamic writers who favour its view of the falseness of the Holy Trinity and other Christian doctrines, this very long work shows us the interesting image of Judas Iscariot being crucified in Jesus' place.

According to the story, Judas' appearance was transformed to that of Jesus at the time of the arrest of Jesus. Everyone thinks it is Jesus who has been crucified. The gospel then tells us that three days after the burial, Judas' body was stolen, eliciting the view that Jesus had risen from the dead. Jesus, meanwhile, in the Third Heaven, gets permission to come back to earth to tell his family and his disciples the truth. He then re-ascends after promising he will return again as a just king.

If this work were not – from internal evidence – so clearly a forgery, one could speculate on whether the author or authors were familiar with the Gnostic image of Simon of Cyrene being crucified in Jesus' place. One might also speculate on whether the likeness between Jesus and Judas was occasioned by stories of Judas the twin, even Judas the twin brother of Jesus.

The earliest manuscripts of the work are in Italian and Spanish and date from the 17th century. The Gospel of Barnabas is generally held to be a pious fraud in favour of an Islamist polemic, dating back no earlier than the 14th century and no later than the 16th century. Nevertheless, there is still something rather haunting in the image of a crucified Judas, however fictional its origin.

The Eastern Orthodox Church has continued the ancient tradition of Judas the betrayer of Christ. In that Church's hymns of Holy Wednesday (the Wednesday before Easter) the figure of Judas is contrasted vividly with the alleged prostitute who anointed Jesus' head at Bethany. The story of Judas condemning the 'waste' of money involved in the anointing is taken from John's Gospel. Believers are encouraged not to follow the example of the wayward disciple but to embrace the repentance shown by the woman with the alabaster jar.

The betrayal of Judas is also memorialized in the Orthodox Church with a Wednesday fasting from meat, dairy products and olive oil. Before taking communion on that day, the prayers demand that 'I will not reveal your mysteries to your enemies, neither like Judas will I betray you with a kiss, but like the thief on the cross I will confess you.'

We must travel a long way to find sympathy for Judas. The power of the Church to frighten its followers away from thinking about things for themselves has diminished since the 18th century. In the wake of this agony of the Western soul has come a willingness on the part of some thinking writers to see the figure of Judas without automatically seeing a bad man.

Judas – Mirror of the Times

It is a curious fact and something of a tribute to the man himself that Judas Iscariot appears in the arts, especially literature, as a kind of lodestone for the disquiets of the times. When an author wishes to make oblique comments about things that are disturbing, or simmering under the surface of the culture, the figure of the great betrayer seems to leap into consciousness.

Judas is a kind of one-man Amnesty International. He seems to make us aware of something hidden, locked up or repressed in our culture. His transgressive status helps of course. Did he betray God? Or have we misunderstood? Is Judas Satan's slave, or are we?

In English composer Edward Elgar's oratorio *The Apostles*, Judas' motive is to force Jesus to declare his divinity. Judas wants to see Jesus establish a kingdom on earth. In this sense, Judas seems to represent a twisted romanticism. Elgar has been associated with the symbolist movement in the arts: a kind of spiritist romanticism that tried to depict the spiritual undercurrents – and spirits (malevolent and otherwise) – of a spiritually warped and potentially explosive time. The end result was a massive sense of foreboding. The ghosts were starting to move in to the allegedly 'enlightened' chambers of Western culture.

Perhaps Judas' earthly dreams also reflect the concerns at the beginning of the 20th century for the potential for global conflict. Germany exhausted the world in its desires for earthly empire. Mussolini was likewise engaged in outsize imperial ambitions. Judas in Elgar's work represents the dark side of imperialist romanticism – the tendency to go too far. In trying to realize the earthly paradise, we only become aware of our greater need for spiritual integrity. We do not need to conquer the world; the world has conquered us already.

Mikhail Bulgakov (1891-1940) wrote his satirical work *The Master and Margarita* on Stalin's Russia in a world, you could say, where Elgar's Judas has been allowed to have his way – the Soviet Union in the 1930s. The earthly paradise and communist empire turns out to be a hell of deceit, cynicism and overwhelming cruelty. Stalin is the anti-messiah whose God is raw power.

Instead of Stalin at the top, Bulgakov gives us Pontius Pilate talking to his head of the secret service. Judas Iscariot has been found to be unacceptable to the state; his days are numbered – but nothing will be recorded. The secret things that happen have not happened. The conversation between Pilate and his head of secret operations is drenched in black humour. Judas has been marked, it is said, for an early grave. 'I expect you to do your best to help him,' hints Pilate.

Later, Judas is reported to be dead: 'A shame, I understand you did your best ...' Perhaps the line, 'he might have killed himself?' sounds like a workable cover story to wipe clean the 'good reputation' of the conscienceless state. Thus begins the rumour we know from the biblical account of Judas' suicide. Here, Judas is the victim, caught up in events that transcend his power to alter them. He is an individual; as such, he is nothing.

The author has sensed something peculiar about the accounts in the Gospels surrounding Judas negotiating with his superiors. Reflecting events in Russia during the Stalinist terror, Judas becomes one of many dupes of the insatiable lusts of absolute power that corrupts absolutely. Judas was dead before he was born. There will be no grave to mark his incidental existence. Take the 'will to power' beyond the level of the individual, and the individual is crushed. 'Collective' action is a euphemism for tyranny.

It is Jesus' will to power that is in part the subject of Robert Graves' intricate novel, *King Jesus* (1946).[1] Perhaps its sacrificial themes were influenced by the masses of sacrifices made during the previous seven years. The Second World War called for millions of individual acts of sacrificial courage. In seeing Jesus as the sole legitimate heir to the Davidic, messianic throne, Graves was ahead of his time. The idea would re-surface in Baigent, Leigh and Lincoln's bestselling *The Holy Blood and the Holy Grail* (1982).[2] What if Jesus was part of a dynasty?

Graves takes no interest in a bloodline stemming from Jesus. He is interested in the effects such a claim will have in his own time. Graves' Jesus is the secret son of Herod Antipater, deeply aware of his messianic responsibilities to his country. He realizes, however, that there is no realistic possibility of his defeating the Romans by force. While the Zealots think a miracle will save them if they try – by force – to save themselves, King Jesus looks to a spiritual solution. He must fulfil the prophecies of Zechariah in order to realize the beginning of a new kingdom of God.

He conveys his message to his disciples in an indirect way: one of his disciples is going to have to slay him with a sword. The disciples do not understand what he is talking about. Judas, however, is the exception. He understands what needs to be done. He knows that humanity cannot be saved unless he plays his thankless role in engineering Jesus' death.

Graves, a man familiar with the Gnostic tradition, posits a realistic interpretation of the events surrounding Jesus' life and death, in tune with the greater realism of the post-war world. Romantic dreams will not flow well into the modern world (apart from advertising and the movies), but the need for hard spiritual choices and definitive actions will go on. Why should Jesus' messianic claims not be taken in their full, literal sense? The messiah was regarded as a politically significant role; this is clear in Matthew's Gospel, in which King Herod the Great is determined to annihilate rival claimants, be they even so small as babes in swaddling bands.

Over the crucified Jesus hung the words *King of the Jews*. Pilate's taunt was a political lesson for the Jewish people. Rome is power. The Catholic Church perhaps learned the lesson the Zealots failed to grasp; the latter expected a supernatural miracle, the Church had time on its side. Modern Israel has learned the lesson: miracles are for the holy – and there will never be enough of them.

Robert Graves demythologized Jesus' earthly career without robbing it of spiritual meaning. The Churches have not been so successful. *King Jesus* deserves wide appreciation. It has undoubtedly been influential on a number of post-war writers.

It appears to have influenced Hugh J Schonfield's 1960s revisionist text, *The Passover Plot*,[3] a conspiracy book before its time. Schonfield was one of the first to take inspiration from an imaginative novel and try out its implications directly on the recorded tradition. The result was for many Christians in the mid-60s a disturbing read. *The Passover Plot* presented itself as a rational hypothesis that had a claim to be taken as fact, if it could be proved.

Schonfield looked at the events surrounding the Crucifixion and noticed that there are signs of a pre-arranged 'operation'.

Rather than the events unconsciously fulfilling ancient prophecies, there was a conscious, mechanical and deliberate attempt to engineer the prophetic events into shape.

Many theologians had taken the view that the perception that Jesus' life and death 'fulfilled the prophecies' was a perception that dawned on Jesus' followers after the events. Thus, Matthew's continual telling that this or that event, or saying, was 'in fulfilment of the scriptures' was a literary device. So sure were theologians that this process post-dated the events themselves, that it was – and is – widely believed by scholars that where the Gospel writers had no tradition of Jesus' actions, all they needed to do was find a useful sequence in the Hebrew scriptures. For example, the story of the 30 pieces of silver was added later to the events sequence, once the decision had been made that it must refer to the betrayal of Judas Iscariot.

You could take a line from one of the Psalms and add Jesus or one of his disciples to it. Since the Old Testament testified of Jesus, then the history must have been 'pre-written'. Taking the latter idea to its logical limit, Schonfield made the case for Jesus deliberately *fabricating* scenes of prophetic fulfilment. The events of the Passover were a plotline, a kind of act. Therefore, Judas was playing a part, consciously. It had to look like he was betraying the good shepherd.

According to Schonfield, the disciples in general did not have a clue what was going on. Like the men in The Gospel of Judas, they were so blinded by their own ideas, they failed to see what was going on before their eyes. Schonfield's basic ideas still pack punch.

Schonfield has been criticized for failing to see that while he recognized Judas' actions as fulfilments of prophecy, he did not acknowledge that thereby the prophecies really were fulfilled in history. Did it matter how the prophecies were fulfilled so long as they were fulfilled? A fascinating question: when is a prophecy not a prophecy? Is conscious fulfilment of prophecies true fulfilment?

Take this scenario, for instance: if I push the Armageddon Button and thereby launch an apocalyptic war (knowing that I am deliberately trying to fulfil The Book of Revelation), have I *fulfilled* prophecy – or have I abused it?

It is an abiding fear of people confronted by evangelical Christian enthusiasts of the apocalyptic-minded kind that these people are so filling the media air-waves with prophecies, that they are actually – consciously or otherwise – willing someone or something to 'fulfil' those prophecies. It is widely believed that this obsession with the apocalyptic scenario may have influenced Western diplomacy with regard to the Middle East. Some political realism is needed here, I think.

The Passover Plot, appearing as it did within a few years of the assassination of President Kennedy, seems to have set off a strange tremor in the global subconscious that persists to this day. The last days of Jesus were a conspiracy, *right*? Judas knew the *inside story*. There is a clear line of imaginative idea that links *The Passover Plot* with *The Da Vinci Code*, via *The Holy Blood and the Holy Grail*.

The Myth in Action

People want myths. One of the greatest myths is fame. This was a powerful theme at work in Tim Rice's and Andrew Lloyd Webber's mass-selling pop opera, *Jesus Christ Superstar*. Ironic it is that when Rice and Webber began work on the first West End stage presentation, it was reported in the London press that they had asked John Lennon to play the role of Jesus! This was in 1969.

In one newspaper cartoon reflecting the news of John's imminent appointment as Jesus (he was already a *superstar*), a hippy passer-by glances at the news hoarding announcing the story – *LENNON TO PLAY JESUS* – and mutters: *'Who's Jesus?'*

Jesus Christ Superstar is a kind of essay on the perils of fame, especially that fame born of the incessant hunger of popular culture, and centres on the reaction of Judas Iscariot to the 'Jesus Myth' that is growing around him.

This was an astute commentary on the direction of the times by

Rice and Webber. Fame, of course, can come as a 'kiss of death'. The musical posed an interesting question: what happens if we transpose the idea of pop hysteria back to the time of Jesus? What happens then to the myth?

The phenomenon of adulation distorts everything. Could it be, the writers hint, that Jesus' mind might have been turned by all this ecstasy? Mary Magdalene weeps and wails like a girl caught in the grip of a policeman at the edge of a stage on which a pop star is 'singing his heart out'. 'I don't know how to love him,' she cries like a groupie whose idol has left in the early hours without even a goodbye note. People thought the song was romantic – great tune! But the sentiment was truly pathetic. She compares her new idol to her ex-lovers – this one is *really different*! How can she move *him*? 'Shall I bring him down?' 'What's it all about?' What, indeed?

But Judas is watching. He is our narrator, the anxious, the cool, the street-wise, jazz-wise, funked-up political realist: Judas Iscariot, played to the hilt as a hip cat from Harlem. 'What's the buzz?' he asks. What's going on? He is at the birth of a myth, and he knows it. He loves Jesus – or thinks he does. He understands Jesus – or thinks he does. But things are getting out of hand. If this *Jesus mania* goes on any more, the Romans will hit Israel like a ton of bricks. People are going to die. It has happened before, it will happen again. There is going to be widespread despair.

Jesus cannot do what people think he can do. OK, he can do the odd miracle – but there is a limit. He cannot change the world. He, Judas, knows that. Somehow, he has got to put an end to this crazy party.

There is just the hint that Judas might know that Jesus actually wants him to betray him. We can never be exactly sure that this is a betrayal. Judas convinces himself he has got to bring in the chief priests 'for Jesus' own good'. The whole thing had got out of hand. Jesus' fame had become the message. The message had generated the myth. But all around them was poverty and squalor, rats and soldiers, death and dirt. Why could people not see the terrible, brutal facts? *What is all this hippy shit?* Why were they so blind they could not see reality?

This emphatic contrast of image and reality was a powerful re-working of the account in The Gospel of John of the anointing at Bethany. Yes, Judas complained about the waste of money spent on giving Jesus luxuries, while the children starved outside. Jesus' reply that 'you have the poor always with you' just seemed callous to the politically hip-radical-realist, Judas. It sounds a bit callous to us too, even though we still want Jesus to be wise. We want the myth.

Coming out at the gateway to the 1970s, on the back of the Aquarian Age musical *Hair*, *Jesus Christ Superstar* gave us a Judas from the radical ghetto of New York City and the slums of Chicago. Images derived from fantasies of these social sources would dominate the clash in 70s' fashion between romantic waifs sitting in chiffon underwear beside Provençal lakes, and politically brain-washed 'Patti Hurst'-style radical chic.

Then Punk would come to smash the Myth to pieces. It all left a nasty taste in the mouth. Perhaps that is what worldly reality tastes like. You do not need a sledgehammer to crack a nut. Jorge Luis Borges (1899-1986) gave us 'Three Versions of Judas', a short story in his collection, *Labyrinths*.[4] Borges creates a character, a theologian called Nils Runeberg, who decides that much that has been attributed to Judas is false. Take the Judas 'kiss' for example, suggested as a means of identification. Nonsense. If Jesus had all these crowds following him, anyone could see what he looked like. Judas was representing all mankind in making a sacrifice of himself, in parallel with Jesus' sacrifice for all mankind.

Theologians attack Runeberg's ideas. He comes back with more. The idea of God spending only one afternoon on the cross as a sacrifice is 'blasphemous', the fictional theologian asserts. If Judas were chosen to be a disciple, he cannot be all bad. He must have had great moral qualities to involve Jesus' attention. Judas put his own happiness aside to serve his Lord: 'Judas sought Hell, because the happiness of the Lord was enough for him. He thought that happiness, like morality, is a divine attribute and should not be usurped by humans.'

Runeberg also contends that it would be impossible for God to be fully human without being able to sin – and that means sinful thoughts are inevitable. Runeberg's final conclusion is arresting: God did not become Jesus; he became Judas.

The curious connection between Judas Iscariot and pop culture continues. Pop culture is an arena of barely suppressed ideas, the forbidden, the transgressive. In the words of Rice's and Webber's Mary Magdalene: 'Shall I scream and shout? Shall I talk of love – let my feelings out? I never thought I'd come to this!' No, and neither did we. Pop culture requires constant novelty, shocking changes.

In 1965, Bob Dylan toured Britain. One night, he changed his acoustic guitar for an electric instrument and the folk singer became the leader of a pop band. From out of the usually respectful audience – no mindless adulation at a Dylan gig, surely? – came the cry: 'Judas!'

Bob Dylan had *betrayed* folk music! Was he to be damned for all time to worry about his image, chart-position, fame-count, popularity, bank account? Would the 'serious message' be distorted by popular culture?

Oh, so much betrayal has occurred in the world of pop music! Half of the superstars have allegedly betrayed someone at some time. They have 'sold out'. Is this not what the murderer of John Lennon was giving hideous voice to? The betrayal? Surely the sick fan took it on himself to execute the messiah turned Judas! How can singers who speak of a paradise for the peaceful and loving ever think so *low* as to want mere *money*? Politicians betray their voters. Voters change their minds and 'betray' their politicians. It is 'Hosanna in the highest!' one day and 'Damn you, Jack!' the next.

Everyone is betrayed, so everyone is a Judas to someone. Can you trust me? Are you real?

Film Director Martin Scorsese made a film of Nikos

Kazantzakis' *The Last Temptation* and poured all his acquired knowledge of pop culture into it. Pop culture still required Jesus was something of a hippy. The audience was not ready for a Punk Jesus – after all, punk messiahship has passed to Johnny Rotten who has, very properly, spat on the idea.

Jesus must be portrayed as a kind of hippy. It is the beard and long hair thing. Willem Dafoe duly obliged. Was this image of Jesus meant to suggest a cross between Kris Kristofferson and an anaesthetized Charlie Manson? The music was by pop master Peter Gabriel; the editing was fantastic. There is a tastefully shot sex scene between Mary Magdalene and Jesus that upset a lot of people (it was meant to be a tempting fantasy), but the depiction of Judas, contrary to the thrust of the Gospels, barely raised a murmur of protest.

Judas does what the other disciples cannot bring themselves to do; he will help Jesus fulfil his destiny to die on the cross. Judas should share in the glory of effecting salvation for humankind. The basic idea is there in The Gospel of Judas.

Armando Cosani's *The Flight of the Feathered Serpent* (2003)[5] is a novel in three parts, concluding with a portrait of Judas' real identity as spiritual master. Those who loved The Gospel of Judas would have found much to their taste in Cosani's novel. This is how he describes Judas:

> I could never understand this strange man of moderate words, who seemed to enjoy confusing me with his caustic and paradoxical observations upon all things. He gave the impression of being taciturn. However, soon after dealing with him, one couldn't help noticing the extraordinary fact I have come across in my agitated life: he was a smile. He was it from head to toe. He didn't smile, he didn't need to smile; he was all a smile.

The laughing Jesus meets the smiling Judas: we have entered the New Age. One of the fascinating aspects of this novel is the way that

Judas is shown as an identity transcending time; he can manifest in a friend. His fundamental identity is precisely that: as a friend. I wonder if Frieda Tchacos Nussberger has read the novel. She felt so close to Judas while trying to rescue his gospel from various scrapes, I wonder if she felt Cosani and her Judas are somehow the same person?

And so we have come to the New Age – and for it we now have a very old version of a very new Judas. We know we have entered the pop culture of the New Age because in Dan Brown's *The Da Vinci Code* the Last Supper has no really nasty elements of *betrayal* in it. The point of focus is Mary Magdalene; Judas does not play a part. It is Mary – and the spirituality of all women – that is 'betrayed' in Da Vinci's *Last Supper*. It is there, but it must be decoded. The Crucifixion is not important because Jesus had progeny and therefore the Word can be made flesh in every new generation, reborn.

And now, we have come full circle – almost. Like a phoenix from the flames of time arises the one and only, the original Gospel of Judas. Its coming seems to have been prophesied throughout a century of the blackest torment. The 20th century saw the trio of *Judas, Judaea, Jews* of The Gospel of John (6, v70 – 7, vi) all linked together by the Nazi Party in a mass condemnation and caricature of all Jews – venal, ugly, treacherous, damnable and condemned to die.

> He spake of Judas Iscariot the son of Simon: for he it was that should betray him, being one of the 12.
> After these things Jesus walked in Galilee: for he would not walk in Judaea, because the Jews sought to kill him.
> (John 6, v70 – 7, vi)

It may say something for the existence of a hidden balance in the world that while the last century has seen anti-semitism reach hitherto unplumbed depths of unspeakable depravity, there has also been a slow revolution in the perception of Judas, the hitherto unspeakable Jew.

From a figure that once embodied the very essence of treachery, we have seen Judas come to be treated humanely in the arts: a figure upon whom we can project our own doubts and cultural regrets.

From a figure instantly condemned by the Church, we have come to the Judas of an ancient gospel who is – if we are indeed close to the end of 'time' as we know it – on the verge of a glorious heavenly assumption.

Whether conventional Christianity can prevent such a theological catastrophe we have yet to see. Such may not be a simple task. For as we have seen in this book, there really is more to Judas than meets the eye.

END NOTES

Chapter 1

1 *The Nag Hammadi Library in English*, translated by Members of the Coptic Gnostic Library project of the Institute for Antiquity and Christianity. James M Robinson, Director. 2nd Edition, E J Brill, Leiden, 1984.

2 *Citizen Kane*, RKO/Mercury Productions, 1941. Director/Producer, Orson Welles. Screenplay by Herman J Mankiewicz and Orson Welles.

3 *The Complete Dead Sea Scrolls in English*, ed. Geza Vermes, Penguin Classics, revised edition, 2004.

4 Herbert Krosney, *The Lost Gospel, The Quest for the Gospel of Judas Iscariot*, National Geographic, Washington DC, 2006.

5 *Parzifal*, Wolfram Von Eschenbach, ed. A T Hatto, Penguin Classics, 1980.

6 *The Nag Hammadi Library in English*, translated by Members of the Coptic Gnostic Library project of the Institute for Antiquity and Christianity. James M Robinson, director. 2nd edition, E J Brill, Leiden, 1984.

7 James M Robinson, *The Secrets of Judas, The Story of the Misunderstood Disciple and his Lost Gospel*, Harper-Collins, San Francisco, 2006.

8 Jane Rowlandson, *Landowners and Tenants in Ancient Egypt: The Social Relations of Agriculture in the Oxyrhynchite Nome*, Oxford Classical Monographs, Oxford University Press (USA), 1996.

9 James M Robinson, *The Jung Codex: The Rise and Fall of a Monopoly* (*Religious Studies Review* 3, 1977).

10 James M Robinson, *The Secrets of Judas, The Story of the Misunderstood Disciple and his Lost Gospel*, Harper-Collins, San Francisco, 2006.

11 Herbert Krosney, *The Lost Gospel, The Quest for the Gospel of Judas Iscariot*, National Geographic, Washington DC, 2006, p245.

CHAPTER 3

1   Herbert Krosney, *The Lost Gospel, The Quest for the Gospel of Judas Iscariot*, National Geographic, Washington DC, 2006.

2   Simon Mawer, *The Gospel of Judas*, Back Bay Books (USA), 2002.

3   Pheme Perkins, *Gnosticism and the New Testament*, Augsburg Fortress Publishers (USA), 1993.

4   *New York Post*, Angela Montefinise, 'Canon Fodder: Judging Judas' Gospel', 9 April 2006

5   Adam Gopnik, *The New Yorker*, 'Jesus Laughed', 10 April 2006

6   Christopher Hitchens, '*Why the Gospel of Judas makes sense*', *Slate* magazine, 13 April 2006.

7   Eduard Iricinschi, Lance Jenott, Philippa Townsend. *New York Review of Books*, 'The Betrayer's Gospel', 8 June 2006.

CHAPTER 4

1   Hyam Maccoby, *Judas Iscariot and the Myth of Jewish Evil*, Free Press (USA), 1992.

2   S G F Brandon wrote an essay on the Zealots in his interesting book of collected papers, *Religion in Ancient History, Studies in Ideas, Men and Events*, George Allen & Unwin Ltd, London, 1973.

3   Ludwig Noack, *Die Geschichte Jesus*, Strassburg, 1876.

CHAPTER 5

1   Robert Graves, *King Jesus* (first published 1946), Hutchinson, London, 1983.

2   Baigent, Leigh and Lincoln, *The Holy Blood and the Holy Grail*, Jonathan Cape, London, 1982.

3   Hugh J Schonfield, *The Passover Plot*, Disinformation Company (USA), 40th anniversary edition, April 2005.

4   Jorge Luis Borges, 'Three Versions of Judas' from *Labyrinths*, Penguin Modern Classics, introduced and prefaced by J E Irby, Donald A Yates, André Maurois, New Edition, 2000.

5   Armando Cosani, *The Flight of the Feathered Serpent*, Absolute Publishing (USA), 2003.

Quotations from The Gospel of Judas are taken from *The Gospel of Judas, from Codex Tchacos*, Edited by Rodolphe Kasser, Marvin Meyer, Gregor Wurst, with additional commentary by Bart D.Ehrman, National Geographic, Washington DC, 2006.

Biblical quotations are taken from the King James Bible, the Authorised Version, of 1611.

BIBLIOGRAPHY

Baigent, Leigh and Lincoln, *The Holy Blood and the Holy Grail* (Jonathan Cape, 1982)

Bettenson, Henry (ed), *Documents of the Christian Church* (Oxford, 1977)

Bibliotheca Philosophica Hermetica Publications *In de Pelikaan* (eds Joost Ritman, Frans Janssen) *Hermes Trismegistus, Pater Philosophorum* (Amsterdam, 1991)

Blair, H. A., *The Kaleidoscope of Truth, Types & Archetypes in Clement of Alexandria* (Churchman Publishing, 1986)

Blake, William, *Jerusalem* (Blake Trust/Tate Gallery, 1991)

Borges, Jorge Luis, 'Three Versions of Judas' from *Labyrinths* (Introduction and Preface J. E. Irby, Donald A.Yates, André Maurois; Penguin Modern Classics, 2000)

Brandon, S. G. F., *Religion in Ancient History, Studies in Ideas, Men and Events* (George Allen & Unwin Ltd, 1973)

Burkitt, F. C., *Church & Gnosis* (Cambridge University Press, 1931)

Chadwick, Henry, *The Early Church* (Pelican, 1978)

Charles, R. H. (trans.), *The Book of Enoch* (SPCK, 1984)

Churton, Tobias, *The Gnostics* (Barnes & Noble, 1997)

Gnostic Philosophy – from Ancient Persia to Modern Times (Inner Traditions, 2006)

Cosani, Armando, *The Flight of the Feathered Serpent* (Absolute Publishing, 2003)

Dart, John, *The Laughing Saviour* (Harper & Row, 1976)

Doresse, Jean, *The Secret Books of the Egyptian Gnostics* (Hollis & Carter, 1960)

Eisenman, Robert and Wise, Michael (ed; trans), *The Dead Sea Scrolls Uncovered* (Penguin, 1992)

Eusebius, *Ecclesiastical History* (trans. Kirsopp Lake; Loeb Classical Library, 1975)

Fowden, Garth, *The Egyptian Hermes* (Cambridge University Press, 1986)

Gopnik, Adam, 'Jesus Laughed', *The New Yorker* 10 April 2006

Grant, R. M., *Gnosticism: An Anthology* (Collins, 1961)

Graves, Robert, *King Jesus* (first published 1946; Hutchinson, 1983)

Hitchens, Christopher, 'Why the Gospel of Judas makes sense', *Slate* 13 April 2006

Inge, William Ralph, *The Philosophy of Plotinus* (2 vols; Longmans, undated)

Iricinshi, Eduard, Jenott, Lance, and Townsend, Philippa, 'The Betrayer's Gospel', *New York Review of Books* 8 June 2006

Jonas, Hans, *The Gnostic Religion* (Beacon Press, 1958)

Philosophical Essays (University of Chicago, 1974)

Josephus, Flavius, *The Works of Flavius Josephus* (trans. William Whiston; Nimmo, 1865)

Kasser, Rodolphe, Meyer, Marvin and Wurst, Gregor, *The Gospel of Judas, from Codex Tchacos* (additional commentary Bart D. Ehrman; National Geographic, 2006)

Kee, Howard Clark, *Medicine, Miracle & Magic in New Testament Times* (Cambridge University Press, 1988)

Kelly, J. N. D., *Early Christian Doctrines* (A & C Black, 1977)

Krosney, Herbert, *The Lost Gospel, The Quest for the Gospel of Judas Iscariot* (National Geographic, 2006)

Logan, A. H. B. and Wedderburn, A. J. M. (eds), *New Testament & Gnosis* (T & T Clark Ltd, 1983)

Maccoby, Hyam, *Judas Iscariot and the Myth of Jewish Evil* (Free Press, 1992)

Mahé, Jean Pierre, *Hermès en Haute Egypte* (2 vols; University of Quebec Press, 1978, 1982)

Mawer, Simon, *The Gospel of Judas* (Back Bay Books, 2002)

Montefinise, Angela, 'Canon Fodder: Judging Judas' Gospel', *New York Post*, 9 April 2006

Noack, Ludwig, *Die Geschichte Jesus* (Strassburg, 1876)

Novum Testamentum (Vol. XXVII, Fasc. 3 July 1985)

Perkins, Pheme, *Gnosticism and the New Testament* (Augsburg Fortress Publishers, 1993)

Quispel, Gilles, *Gnostic Studies* (2 vols; E J Brill, 1974, 1975)

Review of *Neues Testament und Gnosis* (Walter Schmithals, 1984) in *Vigiliae Christianae* 39 (E J Brill, 1985)

Roberts and Donaldson (trans.), *The Ante-Nicene Fathers* (Erdmans Publishing Co., 1981)

Robinson, James M., *The Jung Codex: The Rise and Fall of a Monopoly* (*Religious Studies Review* 3, 1977)

The Secrets of Judas, The Story of the Misunderstood Disciple and his Lost Gospel (Harper-Collins, 2006)

Robinson, James M. (ed), *The Nag Hammadi Library in English* (trans. Members of the Coptic Gnostic Library project of the Institute for Antiquity and Christianity, James M. Robinson, Director; 2nd edn; E J Brill, 1984)

Rowlandson, Jane, *Landowners and Tenants in Ancient Egypt: The Social Relations of Agriculture in the Oxyrhynchite Nome* (Oxford Classical Monographs, Oxford University Press, 1996)

Rudolph, Kurt, *Gnosis* (trans. R. McL. Wilson; Harper & Row, 1985)

Schonfield, Hugh J., *The Passover Plot* (Disinformation Company, 40th anniversary edn, April 2005)

Stoyanov, Yuri, *The Other God – Dualist Religions from Antiquity to the Cathar Heresy* (Yale University Press, 2000)

Van den Broek, Roelof and van Heertum, Cis (eds), *From Poimandres to Jabob Böhme: Gnosis, Hermetism and the Christian Tradition* (Amsterdam, 2000)

Van Lamoen, Frank (ed), *The Hermetic Gnosis* (Amsterdam, 1988)

Vermes, Geza (ed), *The Complete Dead Sea Scrolls in English* (Penguin Classics, revd edn, 2004)

Bibliography

Von Eschenbach, Wolfram, *Parzifal* (ed A. T. Hatto; Penguin Classics, 1980)

Wilson, R. McL., *The Gnostic Problem* (Mowbray, 1958)

Gnosis and the New Testament (Blackwell, 1968)

Zaehner, R. C., *Our Savage God* (Collins, 1974)

INDEX

Index

Index

Index